TRAVELER

STREETS *with*
NO NAMES

STREETS *with* NO NAMES

*A Journey into Central
and South America*

Stryker McGuire

THE ATLANTIC MONTHLY PRESS
NEW YORK

To Julith

Published simultaneously in Canada
Printed in the United States of America
FIRST EDITION

Library of Congress Cataloging-in-Publication Data

McGuire, Stryker.
    Streets with no names: a journey into Central and South America /
by Stryker McGuire.—1st ed.
    ISBN 0-87113-433-0
    1. Latin America—Description and travel—1981– 2. McGuire,
Stryker—Journeys—Latin America. I. Title.
F1409.3.M4 1991   918.04'39—dc20   90-29294
                            MCG

The Atlantic Monthly Press
19 Union Square West
New York, NY 10003

FIRST PRINTING

ACKNOWLEDGMENTS

WHEN I DECIDED TO SPEND the better part of a year traveling through the Americas with Julith Jedamus, then my companion and now my wife, I thought that perhaps once our journey was over I would look into doing a book about it. Fortunately, Harold Evans, now president and publisher of Random House, Inc., heard about my plans through a mutual friend, Michael Kramer, the magazine writer. Harry encouraged me to formalize plans for a book before I left the country. I thank him for that—and for putting me in contact with Robert Ducas, who became my agent and a valuable font of ideas. I am grateful to Gary Fisketjon, who was with Atlantic Monthly Press and is now at Knopf, for taking on this project and shepherding it through the early stages. I would like to thank Ed Sedarbaum, my copy editor, for his keen eye and sensible suggestions. I am especially indebted to Ann Godoff, who succeeded Gary as editor in chief at Atlantic Monthly Press, for her guidance and deft editor's hand.

Throughout this enterprise, my editors at *Newsweek* were supportive of my plans even when mine did not mesh neatly with theirs. I am particularly grateful to Rick Smith, president and editor in chief, and to Maynard Parker, the magazine's editor, for generously accommodating my desire to take a sizable period of time off and then return to work.

During the course of our 20,000-mile journey, three families in particular favored us with their uncommon hospitality, their insights, and their stories: in San José, Costa Rica, Dick Dyer and his daughter, Dery, who edit and publish the newspaper *Tico Times*; in Buenos Aires, Argentina, the writer Jacobo Timerman and his wife, Risha, as well as one of their sons, Daniel, and his wife, Ronit; and in Mexico City (and at their ranch at Peotillos, San Luís Potosí), Samuel Del Villar, a lawyer, journalist, and professor, and his wife, Enriqueta, a public relations consultant. I would like to extend a special thanks to: Carlos Jervez, a university student, and his family in Cuenca, Ecuador; Michael Smith, a journalist in Lima, and his Peruvian wife, Teresa; Peter McFarren—reporter, photographer, printer, art collector, publisher, and chef—and his family in La Paz, Bolivia; Jack Aitken, a museum director and hacienda operator in Potosí, Bolivia; and in Buenos Aires, our friends Jorge and Irina Simonelli and their daughters, Gabriela and Alejandra.

Along the way, there were hundreds of helping hands reaching out to us—teaching us, taking care of us, urging us to press on, tugging at us to stay. Some of those hands belonged to four small boys who turned out to be our best guides and whose stories are told in this book: Tomás José Ordoñez of Quiejal, Guatemala; Manuel Pérez Sánchez of

Salquil Grande, Guatemala; Juan Carlos Añasco of Quito, Ecuador, and Erasmo Guanaco Vilca of Yanque Nuevo, Peru.

Finally, I have no doubt to whom I owe my greatest debt of gratitude. Without Julith, the trip, this book, and so much more would never have been possible.

CONTENTS

Introduction: War Math

I SPENT TOO MANY MONTHS in Nicaragua during the civil war of 1978–79. To be able to work, at least as I saw my work then, I kept my psychological distance from the demolished bodies. I was determined to be as good a spectator as I could without being drawn too deeply into what was going on around me. I felt that I had to keep my distance in order to tell the story. I felt that if I let down my guard, the story would come rushing in and so overwhelm me that I would be left wordless.

People who actually fight wars and don't just cover them tend to deal with untenable reality in the same way. But the reality of what happened, however repressed, is always around the corner, waiting to come back in a damburst of memory, or worse. Vietnam veterans say memory's trigger can be an odor: gasoline, which smells just enough like napalm to fill the mind with an explosion of flames. Or, they say, it can be a sight: something special about the shape of a forest trail as it rounds a bend might summon up an awful jungle ambush.

For me, it was a sight. One day in 1986, several years after my last visit to Nicaragua, I was at Gettysburg. I had bicycled past the scores of monuments to this regiment and that regiment that line the two ridges—Cemetery Ridge and Seminary Ridge—overlooking the memory-soaked battlefield from my own country's Civil War. A stupid bit of war math came to me: the number of people who died in battle here in Pennsylvania on three July days in 1863—51,000—happened to equal the number of deaths, most of them civilian, in the civil war in Nicaragua. Soon I was walking up on the hill where the Confederate and Union soldiers were actually buried. Their tombstones—tiny cement squares stuck flat into the soil—formed a mosaic of sterile sod in the earth, fanning out from the point where Lincoln gave his most famous speech, the address he had written on the back of an envelope. The sheer force of all that death finally kicked in my personal door to Nicaragua. And that war all came rushing in, a riptide of feeling. This time I let myself go with it. I was drawn to a place that was calm. And I walked away.

Gettysburg was one of many things that helped me decide to take some of the distance out of my life, to set aside for a while my work at *Newsweek* and to see people and places from a different angle. I wanted a break from my usual *modus operandi:* landing in a country with a notebook that looked empty but was actually replete with preconceived notions. I wanted less detachment. I wanted to see places from the ground up. I wanted to meet people by happenstance, not make appointments with them.

So I took a long trip south. In a car, I went to places I

knew by some measure well but wanted to know differently, and I went to places I knew something about but didn't really know at all.

The distance and detachment that I wanted to take out of my life had been widening in recent years. Following my time in Nicaragua, I had gone to Houston as a reporter and then on to New York as an editor. By 1986 I had spent three years practicing my craft of journalism most closely not so much with people as with the green-tinted screen of my Atex computer. I would stare at the screen and wrestle with some phrase flung in from London or Nairobi. And I would wonder why I wasn't doing the flinging. At thirty-nine, the really telling word in my title—Senior Editor—started to be the first one.

I had an office with a couch, which, as my eldest son Shayne enjoyed explaining to his college roommates, was there for catnaps during the legendary Friday night editing marathons. Shayne—himself an incurable romantic who was born to me and my first wife during my freshman year in college, in 1966—could still squeeze romance and excitement out of my job: the responsibility of deciding what stories would run, how they would run, where they would run, when, at what length, with what artwork. I was having a harder time feeling the excitement; it paled beside what I got as a reporter out in the field.

I explained to a lawyer friend what it was like: You're a partner in an important Wall Street law firm, but your work is confined to the cluttered table in the office library. You don't set foot in court. You don't talk to witnesses. You don't even take depositions. You direct the casework by reading court transcripts. Your contact with the real world becomes limited to cramped Manhattan restaurants, the high ceilings and nice molding of a co-op near the Promenade in Brooklyn Heights, and a weekend farmhouse close enough to the city so that, after the week's work, you can drive to it Saturday night on four hours of sleep without killing yourself or your girlfriend or some family on a hamburger outing at the Red Rooster in Brewster along Route 22. For this, you also used to get a potted plant in your office as well as the couch. Budget constraints have done away with the plant.

My escape routes from this midlife career bog were few. I could wheedle, cajole, and maneuver for a new job with *Newsweek* out in the field. To execute this option would be not only time-consuming but also a half measure that would not give me the full break from work that I was looking for. My other option was to just take off, severing my ties with work and risking penury while fulfilling an old dream to drive through Latin America. I chose the dream option.

I tried to lower the risks of penury. I worked out what most people thought was a terrific deal with *Newsweek*. I wasn't so sure. I would—not to put too fine a point on it—quit. *Newsweek,* in turn, pledged to hire me back between twelve and twenty-four months after my departure, whereupon I would resume my tenth year at the magazine. Fine. Except that my agreement with my editor was as porous as the U.S.-Mexico border and in two years *Newsweek* might belong to a Japanese appliance manufacturer. Still, I took the deal.

Though my luck would soon improve, such close observers of my life as my parents were convinced that this trip idea definitely fell into the long-hair category: it's something you do when you're in college, not when your son is in college. They undoubtedly also detected profound psychological significance in the fact that I would manage to turn forty years old thousands of miles away from home, without a regular paycheck and not a business card to my name, and with a girlfriend from Boulder, Colorado, a notoriously flaky venue. I figured that if they could abandon New York and retire to Florida in a place where all the streets had golfing names (Birdie Lane, Bogie Street), then I could celebrate my next birthday in (as it turned out) Quito and go to places where the streets have no names.

Fortunately I did not make the journey alone. Enter the girlfriend from Boulder. Julith Jedamus accompanied me every step of the way—from the giddy, joint conception of a quirky idea through every marvel and setback as we brought it to fruition—as my lover, as my fiancée, and ultimately, as I wrote the final words of this book, as my wife. The trip was like our first child; I cannot imagine moments from it ever ceasing to shine brightly in our memories of our early days together. The idea was born of a shared affection for Latin America, for travel, for discovery, and for the Spanish language. Julith's predilection as a daughter of the Rocky Mountains for strenuous exercise and no-frills travel not only helped to imbue the trip with a pleasantly rough-hewn character but kept it on budget.

Julith and I had met while we were both working for Newsweek International, which publishes the international editions of *Newsweek*. Three months before I left *Newsweek*, she resigned from her writing job to take charge of the early planning for our journey. Throughout the trip I learned much from her own special vision of what we saw together. Her background as an art student, as an omnivorous reader, and as a more literary writer than I complemented my experience as a journalist. Hardly ever did we see anything in exactly the same way. I came to feel that without her I was looking at things with one eye closed, that only with her vision did I attain proper depth perception during our twenty-thousand-mile enterprise together.

The trip evolved pretty much as we had planned it over long, wistful dinners at our home in Brooklyn Heights. Our itinerary by no means took us along the most direct route, nor did it take us to every country in our path. We dawdled and meandered, picked and chose; we hurried where we had to, and we ignored what we wanted to. From the United States, we drove through Mexico and Guatemala. We sidestepped El Salvador and skipped Panama and Colombia. We crossed Ecuador and Peru and kept Bolivia to our left as we headed into Chile and then Argentina. While unwinding in Buenos Aires, we left our vehicle behind, hopped a plane to La Paz, rented a four-wheel-drive vehicle for a long swing through the stark Bolivian altiplano, and then returned to Argentina for a final fling with blissful unemployment before heading home. At the conclusion of our trip, we spent another year and a half in Mexico, where I was sent by *Newsweek;* there I was able to gather material for the book's final chapter, which incorporates our brief drive through Mexico at the start of our journey as well as our eighteen-month sojourn in Mexico at the end.

The trip was only rarely harrowing. We were on our own, self-insured, and had no desire to become fools or heroes through either stupidity or recklessness. I had seen enough colleagues killed in the line of duty in Central America—in a few tragic cases because they crossed the line between enterprise and excess—to learn the importance of caution. I was off duty, so was Julith. This trip was no time for derring-do. We were living off our own money and responsible for our own possessions, including an expensive vehicle. We had invested a lot in this journey. We were not about to lose it through carelessness or unanchored ambition.

So we deliberately set out to avoid certain known dangers along our route. El Salvador was in a perilously unpredictable stage as we made our way south. Along the shadowy margins of the war between the government and the guerrillas, acts of indiscriminate violence could take out anybody who got in the way. The summer of our journey an especially popular guerrilla tactic was to declare nationwide travel bans and then to enforce them by blowing up bridges along the Pan American highway. We were prepared for the unexpected on the trip, but our flexibility did not include extended delays in the Salvadoran countryside waiting for a bridge to be rebuilt. We skipped El Salvador. We swung east through Guatemala, into Honduras through the back door alongside the spectacular Mayan ruins at Copán, and down into Nicaragua where the war being waged by the U.S.-backed Salvadoran government shook hands with the war being waged by the U.S.-backed Nicaraguan contras.

We skipped Panama for a number of reasons. We knew we couldn't get our car through the Darien Gap, a jungle south of the Canal Zone and north of the Colombian border. The Gap has always been impassable by car or truck (though we did hear that some people had done it by hitching their Land Rover to a team of horses); the section of the Pan American Highway that would have traversed the Darien remains the one that has never gotten beyond the drawing board. We could have driven as far south as Colón or Panama City and shipped our car from there to South America, but we opted instead for spending a languorous month in Costa Rica, imposing on the boundless hospitality of friends and painstakingly negotiating the shipment of our car out of the Caribbean port of Limón.

We had always planned to give Colombia a by. Cocaine trafficking had turned Colombia into the kind of nasty street corner you make a point of avoiding. The place was bristling with guns and thuggery. Before we took off, I talked to a Californian who had recently driven his jeep through Colombia; he counseled caution and urged us to do what he did: get a well-armed army infantryman to ride shotgun with us in our car through the more dangerous areas. Colombia—though life went on with surprising normalcy in some parts, including for much of the time in the graceful capital of Bogotá—had for the most part sunk into lawlessness, and we couldn't afford to get caught up in it.

We shipped our car through the Panama Canal to the pirate port of Guayaquil, Ecuador. With payments of several hundred dollars to agents and fixers, we managed to get the car back on the Pan American Highway heading south. We stuck mostly to the lofty spine of the Andes or to the coast as we made our way from the fetid marshes of coastal Ecuador to the ice floes of southern Chile. All the while, through Ecuador and Peru, the Amazon Basin east of the snowy mountains beckoned to me like a siren's call: dead missionaries floating down Ecuadoran rivers, Peruvian honky-tonks awash in drug runners and oil-company roughnecks, hidden resources that might spell the only hope for poor Bolivia. Pragmatism (and Julith's high-mountain aversion to low altitudes and high humidity) kept us from sliding down that slippery slope.

* * *

My vision of this book changed ⸓
between the early planning days and the fin⸓
in 1990. We had already decided to go o⸓
one publisher approached me, suggesting I⸓
version of the Latin American entry in John Gunther's
series of journalistic *tours d'horizon*. Gunther wrote *Inside
Latin America* in the darkening days before the United
States entered World War II, a time when the hemispheric
bonhomie of Franklin D. Roosevelt's Good Neighbor Policy was already beginning to wane.

In his book, Gunther repeatedly mentions Pan American Airways, the U.S. embassy, and the sundry "great" men
of Latin America. It was easy for me to imagine his reporting technique. Arrive (via Pan Am) at the airport. Whisk
off to an embassy-arranged party (a few "Western"—read
U.S.—diplomats, several U.S.-educated local businessmen,
the president of the local Rotary Club, and a nominal
opposition figure plucked from the study carrels of the local
university). Chat about coffee production and the Nazi
menace on the presidential veranda with the local "great
man." Fly off to the next capital. Stir the local color into a
batch of newspaper clippings and predictable reference
books, and—voilà!—a book.

Gunther learned about Latin America this way, and as
a result so did his readers. It all had a familiar ring to me;
the methodology was enough like what I had done at
Newsweek to make me feel queasy—so much so that the
Guntherization deal died a quick and natural death. But the
idea of doing a book lived on. I switched publishers and
was encouraged to do a more personal book.

That fit my own evolving notion of what I wanted to

do. I did not want my book to become a lecturer's podium from which to broadcast sweeping generalizations and condescending homilies about our American neighbors. I wanted to give a sense of what it is like to wander into a strange place and learn about it. I wanted to meet these countries from the ground up, not swoop over them in one of Gunther's Pan Am planes, and I hoped to share that perspective with the reader.

It was not easy. My mind carried a lot of baggage. What knowledge I had was useful, sometimes essential, but it also sometimes obstructed my vision. I found it especially hard to adapt my ground-level approach to Mexico. The clutter was heavy. Mexico and I went way back—to 1970— but as with a couple whose relationship has not been seasoned by living together and sharing responsibilities, casualness had bred familiarity but no deep understanding. My son Shayne had gone to Mexico with my first wife when he was eight and had grown up there. Visiting him there over the years, speaking Spanish with him, hearing his stories—these things made me feel at home in Mexico. During those years I was living in San Antonio, Texas. Many of my friends were Mexican Americans. As a journalist and as a tourist, I made frequent trips to the border and into Mexico.

But what really had I learned? I had digested enough information to speak with some authority about the country, but now that information was getting in the way. I was finding it hard to restrain the journalist in me, to stop taking the grand, panoramic view. I knew too much to let the country take charge and wash over me. I wouldn't allow Mexico to awe me with its physical grandeur, puzzle me with its rich mix of cultures, or scare me with the unknown.

In Guatemala, Peru, Bolivia—places I knew relatively little about—it was easy to become a passive observer. But I was swooping down on Mexico with my prepackaged ideas instead of allowing the country to take me by surprise.

The problem reappeared in my first pass at writing the chapter on Mexico. The "I" in that chapter was, while trying hardest to assert its authority, the most detached. The chapter needed a different voice. In rereading the original chapter on Mexico I found that my voice as a writer seemed most honest and direct, and least inflected, when I wrote about the parts of Mexico I had not been to before. The writing I liked the best were the sections infused with a rush of wonder. As I got south of Mexico City and into unfamiliar territory, I had to worry less and less about filtering my impressions as a traveler through the distorting gauze of past experience. Only then, in the tangled mountains south of the capital, did I begin to sense the quality of mystery that would have dominated all my impressions of Mexico had my old knowledge not gotten in the way.

Solving mysteries is an invigorating challenge, and the trip gave me insights that helped guide me through the Latin American labyrinth. But not always, thankfully. I would hope that mystery permeates this book. I can hardly imagine Latin America without mystery. Without mystery, Costa Rica becomes Connecticut, Chile becomes California. Exploration, not explanation, was the main purpose of this trip. While I enjoy explaining mysteries when I can, I do not believe that a mystery unexplained loses its power to teach.

CHAPTER ONE
Leaving: A Single Light

THE PHYSICAL BEAUTY of what I saw on our trip was sometimes so powerful that it briefly whited out everything else: staring into an impossibly deep canyon waiting for the next flight of condors to swoop by, their serrated wings whistling in the wind; catching the distant, thin-air sound of an Andean shepherd blowing into his quena, his shawl-draped body silhouetted against the fading light; gazing down from a campsite onto a herd of llamas, their babylike sunset whimpers echoing off the stony backdrop of an Inca ruin as they tugged at their tethers; standing at midnight on a ferry deck during the southernmost foray of our journey, moving in almost total silence except for the deep thrum of engines far below and the sharp, remote sound of the steel hull cutting through cold water, studying the pitch-colored fjord slopes and silvered glaciers, and being unable, for one of the very few times in my life, to see a single light, anywhere.

One place in particular affected me this way. Julith and

I were in Ecuador, the first country on the trip that neither of us had been to before. We had flown into Quito, having sent our car by sea to Guayaquil, and found ourselves easily seduced by the newness of everything. Approaching the Quito airport, we peered down the alley of volcanoes that stretch from north to south, our first sense of the awesome grandeur of the Andes. One day we drove up Mount Chimborazo. At the lower altitudes, the volcanic soil is rich and black, planted with potatoes and barley and wonderfully pungent onions—they smelled so to us even as we drove by in the car—and crisscrossed by irrigation ditches dug as the Incas had dug them and running swiftly with the icy water that promises deep snow and glaciers up higher. At two miles high, the amount of cultivated land begins to decline. It's replaced by short grass and grazing cattle and, increasingly, by springy tundralike plants.

Soon we were driving across coarse russet sand at an altitude higher than any mountain in Julith's home state, Colorado. At 15,275 feet we came to a mountain-climbing shelter. From there we walked up to the snow line, the only sounds coming from the wind, from small birds, and from gurgling streams of snowmelt. I can still recall the stab of exhilaration I felt there, with 4,000 feet of mountain still looming over me. I ran back to the shelter, a wild clamber across rocks and around boulders, my exhilaration mixing with a high-altitude champagne giddiness.

I was looking for liberation from a stale work routine, and my real liberators were, of course, people. A war widow in the Ixil Triangle of Guatemala, tired of death, didn't want to answer any questions; and I, suddenly and for a pleasant change, didn't want to ask any. A shoeshine boy taught me more about Quito than I could have learned from anyone else. My introduction to Chile's enchanted Valle del Elqui came from a man I met by extraordinary accident: on a small bridge one moonless night I so spooked his horse that he was nearly thrown into the icy river.

The great shining heights of our trip stand in stark contrast to the early months of 1987 back in New York. That was a time of preparation and planning, the tedium of which was thankfully lost in the euphoria of optimism as Julith and I readied ourselves and our bodies for the trip. We got shot up against various diseases, took a Red Cross first-aid course. We stocked up on pills for malaria (Aralen) and dysentery (Bactrim), and purchased a backpacker's compact Katadyne water filter to go with the rest of our camping gear. We lovingly shuffled and sifted and reshuffled our libraries to come up with the three dozen or so books that would comprise our traveling bookshelf. They would be stored alongside our trip bible—the indispensable *South American Handbook*—and assorted writerly paraphernalia, which in my case included a portable word processor and in Julith's a thick sheaf of black-and-white marbled composition books. We sorted through our clothes, trying to come up with a modest traveling closet that would still serve us during every conceivable season and at every conceivable elevation between Tijuana and Tierra del Fuego.

All of this, along with spare auto parts and a few keepsakes, we stuffed into one large steamer trunk, one medium-size trunk, a footlocker, and a spill-proof plastic box in the back of what had been our first trip purchase: a new Toyota Land Cruiser station wagon, the workhorse that is to Central and South America what the Land Rover is to Africa. It was big and plain white, sturdy and strictly utilitarian. A colleague at work immediately dubbed it "the War Wagon."

We ignored recommendations from alarmists that we pack a gun or at least a large dog, deeming each unnecessary and a terrible nuisance at customs checkpoints. We rejected another suggestion as impractical, although it makes a kind of sense if you want a weapon that can get by customs inspectors: a skin diver's spear gun. We did bring a four-foot-long "cheater bar"—a heavy piece of pipe that, among its less bellicose properties, can extend the length of a normal tire iron and greatly improve one's leverage when removing frozen lug nuts along Peruvian "roads" that used to be railroad track beds.

We slogged through a swamp of paperwork. International driver's licenses (two kinds, neither of them essential insofar as we could determine). International auto insurance (expensive). Health certificates (never requested). Health insurance (never used). A carnet for the War Wagon (think of it as an automobile passport issued by the American Automobile Association).

The bikes—yes, Julith's ten-speed and my eighteen-speed modified mountain bike had to be part of the deal— would go on the roof of the Toyota. We checked with cycling outfitters across the country and found no carrier that would protect them to our satisfaction. So we settled on our old Thule rack, and Julith set out to design weatherproof bike covers. The idea was terrific: a heavy, custom-made vinyl sheath that could be slipped over a bike and laced up on the one open side like a shoe. When the canvasmaker in lower Manhattan showed us the final product, we were convinced that when we came back we could live off the income our brilliant design would surely generate. Then came the trial run.

Dateline: Ashfield, Mass. A glorious early-spring day in the Berkshire foothills. Within a few hundred yards, we learned that our brilliant design would not quite do for a twenty-thousand-mile trip. The snug-fitting sheaths turned out to be more seaworthy than roadworthy, less like covers and, in a crosswind, more like twin sails: when the War Wagon got up to about fifty miles per hour, Julith's tenspeed heeled precipitously, snapped the bike rack, and wound up splayed against the car roof like a big dead bug. Our relatives saw no humor in our suggestion that our creations would make good body bags in case we needed them on the trip. We have found, however, that the handsome sleeves (gray with white canvas trim, brass grommets, and red parachute-cord lacing) make nice covers for porch furniture. The bicycles would go to Buenos Aires uncovered.

We felt lucky just to be doing what we were doing— and we were doing it the easy way. In the 1920s, Aimé Félix Tschiffely, the Swiss headmaster at an English high school in Buenos Aires, rode from Argentina to Washington, D.C.—on horseback (two horses, actually, Mancha and Gato, to whom he dedicated the account of his journey). In the 1950s, an American couple drove an amphibious jeep from Alaska to the Southern Cone. More to the point, every month thousands of Central Americans and Mexicans in search of work make their way to the United States by foot and bus. Still, to some of our friends and family our trip seemed flighty and irresponsible. At least this book project helped give the whole enterprise a grownup sheen.

Another bit of luck came as we spent our final days in the States. Arriving at Julith's parents' house in the mountains outside Boulder, we learned that *Newsweek* had been trying to reach me. This is almost never good news. For me, the words "phone call from *Newsweek*" have the same mnemonic quality as "dentist's drill." At home in Los Angeles in 1978 and 1979, getting that call meant packing, rushing to the airport, and grabbing the Pan Am flight to Managua to see what kind of damage the Sandinistas were inflicting on Anastasio Somoza, the Nicaraguan dictator.

Now, in Boulder, I could feel my stomach tighten reflexively, and I wasn't even in the magazine's employ anymore. As it turned out, it was Bob Rivard, our chief of correspondents, with of all things a job offer: I could take off for nearly a year and return to the magazine as bureau chief in Mexico City. I had planned to be gone for eighteen months and was prepared to spend another six writing at home in Massachusetts. But the prospect of a paycheck, of a job I wanted, of reporting again seemed too good to turn down. Julith agreed. A little subdream—living and writing for six months on a small mountain ranch in Argentina— evanesced: there would no longer be time for that. But, we consoled ourselves, living in Mexico City would be like prolonging the trip beyond even two years. I told Bob yes. We said our good-byes in Boulder on a sparkling morning in June 1987, and headed south.

We followed the Rio Grande toward Mexico. A couple of nights after we left Boulder we camped deep in a New Mexican pine forest near Coyote, between Los Alamos and Cuba. We got to the forest by guessing our way through a network of brick red logging roads, mostly dry but still deeply rutted after a recent downpour. We thought we were at least alone, if not lost. After dark we were set straight.

They sounded at first like giant mechanical beetles chewing their way toward us through the pine. It was a beery caravan of high-riding pickups, the kind the good ol' boys race on a muddy steeplechase on Sunday afternoons in the Lower Rio Grande Valley of Texas. Darting, crossing laserlike beams from unseen headlamps turned the woods into an eerie outdoor discotheque. There was even music. From souped-up tape decks, it faded in and out as the machines negotiated the bewildering crosshatch of loggers' roads. Finally the rains came again and sent the machines skulking back to some distant 7-Eleven for more beer.

The next night we spent in Truth or Consequences, New Mexico, in a typical American roadside motel. Tomorrow we would cross into Mexico. The traffic along I-25 was a steady buzz, too close by. The neon sign of a twenty-four-hour diner flashed metronomically through our window. The room cost us twenty-seven dollars. After a few months on the road, that would strike me as an outrageous amount of money to pay for a night anywhere. Only two or three times on the whole trip would we fork over that much money for a bed. The room had a hospital-clean, antiseptic smell that undoubtedly masked the presence of Legionnaires' disease in the clickety-clacking air conditioner.

A dog-eared brochure on top of the dresser explained how Truth or Consequences got its name. It used to be called Hot Springs. Before there was an I-25, other highways were siphoning off the tourists to other resort towns. Down on its luck, in 1950 Hot Springs made a Faustian bargain with the popular radio show *Truth or Consequences*. As part of a promotional stunt designed to benefit both parties, Hot Springs changed its name and the show's host, Ralph Edwards, did one show from there to celebrate *Truth or Consequences'* tenth year on the air.

By noon on June 16, 1987, we had left behind the Siamese sprawl of El Paso, Texas–Ciudad Juárez, Chihuahua. Soon high walls painted with the word *yonke* (border Spanish for "junk") gave way to . . . nothing. The land there spreads like some impossibly bleak khaki canvas between the two branches of Mexico's Sierra Madre. Deprived of the water that lies to the north—water harnessed by U.S. engineers to coax life out of the Southwestern deserts of California and Arizona—the Chihuahua badlands, like most of northern Mexico, are grim-looking territory. Lonely stone walls wander aimlessly up and down burnt hills. The walls announce some purpose: it must be livestock, but the closest thing to livestock we came across was a horse carcass by the side of the road. A sign insisted that, against all odds, out there somewhere was a ranch called El Milagro (The Miracle). We were on our way.

CHAPTER TWO
Guatemala: The Army's Road

OUR SECOND DAY in the country, we catch our first glimpse of the generals at work in their new Guatemala: a sham democracy in which an elected president basks, if only for the time being, in the international public-relations lime-light while behind the scenes, in the shadowy recesses, the generals pull the strings of power. We had sped through Mexico in a mere three weeks, knowing we would return there to live, and crossed the border into the deepening green of Guatemala. It's July, and the rains are in full bloom. Brief periods of sunshine in the morning give way to strangely thunderless but drenching storms in the afternoon that fill arroyos to foaming and so drench the roads that they seem slick with ice.

We sight the new Guatemala on our way from Huehue-tenango to Chichicastenango. We are driving along a wind-ing eleven-mile stretch of road that leads from the Pan American Highway north to Chichicastenango, the market hub of the Quiché-speaking highland Indians. We spot a band of what at first look like hunters. They are one of the civil defense patrols—the *autodefensas*—outfitted by the army with old but not yet harmless rifles. They are the new first line of defense against the guerrillas who are still making it this far south from their mountain bases. Like the presidential sash fastened to the chest of an elected civilian, these "people's patrols" help bolster the notion that popular rule has supplanted the bad old days when the army would put a general of its own in the president's office and send its own patrols out to battle the guerrillas.

In fact, much less has changed in Guatemala than meets the eye. Every move we make to the north and east of the Pan American Highway brings us closer to areas that were fought over bloodily just a few years ago. The only sign of the army we've seen so far was a troop carrier speeding by in Huehuetenango. Up the road from Chichicastenango we pass our first military base, at Santa Cruz del Quiché, the department seat. There's just a suggestion of extraordinary alertness: machine guns in the watchtowers, soldiers on guard duty dressed in battle fatigues. The areas north and east of here have the feel of an old battleground: homes that are still abandoned, a skittishness among the people in the smaller towns. Rebel slogans hurriedly painted on walls on the outskirts of Santa Cruz del Quiché have faded a bit. So too have the signs of tension. But the tension is there still, and so too are the rebels.

Santo Tomás Chiché, an Indian town, is east of Santa Cruz del Quiché, a mestizo town. On the road into town we pass a number of civil defense guard posts, pretty blue-and-white Guatemalan flags fluttering in the breeze. Closer to town is a schoolhouse; two hands painted on the wall, one light and one dark, clasped in a handshake, announce that this building was a project of John F. Kennedy's Alliance for Progress. (The handshake is a perfect symbol for American bounty and bumptious goodwill. There's something about a firm handshake that seems so very gringo in the more Indian countries of Latin America. When a Quiché gives you his hand, it's limp and reaches yours with some tentativeness, as if he fears you might be taking something from him.)

We've come to Santo Tomás Chiché for the Saturday market, which will be shutting down by two o'clock, in time for the afternoon rains. Corn and potatoes, peaches and apples, pigs and goats tethered by their owners. The market—the fact that it is taking place—is a sign of the cautious revival of this town. In 1981 more than half the townspeople of Chiché fled the fighting around them. A young man in a "California" T-shirt—two uncles of his are working without papers in the United States—tells us the story. Those who fled took what they could and went to Santa Cruz del Quiché, or to the Pacific Coast to work on the banana plantations, leaving their homes behind; the people who stayed watched after them. Two to three years later they began to come back.

The army has organized the men into civil defense patrols. They serve three times a month, a twenty-four-hour shift, always out in pairs. The army gives them weapons, often rattletraps that are at least as dangerous to the user as to the target. But the weapons are nonetheless a token of trust, another calculated strand in the web of seeming cooperation between the army and the people. There are places where the situation is still too delicate to give the autodefensa patrols any kind of weapon. Even armed, though, these ragged patrols are no match for a guerrilla column moving down from the mountains. The patrols serve as a kind of human DEW line—a distant early warning of rebel movement. And if the guerrillas are stupid enough or pressed enough to mow them down, the army scores another point by shoving a wedge of enmity between the townspeople and the guerrillas. Thus far it has been an effective, if cynical, strategy.

Chichicastenango, an appealing mountain town with grand views through shifting clouds, is more than just a trading center. It reflects the cultural schizophrenia that has settled over the Quiché highlands. The town is caught in a sordid tug-of-war over who will dominate the culture of Chichicastenango: the Indians, who are not so far removed from their Mayan past; the ladinos, Guatemala's mestizos who dominate the commercial class; and the tourists, who swarm obstreperously up in shiny buses from Guatemala City and Antigua at the weekend to rummage through tented Indian market stalls and ladino-run curio shops.

The town has the solid feel of a mercantile crossroads: houses built to last in the near-permanent foggy chill at 6,795 feet, the bustle of goods and money trading hands. But the image that lingers is this: on the broad plaza between two churches—Santo Tomás and Calvario—the Quiché women, famously able merchants, running their market stalls like tight little ships; off to the side, sometimes even at the women's feet, a Quiché man lying rumpled at the curb, wasted by aguardiente, the ethyl alcohol distilled from cane sugar.

Inside the Iglesia de Santo Tomás, the religious syncretism that we will see throughout our journey is in evidence. In church, the Mayan traditions—chanting in Quiché, the burning of native wood, pre-Columbian reliquary—over-power the veneer of Catholicism. But in the tourism-driven economy, the Quiché Indians come out on bottom. At the Mayan Inn, an otherwise admirable and attractive hostelry run by ladinos, each room distastefully comes with its personal Quiché houseboy. Our "boy"—they are indeed called *muchachos* by the management, as in, "Your boy will help you with your bags"—is older than I. He dresses in black knee breeches, an embroidered short-waisted jacket in red, a sash of woven cloth, and a boldly colored kerchief around his head. It is traditional garb, and quite handsome, but in the context of a hotel it seems a costume. He will serve us at our table. At the dinner hour, between trips to the kitchen, he will pad back to our room to get a wood fire going in our fireplace and turn on our lights. (When we retire for the evening, we will notice from our window that only one house in view has electricity.)

It's a one-and-a-half-hour walk along a well-worn foot-path from Chichicastenango to the village of Quiejel, up and down ravines amidst dripping-wet foliage. Halfway there, we encounter an autodefensa patrol of three men. They ask us why we're on our walk and when we'll be coming back. A little later we cross paths with another man, who strikes up a brief conversation. He wants to know three things: if we've talked to the patrol, where we're from, and whether we've accepted the Gospel. The last question is not so unusual in the Guatemalan countryside, where the evan-gelical movement, inspired and often funded by missionary organizations in the United States, has been waging its own, peaceable guerrilla war. It has made tremendous in-roads into nominally Catholic territory. In Chichicasten-ango, there are several storefront fundamentalist churches;

on a quiet evening they can be found easily by listening for the hymns—in Spanish, no chanting in a Mayan tongue here. Jimmy Swaggart—not yet fallen from grace for his sexual antics—is a fixture on TV, his histrionics expertly interpreted.

Just about when Quiejel is in sight, we meet up with a boy named Tomás José Ordóñez. We're looking for a soft drink, and Tomás guides us to the highland equivalent of a 7-Eleven convenience store for this village of four hundred people. The woman who runs it carts her merchandise over from Chichicastenango: yarn, handkerchiefs, Mejoral aspirin, snacks. We buy a bottle of Canada Dry club soda for one quetzal. (The quetzal, named for the extravagantly beautiful Guatemalan national bird, is worth thirty-eight cents; until two years ago it was on a par with the dollar.) In a small courtyard, near a woman sorting through beans, a barefoot baby, dressed in a T-shirt emblazoned with the Puma tennis shoes logo, plays with a rattle. Up against one shaded wall, snoring in loud, TV-cartoon sputterings, two Quiché men are passed out beside an empty bottle of Quetzalteca Especial aguardiente. It's not quite noon.

The woman behind the counter wears the traditional huipil, an embroidered blouse, and a wraparound skirt of woven wool, long and slender. Though more and more synthetic fabrics and dyes are being used, the design of each piece of clothing is a telltale; at the very least, it identifies the village the wearer comes from. (The army, in fact, has been trained to identify different huipiles as a way of monitoring Indian movements from town to town.) All the Quiché women we have seen wear pretty much what Quiché women have worn over the centuries. The men are much less resolute in carrying on such traditions. For years they have traveled by bus and truck seeking seasonal work—down to the coastal lowlands to pick coffee or bananas; following the sugarcane harvest between August and January—and so have mingled more with the ladino culture. For comfort in the coastal heat, but also yielding to pressure to conform to ladino ways, the Quiché men have all but abandoned their traditional clothing except at ceremonial occasions or to please the tourists who have come to see authentic Indian garb.

Before he died, Tomás's father worked the cane fields every year. Almost certainly Tomás will too. Tomás, who is eleven years old, says his father died of *calambre,* a catchall term for any number of stomach disorders. From his father, Tomás inherited a small parcel of land and an ax. He lives with his mother, who tends seventy-five chickens and a bean field. Tomás quit school to set himself up in a small business. With his ax he scavenges the badly deforested hills for wood. He bundles the wood into a load the size of an adult's backpack. Six days a week he hefts a bundle onto his back, holds it in place with a traditional cloth sling braced high up on his forehead at the hairline, and carries it up and down the trail into Chichicastenango, where he sells the firewood door to door. Doing this, Tomás makes about twelve quetzales a week. An ax costs about twenty-two quetzales.

On our walk back into Chichicastenango we run into our autodefensa friends again. Now that the element of surprise is absent from these encounters, this patrol looks to us like a small troop of superannuated Boy Scouts. Except for the guns. The patrol has grown to four men. Three carry old bolt-action Mausers. One carries a twelve-gauge shotgun. They tell us that the army, whose standard infantry rifle is the Israeli-made Galil automatic, rations ammunition to them in small quantities. That worries them, should they ever have to shoot it out with the guerrillas. (Their fears are well founded. The army, however, is not about to arm the civil patrols well enough to create a potential threat to its own troops, nor does it want large quantities of ammo or good weapons falling into the hands of the guerrillas.) In the manner of someone uncomfortable with his own authority, the patrol leader informs us that he must ask us to do something that he forgot earlier. He gives us a green Bic pen and schoolboy's notebook, and entreats us to write down our names and passport numbers.

Among those of us who have covered Central America since the late 1970s, Guatemala has always loomed as an especially dark and foreboding place. When the civil war in Nicaragua ended, in 1979, many of us expected that the next war would have us working out of Guatemala City. We ended up going to San Salvador instead, but we still expected Guatemala to blow sky-high. Then came elections and the chimerical democracy that bought time and international prestige for the Guatemalan generals. None of this has diminished the sense that someday the tensions coiled so tightly beneath the surface in Guatemala will find a bloody release.

Guatemala looks the part. The countryside gets very remote very fast. The year the CIA helped to overthrow the reformist government of Jacobo Arbenz Guzmán—1954—American military cartographers provided detailed aerial photographs to Guatemala's National Geographic Institute. The resulting contour maps are handsome portraits: tight gnarls and broad swirls capture every rise and fall from the banana plantations along the narrow coastal lowlands of the Pacific Coast, across the cragged highlands, and on to the two great valleys that swoop down through old banana lands to the Gulf of Honduras and the Caribbean. Even at a scale of 1:50,000, the maps only begin to suggest the ruggedness and remove that one encounters in Guatemala.

How remote? Two months before we crossed the border into Guatemala on July 9, President Vinicio Cerezo needed to send some troops from Guatemala City to Playa Grande, in an area where leftist rebels were still active. He asked the United States to provide helicopter transport. (He said Guatemala's entire fleet was out of service; whether it really was or wasn't, the claim is nonetheless credible.) To move the troops by truck would take eighteen hours, he said. Playa Grande is eighty-five miles north of the capital—closer than Philadelphia is to New York. And the rainy season, when roads are often washed out, had not yet begun.

Guatemala is, after Bolivia, the most Indian of Latin American countries. Most of its nine million people are confined to a southern strip of lowlands and highlands no wider than one hundred miles. Nearly one in every five Guatemalans lives in or around the capital; no other city is even a tenth the size of Guatemala City. In the north, no more than fifty thousand people inhabit the undulating mesa of El Petén, the ancient Mayan lands that comprise one-third of Guatemalan territory: twenty-three thousand square miles. Step outside Guatemala City, the cobbled tidiness of Antigua (the old capital of colonial Central America), or the populated corridor along the Pan American Highway, and you slip into another Guatemala, into a place of Conradian darkness.

* * *

May 10, 1987. On the eve of our trip into Guatemala, another Amnesty International report on Guatemala: In twenty years of military rule prior to the democratic election of President Cerezo last year, a hundred thousand Guatemalans were killed for political reasons; another thirty-eight thousand disappeared. This in a country with a population roughly equivalent to that of metropolitan Paris. Most of the deaths are attributed to right-wing death squads and the military's counterinsurgency campaign against a quarter-century-old leftist guerrilla movement. "Human rights remain at risk," says the Amnesty International report.

The traveler, as a rule, is not at risk. Most travelers won't even see the thuggish side of Guatemala, much less be affected by it. The Guatemala they see is the Guatemala after the beating. The army and its paramilitary allies did their dirty work behind closed doors for a while. Now they've opened the doors: See? Nothing. It can especially seem that way since the army decided to camouflage its airtight control of Guatemala by dressing up the country in the smart suit of democracy. They let Cerezo be elected instead of assassinating him, or allowing the civilian right to do the job (the right had tried to kill Cerezo several times). They toned down the gunplay. They still run the country, but in a less outlaw way.

The last time I was in Guatemala, in 1981, the country was in its dark ages. That year I reported some things about right-wing activity in Guatemala that the government did not approve of. Some weeks after I left Guatemala and *Newsweek* published the story, a colleague of mine, George Nathanson, who at the time was doing work for CBS, was detained on arrival at the international airport in Guatemala City. He was taken to a small office staffed by G-2, the army's intelligence apparatus, questioned, and sent out of the country on the next plane. While he was at the airport, Nathanson saw his name on a list that G-2 kept, and he saw mine, in the *M*'s, right above his. Word got around that this was some kind of death list. It wasn't. It just meant that I could not get back into Guatemala until the government changed and the blacklist was forgotten by the new regime.

This time around I am seeing a lot less of the classic bullyboy behavior of a Latin American dictatorship than I expected. I had read that there were four military checkpoints between La Mesilla, on the Mexican border, and Huehuetenango. They are gone. Gone, too, are the bridge sentries along the Pan American Highway; they used to be posted there to ward off guerrilla demolition teams. Now what we see is the fading pastiche of democracy come and gone: on the boulders, trees, and telephone poles of Huehuetenango department and neighboring Quiché, guerrilla slogans compete with electoral graffiti left over from last year's presidential campaign.

But for all the worthy intentions and dogged patriotism of Vinicio Cerezo and the rest of Guatemala's nonviolent opposition, this army-issue democracy is a sham. The country knows better than to trust the army. The country is wary—as wary as President Cerezo, who beneath his suit jacket packs a .45 in a shoulder holster.

I first met Vinicio Cerezo in March of 1981. Earlier that same day I met the man who Vinicio said tried to have him killed. Mario Sandóval Alarcón was then the head of the National Liberation Movement (MLN). In the surreal world of Guatemalan politics, the MLN was not the leftist organization its name suggested it might be. It was far to the right, a paramilitary group that itself claimed to be nothing less than "the party of organized violence."

I was to meet Sandoval Alarcón at party headquarters. The place was eery. You half expected a film director to stand up and yell, "Cut! Take five!"; the actors would then turn their weapons in to the prop manager and go on a coffee break. This was the headquarters of a political mafia; there was no attempt to make it look like anything else. Thugs whom slicker Central American right-wingers would have disguised as "aides" carried sawed-off shotguns, shouldered M-16s, or had Uzis slung loosely, waist-high. Lookouts, pistols jammed jauntily in their belts, leaned against doorframes.

This was before image making ruled in Guatemala, before the generals got p.r. religion. His followers even called Sandoval Alarcón "the Godfather." Being the Godfather of the party of organized violence would have been sinister enough. But Sandoval Alarcón had throat cancer. The doctors had operated, and now he had to talk through a voice box—hoarsely, over a bass electronic hum. We met downstairs. Sandoval Alarcón was wearing a jacket and tie. His shirt was open at the neck to accommodate his voice box; from a distance, the protruding bit of voice box gave the impression he was wearing a bulletproof vest. His hair was slicked back, he had a trimmed mustache, and there was something about his eyes that made him look permanently surprised. As Sandoval Alarcón escorted me upstairs to his office, we filed past a murky, windowless chapel lighted only by votive candles.

It got stranger.

At a landing halfway up the stairway I was confronted with a likeness of none other than my own new president, Ronald Reagan. Hung on the wall was a poster from the movie *Bedtime for Bonzo:* the Hollywood Reagan feeding a chimpanzee with a baby bottle. Printed on the poster was a slogan, in English: THERE IS A SIMPLE SOLUTION FOR EVERY PROBLEM.

Sandoval Alarcón approved of the White House Reagan. He had celebrated the night of Reagan's election four months before. Some Guatemalan rightists even hired a band to serenade the marine guards over at the American embassy on Avenida La Reforma. The marines could also hear fireworks going off in celebration outside large homes in Zona 10, one of Guatemala City's poshest neighborhoods—which must have been unsettling in a city where such staccato outbursts, though not unfamiliar, usually suggest darker events than a U.S. presidential election.

Sandoval Alarcón spoke venomously of Jimmy Carter. Carter, who long after Reagan was gone would continue to be warmly regarded around most of Latin America for his adherence to a strict human-rights policy, cut off U.S. military aid to Guatemala in 1977 to punish the government for political assassinations, disappearances, jailings, and torturings. Sandoval Alarcón would have liked Reagan to resume military aid. Some of Sandoval Alarcón's more p.r.-oriented friends, members of a business association called Friends of the Country, hoped the aid spigot might reopen if they improved their country's image. To better the odds, they retained the services of the consulting firm where Michael Deaver, perhaps Reagan's closest aide in the White House, had been a partner.

Sandoval Alarcón was not big on public relations. The

language of public relations was too soft to convey the hard facts of his world. His world was a Manichaean one. Some of his critics doubtless saw Guatemala in the same way. They disagreed strongly with the Godfather, however, about the side he chose to be on. Sandoval Alarcón almost certainly must have been heartened when Reagan, later in his presidency, would characterize the Soviet Union as an "evil empire." He was on the same side as Reagan in the superpower "Star Wars" (and with his Darth Vaderesque voice, he fit the bill). Sandoval Alarcón's world left no room for doubt or mealymouthing. Reagan was a hero. Carter, to Sandoval Alarcón, was Fidel Carter. Cerezo was a Communist.

It didn't take Sandoval Alarcón long to summarize his Weltanschauung for me. But the logical conclusion of what he'd told me wasn't really clear until he walked me back downstairs. We didn't turn to the right, past the chapel and out onto the street. We turned to the left. We went down the hall to an interior courtyard. On the far side was a wall. Names were painted on the wall in six-inch-high block letters. Who were they? Party traitors, Sandoval Alarcón told me. And what—even as I asked the question, the scary answer was forming in my thoughts: I was pointing at names that had been crossed off the wall, like milk or eggs on a grocery list—what about those names?

Sandoval Alarcón: "They were forgiven."

Somebody had tried to "forgive" Vinicio Cerezo a couple of weeks before, on Saint Valentine's Day. When I saw Cerezo that night, after my meeting with Sandoval Alarcón, he said it was the MLN who had tried to rub him out. He was at an intersection, inside a car, when men opened fire on him from other cars. Police squad cars parked down the street didn't budge. Cerezo's car sped away.

Cerezo and I were meeting in one of the safe houses he used in those days in Guatemala City. It was a nondescript house in a middle-class neighborhood. Charming and good-looking—an all too facile contrast to Sandoval Alarcón, frankly—he still exuded the boyish enthusiasm of a political idealist; by the late 1980s, that quality would be drained from him, and a sour, hangdog expression would find its way into his photographs. We talked not only about assassination attempts, but also about the Guatemalan army's increasingly sophisticated counterinsurgency tactics that were being used against the radical guerrilla left. Under tutelage from the Argentine military, at that time in the last stages of the Dirty War, the Guatemalans were using computers to track down guerrilla cells in the capital by identifying residences that had abnormally high electricity bills: the manufacture of explosives consumes a lot of power. As for the nonviolent opposition, Cerezo saw doors closing on every possible democratic solution to his country's plight at the hands of the generals. "I have spent seventeen years looking for a democratic solution," he said. "But when one is not listened to and when one is threatened constantly, one begins to despair."

The dragnet that nearly swept up Cerezo was part of a purge being carried out by the government of Gen. Romeo Lucas García, who came to power in 1978. Between late 1980 and early 1982, 238 members of Cerezo's Christian Democratic Party had disappeared. Lucas had openly drafted into this war not just the army but also paramilitary groups. There was a brutal candor to what was happening.

Guatemala was already isolated internationally, the military already cut off from its U.S. gravy train. Forget public relations. So one of the death squads called itself the Death Squad, and a secret anti-Communist army called itself the Secret Anti-Communist Army. At one point, the federal government was even issuing press releases for these groups: between January and October of 1979, the police announced shortly thereafter, the Death Squad had killed 1,224 "criminals" and the Secret Anti-Communist Army 3,252 "subversives."

It was in 1979 that the military decided to assassinate two of Guatemala's most prominent opposition politicians. Alberto Fuentes Mohr, a former foreign minister, had recently registered his new Social Democratic Party; he was machine-gunned to death as he drove by a military base in the capital. Manuel Colom Argueta, a former mayor of Guatemala City, had just registered his own new center-left party; he was murdered on a busy downtown street while a helicopter hovered overhead.

The arms-bearing opposition, and its supporters in the countryside and anybody else who got in the way, would feel the brunt of Lucas's campaign. The leftist insurgency in Guatemala was the oldest in Latin America, and yet by the end of Lucas's regime, the number of leftist guerrillas would be cut back from its high of ten thousand to two thousand. That's one set of figures. Another would place the guerrillas' historical maximum strength at six thousand, the low at three thousand. Yet another estimate placed guerrilla strength at only eight hundred by the end of the eighties.

Nobody knows which of these numbers—if any—are accurate. Taken together, they suggest the chaos of Guatemala during the eighties. Taken separately, as they were promulgated, they seemed oddly reassuring in their precision—to the government, to the populace, to journalists. The numbers gave the impression that somebody really had a sense of what was going on in Guatemala. In fact, nobody did. Beyond the numbers lay the grim, seemingly unstoppable reality that Guatemala's rulers were inflicting upon their own people: wave after wave of political violence.

Blatant fraud in the 1982 elections persuaded junior officers in the military to overthrow Lucas. They installed a provisional junta to run the country. Efraín Ríos Montt, who headed the junta, was a general and a fundamentalist Christian, and he brought down on Guatemala his own peculiar mix of the cross and the sword. Urban violence receded a bit as he concentrated his efforts on the war against the leftists in the countryside. Two years later, having alienated senior officers by disdaining the traditional army hierarchy, Ríos Montt was ousted by the military, his main legacy being the civilian defense patrols. His defense minister, Gen. Oscar Humberto Mejía Victores, took his place.

The army changed course. The debilitating coups were threatening its own ranks. The economy was deteriorating fast; internal turmoil and the stench of repression were scaring off foreign investors, hobbling the domestic economy, and keeping U.S. aid at bay even under Ronald Reagan. Besides, the leftist guerrilla movement was a smoldering shell of what it had been.

The army reasoned that with Reagan riding high and about to begin a second term in office, it could make the Guatemalan government an appealing repository for U.S. aid once again by slapping on a fresh coat of democracy.

Presidential elections were set for November 3, 1985. Even when it became clear that their candidate would lose to Cerezo, the generals allowed the process to go forward. They gambled that their power was so entrenched that no mere civilian government could uproot it and that, moreover, their mailed fist could be more effective if slipped into the velvet glove of democracy. It was a safe bet. Within two years, U.S. military aid to Guatemala was back up to pre-Carter levels. The generals had learned well the art of public relations.

Immediately following the Chichicastenango section in our *South American Handbook* there is this note:

> WARNING. In the Quiché region N of Chichicastenango there is still sporadic guerrilla activity N of Nebaj, but it is reported that the situation is improving. The main towns (Chichicastenango, Santa Cruz del Quiché, Sacapulas, Nebaj, etc.) are again safe to visit.

I like the idea of getting into an area that's a little rawer than what we've been seeing. I even like the idea of "sporadic guerrilla activity" as long as a lull coincides with our visit. Mostly, however, I like the "again safe" part. I've heard about Nebaj. My image of Nebaj is that it stands at the edge of something, a place along a border between the known and the unknown. What we've seen so far in Huehuetenango and Quiché departments has afforded us glimpses of the army's war on the left during the early 1980s and of the spruced-up counterinsurgency strategy being carried out in the late 1980s under the cover of the army-issue democracy. From Nebaj, out there on the edge, we should get a better view.

Nebaj will take some planning. We'll need good maps, sound advice, and some names. We'll need to lighten the load in the Toyota and deposit the bikes somewhere. We'll need water and a few emergency provisions. As if to strike a particularly discordant note to the Nebaj leg of the trip— which will be our last major foray in Guatemala—we've chosen Antigua as the place to do our planning.

Most Latin American countries have their own version of Antigua. The countries that don't—war-torn cases like Nicaragua or economic basket cases like Bolivia—are the exceptions that prove the rule. In Mexico the place used to be Cuernavaca; now it's San Miguel de Allende. In Ecuador it's Cuenca. In Peru it's Cuzco (although the xenophobic Sendero Luminoso guerrillas are trying to change that). If the country doesn't have a city to fit the bill, the capital will have a neighborhood that will do. There will be an ancient church on every corner, a language school (usually called an "institute"), a tavern that has a name like Harry's American Bar, a restaurant that serves hamburgers and pizzas just like home (and is usually filled with Scandinavian students whose packs, practically the size of Denmark, take up half the seats). You know those ridiculous strips of paper some hotels still insist on looping around the toilet seat? So that when you check into your room you'll see the strip of paper and the word "Sanitized" in friendly, cursive letters and you'll feel safe and comfortable? Antigua is a "Sanitized" city: safe for tourists.

The other thing about these places is that they tend to be quite pleasant, historically interesting—and reassuringly ordered, a welcome comfort to the road traveler. When we drive into Antigua, workmen are kneeling reverently over cobblestones, refitting them into their original pattern. After some bouncing around among crowded hotels, we end up staying at, and very much liking, the Aurora, with inexpensive rooms around a courtyard of flowers. Down the street is the Panadería y Pastelería Doña Luisa Xicotencatl, which is, understandably, just called Doña Luisa's. If you're secretly and somewhat self-consciously looking for an ethnic break—and want to read a two-day-old *New York Times* over your pancakes—it's worth navigating the sea of backpacks and piled-high language-institute texts to find a berth there. More to the point, for us, across the street from Doña Luisa's we find a cubbyhole of a bookstore with photocopies of the Nebaj-area contour maps we've been looking for.

The bookstore is owned by a Brit of long-standing residence in Guatemala, Mike Shawcross. Shawcross runs a foundation that works with the Quiché Indians of the highlands, who, as we saw in Santo Tomás Chiché, are often caught in the crossfire between the army and the various guerrilla groups. He's knowledgeable about the Ixil Triangle, in which Nebaj is located, and is a good and patient briefer. Because of his work, and because fund-raising for Third World foundations and dealing with sometimes corrupt bureaucrats in-country can be a tricky business, Shawcross has had to fade a lot of heat; he's been accused of being everything from a guerrilla sympathizer to a government spy. I figure that anybody whose only request is that I take clothing, good shovels, and plastic soccer balls on his behalf up to the Quiché of Nebaj can't be all bad.

In the darkest days of Guatemala's war on the guerrillas, whole areas of the country were closed off to outsiders.

Thus curtained off, the army during the Lucas regime of 1978–82 blazed across northern Guatemala in an all-out and indiscriminate effort to wipe out the rebel forces. The idea was not just to hunt down the guerrillas and eliminate them, but in addition to deprive them of fresh recruits, food supplies, and any other support they might be getting. This meant going after peasants, villagers, and townspeople—not only in the deep mountain fastnesses in the roadless northwest where the guerrillas had their bases, but also along a broad swath of more populated highland communities. These were areas through which the rebels passed on their way to raids on military outposts. They were areas from which the rebels might get food or horses or new men and women willing to take up arms against the government. It meant evacuating whole mountains and deep-cut valleys, torching village after village to leave no haven for the rebels and to leave nothing standing for the villagers to come home to. It meant killing those who resisted the army, and it meant exposing to guerrilla reprisal those who obeyed the army. It was a classic scorched-earth military strategy, and it included the Ixil Triangle.

People poured out of the highlands. Most stayed as close to home as they could, settling at least temporarily in squalid camps outside the larger towns, the traditional market hubs like Nebaj and Santa Cruz del Quiché. Many went further—into cities like Huehuetenango or Quetzaltenango, or down to the coast, or on into Guatemala City, where already a fifth of the country's population lived. The exodus spilled over into Mexico: by the mid-1980s there were in Mexico two hundred thousand or more Guatemalans who had fled for political or economic reasons.

Perhaps a tenth of the Guatemalans who have fled their

country over the last decade are still, in 1989, biding their time in a string of refugee camps in Chiapas on the Mexican side of the border. When I spent some time there in 1988, after our trip, the Guatemalans told me that most of them had come from the northwest corner of Huehuetenango, an area of softly rolling, lush green hills. People from different communities and language groups have been jumbled together, and as a result the children grow up speaking, in addition to Spanish, at least two Mayan dialects to be able to communicate in the camps. The Mexican topography is familiar to the Guatemalans, and many Mexican Indians in the neighboring communities speak the same Mayan dialects as the Guatemalans. The twenty-odd camps are much less grim than other refugee way stations around the world. Some of the smaller camps—tidy pole huts with corrugated-tin roofs clustered around two-room schoolhouses, a rushing stream below and pale green hills above—look a little too much like exhibits at that sad tourism invention, the living museum.

These Guatemalans, hoping their stay here is as temporary as the camps look, wait for word that it is safe to go home. But the hope and promise that blew across Guatemala with Cerezo's election is fading, and they feel it. Many, especially the younger men and women, have stopped looking to the south. They look instead to the north—to Mexico and, beyond, to the United States. That is where they see their future. And little wonder.

Guatemala has been building to this sorry state since 1954. The United States was wary about the rise to power of any government displaying the slightest tilt toward Communist ideology. The new Guatemalan government of Jacobo Arbenz, elected in 1950, aroused suspicion in Washington. President Arbenz, an army colonel, was not himself cut from radical cloth. He was a left-leaning reformer who had enough sense of history to know that his country needed to undertake serious land reform in order to stave off serious unrest in the future. (The Agrarian Census of 1950 had established that 70 percent of the arable land was in the hands of 2 percent of the landowners.) But Arbenz's wife was a Communist, and his agrarian-reform department employed a militant young leftist by the name of Ernesto ("Che") Guevara. More to the point, the Arbenz government began expropriating vast, albeit unused, banana lands belonging to the United Fruit Company, which in those days wielded inordinate political and economic power in Central America and the Caribbean.

In June of 1954 Guatemalan exiles supported by the CIA invaded their homeland and easily overthrew Arbenz, triggering a ruthless struggle between the left and the right and polarizing the country more and more with each passing assassination and coup. The army, mimicking the McCarthyist witch-hunt then going on in the United States, scoured records of groups that had supported Arbenz and compiled lists of seventy thousand people whom they classified as Communists. On the basis of such enemies lists, updated and refined over the years, the military conducted its purges of the left. It did so with a vengeance. "There are no political prisoners in Guatemala, only political murders," a former vice-president of the country, Francisco Villagrán Kramer, once commented.

The Marxist-led guerrilla movement took root in the early 1960s. Over the next decade, the army badly defeated the rebels and reduced their numbers, but could not wipe them out. By the late 1970s the guerrillas were back up to strength, drawing recruits and logistical support from the Indians of the highlands, who themselves were turning on the government in response to its brutal repression and a crumbling economy. The army tamped down the guerrillas again, steamrolling across the Quiché and Huehuetenango departments and systematically destroying guerrilla sanctuaries. The rebels rose again; this time three guerrilla organizations united protectively under the single umbrella called the Guatemalan National Revolutionary Union. Peace talks began and ended, inconclusively.

It was a cycle of violence that left no one untouched. The week I talked with Cerezo in 1981 about the Saint Valentine's Day attempt on his life, a Guatemalan coffee planter named Frank Brauderer heard a strange noise out on his plantation, Nuevo Quetzal. He discovered a guerrilla band burning his helicopter. When he turned and tried to flee he was dragged from his truck; fifty submachine-gun slugs tore him apart. The rebels left a note by Brauderer's body: "This is just the beginning." In fact, the cycle has only beginnings and no end.

Now, by the time of our trip, the widening gyre has spun crazily into the surreal, into a mad Land of Bizarro where what is isn't and what isn't is. Maybe the Godfather of the party of organized violence was right to put his faith in the slogan on the poster of Ronald Reagan bottle-feeding the chimp Bonzo; maybe there is a simple solution to every problem: on October 27, 1987, three months after our visit to Nebaj, with Cerezo sitting as a democratically elected president of a country locked in the control of the generals, the Guatemalan foreign minister, Alfonso Cabrera, would tell the world there was no need for a cease-fire between belligerents in his country because there was no war.

* * *

Three months earlier—on July 19—we arrive in Nebaj amid something along the lines of a war. There are army troops along the roads and at ubiquitous street-corner guard posts, behind low fortifications of sandbags and boulders. People who have spent time in villages outside of Nebaj report hearing occasional gunfire at night. Among bus schedules and historical sketches, our guidebook notes: ". . . N[orth] of the town is still not safe. All houses have been burnt between Nebaj, Chajul and Cotzal; no one lives in this area and most traffic is accompanied by military personnel." Not exactly the Battle of the Bulge. Nor is it peace.

Nebaj is tucked away in a spectacular landscape. We're thick into the rainy season now. Billowing banks of clouds, most leaden and dull but some puffed up and backlit, trade places almost languorously in the low sky. As they pass each other high in the valleys, like wary freighters in a befogged narrows, the clouds truncate the views. With your depth perception thus hobbled, mountains and ravines are tele-scoped in a tangle of sharp angles. The lambent green of the foliage is overpowering. Crops are not so much terraced as miraculously anchored to the drenched sides of hills. The earth is so saturated that the rain runs off in a rush, joining forces as it tumbles down into the valleys to crash into foaming streams, silver threads forming silver ropes. Wood is black with wetness. What is not green or black or water is turned to gray. People are gray objects leaning into the rain. What cannot be dried over a wood fire remains wet. What the rain cannot reach, its constant thrumming sound does. And the chill will be in the air as long as the rain is.

Nebaj is as I had pictured it: on the edge. If you look

at a good map of Guatemala and find the departments of Huehuetenango and Quiché, northwest of the capital, you'll see three river systems that flow down from the northern border with Mexico until they run into mountain barriers: the Ixcán and Xaclbal rivers, and the Txeja and Copón branches of the Chixoy. You'll see that from below, from the south, a spidery network of roads reaches northward toward the same area. The roads start out paved, they turn to dirt or to stone, and then they too peter out up against the mountain barriers. You can draw a U-shaped line connecting the points where the rivers run out and the roads stop. That is the edge.

We've come to the edge by way of Route 3, up over a 8,176-foot pass—high for this end of Central America—and down into the tight valley where Nebaj sits along the Río Las Cataratas, the Cataract River. Like the rest of the roads up here, Route 3 is unpaved. It branches off Route 7W, also unpaved. They are both so-called all-weather roads. Attaching numbers to these roads—3 and 7W—imbues them with a structural soundness that is misleading. Perhaps you've started imagining highway medians, rest areas, and viewpoints. Stop. Not even guardrails. No painted lane dividers. No lanes, if you're thinking plural: one lane, widened by half occasionally for emergency passing. The only road sign you're likely to see is one that says ALTO; that's not STOP as in you're urged to stop at this dangerous intersection, but rather STOP at this army checkpoint—or else. These roads are exactly what the maps say they are: passable all year round and, like 80 percent of Guatemala's roads, unpaved. No more, no less. They differ from the unpaved *seasonal* roads in that they do not disappear from the face of the earth when it rains.

The stretch of Route 7W that traverses Quiché department forms the bottom part of the U-shaped edge. It is reputed to be the most scenic drive in Guatemala. It is certainly the most stunning road we've been on: we will soon be taking it from Cunén, near Nebaj, east until it ends, near Cobán. It crosses some very rough country, and were it not made of indestructible cobblestone, the tungsten steel of road building, it would almost certainly not withstand the rains. The problem with the cobbles is that after a while—it took us six hours to do sixty-six miles—you begin to feel as if you're driving over railroad ties; your hands, as if "asleep," feel tingly, numb, and like somebody else's hands all at the same time.

Crossing bridges in Guatemala, we've frequently seen a pair of steel girders lying like giant crutches along the side of the road: spare bridges. Here on 7W we finally encounter one in place.

We've come upon a large emptiness that once was occupied by a bridge—apparently not an all-weather bridge. The rains have swept it away. In its place, two steel girders stretch across a fifty-foot chasm, the space between them, fortunately, just right for the Land Cruiser's wheelbase. I line up the wheels so that they fit into the deep grooves of each girder. Intellectually, this all makes sense, but I'm a nervous wreck. It doesn't help that one girder is disconcertingly bowed in the middle. Julith stands at the far end of the bridge to let me know should the wheels come out of their grooves. As I drive across, one side of the car sickeningly rises and falls in a smooth arc as the wheels on that side traverse the bowed girder.

Nebaj is a market town and, during daylight hours on Thursday and Sunday, has some of the hubbub of a commercial center. On other days, it's quiet except for the rain, and the buses and trucks that have come to the edge. Nebaj is also an army town—there's a good-size post here, a barracks, motor pool, and a fuel depot—and this lends the place a certain grimness. There's a constant light charge of tension in the air, like the rain. Soldiers walk the street in pairs: olive-drab ponchos if they're lucky, protruding rifle barrels that glisten in the wet, green fatigues, boots noisily sucking mud from the street. The soldiers are dark-skinned and short and mostly young, like their guerrilla enemy; no one looks like the son of Guatemala City's upper crust. The houses are gray and wet and unpretty, their doors closed against the chill. Over by the church, in meeting rooms out back, Ixil men are drinking beer. Given the rain, the popular gathering spot is the town gym. The bright lights and the noise—the sounds of partisanship, the sharp squeak of basketball shoes—are a surprise. Soldiers watch in small clusters, off by themselves, ponchos and weapons at rest.

Nebaj is a staging area for the off-and-on war just to the north, just beyond the edge. The town is an outpost not just for the troops, but also for the civilians who traffic in war—the fuel suppliers, the dry-goods merchants, and, periodically and briefly, the reporters: the world's nanosecond attention span demands no more consistency than that. All these places have The Hotel. In Managua during the fighting of 1978–79, it was the pyramidal Inter-Continental, where Anastasio Somoza came sometimes to drink vodka he pretended was water. In San Salvador, it is the Camino Real; there the war is so permanent that a floor of rooms has been turned into offices for the foreign reporters who are based in the capital. In Beirut, it was the old Commodore until it was made uninhabitable by artillery. In Nebaj it is Las Tres Hermanas.

Our guidebook says Las Tres Hermanas is "delightful." The word "delightful" should be taken very loosely, as if you've come across it in the real-estate classifieds. ("Dlghtfl bsmnt apt, Lwr E Side. Nds work.") It is delightful in the sense that it is not an open field exposed to the elements and in that it is run by three charmingly batty sisters (las tres hermanas themselves), aged ladinas who, especially when they are toiling over boiling cauldrons at their wood stove, seem to have flown straight off the pages of *Macbeth*. Las Tres Hermanas consists of several windowless, BYOP (bring your own padlock) rooms. The rooms open onto a Spartan patio that features a communal spigot (singular, cold) and washbasin. On the far side of the patio is a bathroom that would look exactly like a jail cell if it weren't for the bathtub in one corner. Water for the bathtub, if you insist, can be heated in the empty oil drum outside, over a wood fire. While the beds are not perfect (we're carrying plastic drop cloths for just such occasions), the price is right: $1.50 per person per day, including three meals prepared under the personal supervision of las tres hermanas.

When you arrive at a place as remote as Nebaj you always expect to be the only outsider in town. You rarely are. When we pull up to Las Tres Hermanas in a blinding downpour there are four tourists from Spain seated at the table having lunch. Then, having spotted a new vehicle rolling into town, come the curio hawkers, the guides, the interpreters (Ixil to Spanish), the laundresses, the fixers, and the shoeless shoeshine boys. The more entrepreneurial of the lot carry spiral notebooks or carefully folded sheets of writing paper: references in sundry languages from visitors to Nebaj who have come and gone.

Our guidebook says that nobody lives north of Nebaj anymore. The army is changing that. The army is repopulating the areas they had emptied with the threat of the gun and the torch. They are taking back the wilderness from the guerrillas and from the Quiché villagers, and taking it back on their terms. The army cleans an area out, sanitizes it, puts in a camp for the troops, builds new homes to replace the burnt ones, and tries to bring the people back to these "model villages," these "poles of development."

Acul—on the far side of Chochol's peak from Nebaj, over the edge—was the first of the model villages to rise out of the ashes of the scorched earth. The army would have you think of the immortal phoenix of Egyptian mythology, the beautiful blood red bird consumed by a desert fire only to arise renewed. Don't. Try Spanish colonial history in Guatemala: moving the *indios* (Indians) out of their huts deep in the hardscrabble hills and into small compact communities so the crown's agents could keep track of them, collect taxes from them. Acul is a stark grid of white cinder-block houses. The houses are numbered. You don't want to lose track. The streets are straight. Lines of sight are important. The streetlights come on at night. Seeing at night is important. There's an army post down the road. The pattern and purpose are obvious. An army post here on the hill, a "pole of development" down there: watchtowers over the watched.

North from Nebaj, we first notice something strange about the roads: fresh gravel clinking and pinging against the undercarriage of the Land Cruiser. The road from Nebaj to Salquil Grande is broad. It may not have a name but it is considerably wider than Route 3 or Route 7W; it is gently sloped from the center, and drains well. It's a good solid road: Why? Could a road builder have been misled by the "Grande" in Salquil's name? A bizarre comparison occurs to me: what I'm seeing is like the roads put in by developers in the early stages of building a housing subdivision in the middle of nowhere. Except this isn't the Arizona desert.

The road that branches off to Acul is not bad either. It certainly makes it easier for the neighboring Hacienda San Antonio, whose well-to-do owners were driven out by the guerrillas a few years back, to get its coveted cheese down to Guatemala City for sale; the owners, who now live in the capital, have started coming back on weekends now that the army has full control over the area and the guerrillas are rarely a threat. The roads to Salquil and to Acul aren't totally new; they show up as dotted lines on the 1954-vintage contour maps, the ones made on the basis of U.S. aerial photography. But now the roads are wider, better. Buses, trucks, troop transports—they can all travel these roads more easily now.

These are army roads. They are part of the strategic infrastructure designed to take back the wilderness: army posts and army-issue model villages and army roads to link them. The army can watch the villages and the roads, and the villages can send their autodefensa patrols out to scout the forbidding mountains. The army can hire the village men to build the roads. The army and the people: partners in development, partners in keeping the army's democracy safe from the guerrillas that remain in these mountains over the edge. The roads are part of the army's arsenal. The army is driving them like stakes into the heart of Guatemala's darkness.

When we get to Salquil Grande the good road ends abruptly, on the crest of a hill. There's a monument to the road we've just come on. The kids around here call it La Muñeca: The Doll. The Doll looks something like the Tin Woodman in *The Wizard of Oz* and is about the same size. The Doll has a Galil rifle in one hand and in the other a shovel of the sort Guatemalan road crewmen carry to work their way through the heavy, gummy earth. There's a plaque. "The Nebaj-Tzalbal-Salquil road. 23 kilometers. Work completed November 1986. Built by the Army Corps of Engineers of Guatemala." The plaque is dated January 1987. Seven months ago.

The road, in fact, won't end here. It stretches out ahead of us, sans base fill or gravel, a raw cut in the dirt where a path once was. It will go at least as far as Quejchip and perhaps well beyond. We're headed for Quejchip because the army burned it to the ground in the early 1980s, and we've been told the villagers, encouraged by the army, have just begun to trickle back to what's left of home. So we press on.

We had left Nebaj early, hoping to miss the rains. So far we've been lucky. Up here at nearly 7,900 feet the views are glorious all around. Mountain ranges are stacked up like countless combers about to break over a distant reef. It's almost warm. Only the constant rush of water down the waterlogged hillsides everywhere presages the clockwork afternoon downpour. Beyond the graveled section, the road looks muddy but passable. We turn the wheel hubs, and I put the truck into four-wheel drive. My judgment was way off, as I realize when we get a hundred yards beyond the gravel and start up a slight incline. The wheels spin with an awful whine. I throw the truck into low-low four-wheel drive, which always seems to give it tank treads, and back it up to The Doll. We leave it there, its wheels looking like fat chocolate-covered donuts.

We decide to walk to Quejchip. It's not far—not much over two miles—but it will take us two hours of slipping and sliding along a slick carpet of russet mud. An Ixil woman comes up behind us and passes us. (She's in her bare feet and carrying her plastic sandals: ah, so that's it.) The woman is carrying lunch to her husband, who works on a crew that is cutting the road through to Quejchip. The lunch is in a straw basket, which I offer to carry for her, hoping to get her to slow down to my pace. She and her husband own a small piece of land in Quejchip, but they live in Salquil. She says the army evacuated Salquil several years ago. Part of the town went "with the army" to Nebaj. Part of the town went "with the guerrillas" to the mountains. She and her husband went to Nebaj, and came back to Salquil two years ago.

The army came back with the people. There's a camp on the hilltop to our left, on the far side of Arroyo Quejchip. It has a clear view of the road under construction, of the south side of Salquil Grande, and of Quejchip. In addition to the barracks and guard posts in the larger towns, and the military checkpoints at the smaller ones and along the road, this is the second full-scale encampment we've seen since leaving Nebaj. This one, behind a low wall of stone and wood, is like a fort. A fence of wire, wood slats, and tree branches marks the outer perimeter: the slats and branches look like a string of small *x*'s from an electric typewriter with a stuck key. As a crude warning device, empty ration cans have been placed upside down on top of many slats and branches: they'll make a racket falling if someone tries to slip over or through the outer perimeter. This feature was added because about a year ago three guerrillas got close enough to the camp to throw three homemade contact bombs into the compound, harmlessly as it turned out.

We've seen several road crews along this impossibly muddy track. They're taking advantage of the good weather. The last crew we see is the biggest—about twenty men. They're within earshot of Quejchip. The men come from there or from nearby Palob. It's noon, and a number of women are on hand, having brought lunch. We reach them after having made a disastrous decision to trespass through a hillside cornfield rather than fight the mud of the road-in-progress. The cornfield was much steeper than we calculated, and we ended up having to hang on to the corn as if each stalk were a mountain climber's piton. Right below us, the lunch crowd pretends not to notice our most undignified descent through the noisy rustle of corn plants.

The men all wear slip-on, calf-high black rubber boots and carry shovels just like The Doll's. Generally they work from six in the morning until noon, thirty days a month, weather permitting. On a sunny day like today, to make up for the short bad-weather days, they'll work a bit longer after lunch. They work under army supervision. They make the equivalent of seventy-six quetzales ($28.68) a month. Half they get in cash, half in food: corn, flour, canned fish, and cooking oil. The job will strengthen the men's bond (and their families') with the army: partners in progress as roads push northward and the people come slowly, hesitantly back to their villages. The army, watching over the road crews, can keep track of many of the able-bodied men in the area, each man a potential enemy fighter.

Quejchip is up ahead in a clearing, at the foot of rugged but graceful hills studded with too few pine trees. From the vantage point of the path that leads into town, as the first few thatched houses come into view and a few children can be seen at play, the setting is lovely. What happened here is not immediately apparent. What happened here was that four years ago the army came. The army told the people to grab what they could and to leave Quejchip. The people did. Standing where I stand now, some of the people of Quejchip could see their village in flames, the soldiers darting about, arms reaching here and there, the fires catching and growing and then getting smaller again. I keep seeing TV images from Vietnam: arm straight and held high, the click of a Zippo lighter being flipped open, the fire catching. I'm sure the Guatemalan army didn't use Zippo lighters.

The children we could see from a distance are playing behind what looks like a three-foot-high concrete wall enclosing a rectangular area. It turns out to be the foundation of the old one-room schoolhouse. Only the concrete part survived the fire. The kids say that those black stains here and there in the concrete were burned in by the fire. I don't know: the stains could just be discoloration over time, perhaps from the rains to which the concrete was exposed after the roof and wood frame burned up.

No part of any other building in Quejchip survived the fire: just the foundation of the old schoolhouse, which stands as a concrete monument to what happened and which gives the children a place where they can play, like a tiny memorial park.

I'm sitting with some men of Quejchip beneath a

thatched roof held up by four sturdy poles. This serves as a meeting place and, when an itinerant priest makes it by, as a church. The men—three young men, and one elderly man named Pérez—want two things from the government more than anything else: a new school and a potable-water system. There's a spring up on the top of that mountain— Pérez points up the side of a hill to the north—and the people would like to have a water line put in that would bring it down to the village. That way the villagers wouldn't have to hike up the mountain to fill their water jugs, which look like flat-bottomed pottery amphoras but are made of plastic.

The government won't give them a school and a teacher unless they have more people. Twenty-six families have come back. They started coming in March and April, before the rainy season. They are building new homes: pole and thatch huts, a single room with a dirt floor and a dried-mud hearth in one corner. Maybe sixty families will be back by the end of the year. There used to be "many more," says Pérez, waving an arm toward the higher reaches of Arroyo Quejchip. (Even in 1954 there were more than sixty families, judging from the exquisite detail of the National Geographic Institute contour map, which identifies each dwelling in and around the old Quejchip.)

If they have more people, says old man Pérez, the government will also build them new houses, better houses, and give them electricity. (I can't help thinking of Acul, of a "pole of development" down here by the Arroyo Quejchip and the army camp up high on the distant hilltop.)

After the army came, some of the people of Quejchip went to the mountains. (As far as the army is concerned, that means they are guerrilla sympathizers.) Some went to

Nebaj. And some went to the coast to find work. After a year or two, some of the villagers came back to Quejchip, but only to work their land and their crops of corn and beans. They felt it was too dangerous to stay, and they lived in towns like Salquil Grande, back from the edge. Some of the townspeople of old Quejchip still prefer to come back just to work the land, not to stay. "They're afraid," says one of the younger men, Miguel Vamac. Then why come back? "This is our land."

Miguel Vamac, who is thirty-three years old, is quite a rarity around here. You don't see many young men. Many are in the army. Some are with the guerrillas. To avoid either of those fates, many more have moved away and dropped out of sight, often heading to Mexico or the United States to find better-paying jobs. And many are dead, almost all victims of the fighting in one way or another: they were army soldiers who were killed, guerrilla fighters who were killed, or they were caught in the middle, killed by accident or because they were suspected of collaborating with one side or the other.

Almost all the young men I've seen today are on road crews. A lot of the young men I haven't seen are up in the hills on autodefensa patrol duty. In this area, they go out in patrols of eight men each—bigger than the patrols we saw around Chichicastenango. There's another difference: the army doesn't give the patrols out here, over the edge, any firearms. "Our patrols are too small," says Vamac, "and the army is worried that the guerrillas will come and steal the weapons." The army is also worried that young men like Vamac will turn and use the weapons against Guatemalan soldiers. So the small platoons from Quejchip and Salquil and Palob, armed with machetes, roam the hills on the lookout, eyes for the army in the search for guerrillas. They are also cannon fodder. If the guerrillas hit a patrol and open fire, the gunfire will make a racket that the army can hear. Men like Vamac serve the same purpose as the tin cans around the army camp overlooking the Arroyo Quejchip.

I ask Vamac: Isn't it strange that you are all now cooperating with the same army that made you leave your homes and burned your village down?

"We try not to think."

Vamac is not being dense or disingenuous. Obviously he is not happy with the arrangements that have put him virtually in the service of the army. But I don't think it is fear of the army that has brought him back to Quejchip. Yes, I think he's afraid of the army, and I think he's afraid of the guerrillas. But I think that mostly he's afraid of not being here, of not being home. "This is our land," he had said earlier, and he is deadly serious about that. If that means accepting a compromise solution that plays into the army's hands, if that's what it takes to be able to work this land and live on it, then so be it.

Quejchip is weary of war. One out of every five mothers here is a widow. Hilaria Hernández is one of them. She says her husband was killed by the guerrillas in April 1984. She doesn't say how. She doesn't really want to talk about it: she doesn't say that either, but you can tell. It's not so much the sadness; she's just tired. None of us says anything. The inside of her hut is smoky from the wood fire in the corner. There is no chimney. The smoke rises, listlessly, and most of it escapes through the wood poles and through the crack between the poles and the thatched roof; the rest floats through the room in filmy veils, catching the sunlight that filters in between the poles.

We really should be getting back before the rains.

We had met a boy earlier who promised to lead us back to Salquil—avoiding, I hoped, the slipping and sliding that had befallen us on the way in. His name is Manuel Pérez Sánchez. He is nine years old, wears a football jersey with a big "32" on it and a cowboy hat. Manuel's mother has moved back to Quejchip. He is going to Salquil because he lives there with an aunt so he can go to school.

When Manuel was five years old his father was killed up in the hills. His father had a horse and used to ride from village to village selling rope and cook pots and knives. First Manuel says it was the guerrillas who killed his father. I think he's saying that because he thinks it's what I want to hear. Then he says nobody knows for sure who did it. Maybe he doesn't want to say the army did it. Who knows? All Manuel knows is this: one day his father's horse came down from the hills and into Quejchip, riderless, pots jangling.

With Manuel leading, we've again reached the place along the footpath where some of the people of Quejchip stood and watched their homes burn. Someday soon the new road will come right through here: the army's road.

CHAPTER THREE
Nicaragua: Streets with No Names

WITH GYM BAGS SLUNG over their shoulders, the men milling about the tractor-trailers at the El Espino border crossing look like paunchy ex-soccer players off to an old-timers' match. They are money changers. Money changers are a common sight at most borders; like their pin-striped and suspendered counterparts on Wall Street, they make their living off fluctuating exchange rates. But a gym bag in lower Manhattan means: Downtown Athletic Club. Here at El Espino, on the last Sunday in July 1987, near the headwaters of the Río Coco in Honduras, it means: Nicaragua.

The gym bag has become the Nicaraguan wallet. Nicaragua's currency, the cordoba, has been free-falling against the dollar at the rate of five hundred to a thousand "cords" a week. I give one of the money changers a hundred-dollar bill. The man reaches into his gym bag. It's filled with thousand-cordoba bills, the largest banknote in general circulation. He gives me seven stacks of cords and half of an eighth stack: 750,000 cordobas; 750 thousand-cord bills, a foot-high stack. Last month the central bank issued a special five-thousand-cordoba note that will be used only by the Managua government to pay for essential imports. At the official exchange rate, the new note was worth seventy-one dollars the day it was issued; that same day, on the black market, you would have received seventy cents for it.

Poor, sad Nicaragua. The last time I was at a Nicaraguan border crossing was at the end of a week filled with so much hope. It was July 1979. Anastasio Somoza Debayle had fled, his jet carrying away the coffins of his father and brother, and roaring over the unmarked grave of the man his father's National Guard had executed a half century ago and whose name would be borne by the new government: Augusto César Sandino. Two days later, on July 19, the revolutionary junta paraded into Managua, four men and one woman aboard what seemed the perfect counterpoint to months of tanks and rocketing planes and refugees streaming into abandoned schools: a big red fire truck.

The following Sunday, with the airport closed to most traffic, I wangled a tank of precious gas out of the U.S. embassy. Mark Starr, who was then working for the *Chicago Tribune* (he is now with *Newsweek*), myself, and a couple of friends headed in a rental car toward the Costa Rican border. We were convinced, along with my colleagues who for the past eleven months had covered the war, and along with the Nicaraguans who had endured it, that this tortured nation had seen its worst days, that with a little luck a period of postwar reconstruction would give way to better times.

We drove past Masaya, where in the Indian barrio of Monimbó the revolution had begun; Diriamba, where I remembered hearing the church bells peal in celebration as the Sandinista victory became apparent during that last heady week; Rivas, which the rebel columns from the south took as they pressed toward Managua to meet rebel columns from the north. Every town we passed had been a battleground. Now finally they could get on with living.

When we got to the border crossing at Peñas Blancas, the scene was one of giddy confusion. Mark and I had been here before. The slim strip of borderland between Lake Nicaragua and the Pacific had been a key crossing point for Sandinista troops and supplies coming up from base camps hidden in Costa Rica. One time, we found the whole customs and immigration operation on the Nicaraguan side abandoned, so rough had the fighting got down here; we simply lifted the barrier and drove on through. Now the offices were not only open, but bustling with activity. It was manned by Sandinista soldiers who suddenly had become budding government bureaucrats; overnight, they traded their weapons for rubber stamps.

They were mostly young and new at their job, unprepared and clumsy—a foreshadow of what much of the incoming Sandinista bureaucracy would look like as they began the task of getting Nicaragua back on its feet. But what I most paid attention to was the brand-new stamp that went into my passport. They had taken the sun motif from the Nicaraguan flag and made it the symbol of a new era. Below the rays of a dawn rendered in blue stamp-pad ink, the new Nicaragua bade farewell in verse: "May the sun of liberty shine on you." The imprint was big and brash. It took up a full page. It was grander than the stamp of any other country that had made it into my passport. And it outshone them all. As indeed it should have, at the end of that first hopeful week.

And now.

It's getting late. At midafternoon we had gone through Choluteca, the last Honduran town of any consequence before the border. We scavenged for hotels, including the temptingly named Pierre, but once we surveyed the offerings we decided to press on. In so doing, we were bound to break a trip rule we'd imposed on ourselves before we left the States: don't drive after dark. Apparently the truckers who drive this route have the same rule when it comes to driving in Nicaragua. It's understandable: It didn't help that three weeks ago, near a place called Quebrada El Zapote to the east of here, a truck that was being used for public transportation was ambushed by anti-Sandinista contra guerrillas, who killed eleven civilians and wounded five others. This afternoon at El Espino, all the semis, their engines idling restlessly as Honduran customs officials process the paperwork, are parked facing away from Nicaragua and into Honduras—headed north. There are no passenger cars—in either direction.

We are on the far western fringe of the contra war battle zone, and not in any real danger. The El Espino crossing serves the Pan American Highway. Of the three major Honduras-Nicaragua crossings, it is the only one open these days. All three crossings are on the Pacific side of Honduras and Nicaragua. To the east of us are vast stretches of mountains, then plains and coastal lowlands beyond—an area covering more than half of Nicaragua, the largest Central American country, and a third of Honduras, the second largest. From the continental divide down to the Caribbean, this is a sparsely populated region, and roads are virtually nonexistent. In both countries, this was largely a no-man's-land until the contra war broke out in the early 1980s.

The contra war really began the minute Somoza exiled himself to Florida and, shortly thereafter, to what was at the time a favored hangout for disgraced politicians and hoodlums on the run, Paraguay, where he was assassinated on the Sandinistas' behalf in 1980. The day Somoza flew out of Managua and abandoned the fifteen-thousand-strong National Guard, guardsmen scurried out of Nicaragua in a panic. In the field in front of the Inter-Continental Hotel in Managua and next to Somoza's office complex you could see soldiers ditching their uniforms and changing into civvies. In the airport bathrooms they forced civilians to undress and hand over the clothes on their back.

Some of the guardsmen, the ones to whom Somoza had doled out rich government contracts or Mercedes dealerships or gas station permits, landed in Miami condos. The less fortunate, suddenly penniless and unpaid, not to mention unwanted at home, made their own way cross-country and into Honduras. Among both groups, there were plenty of men with time on their hands, men who were trained at war and not much else, and they formed the labor pool that gave us first the secret war and then the contra war, both fueled by Washington's millions.

The war that I thought was over when the Sandinistas' big red fire truck drove triumphantly into Managua never really ended. The guerrillas became the government, and the government became the guerrillas. Fed by the United States and the Soviet Union, the two new armies grew into the most powerful in the region. In the war I covered, a .50-caliber machine gun mounted on a pickup truck was a big weapon. Somoza had a couple of museum-piece Sherman tanks and the Sandies had some antitank weaponry, but the '78–'79 war was in large part a fight between government rockets mounted on a few toylike Cessna prop planes, and teenage rebel street fighters with hunting rifles and homemade contact bombs.

In the contra war, armaments poured off Soviet freighters docked at the Nicaraguan port of Corinto and out of fat-bellied U.S. military aircraft on U.S.-built megarunways in Honduras. The Sandinistas had fierce-looking, heavily armed Mi-17 and Mi-25 Hind helicopters to go out and hunt down contras with, and the *contrarrevolucionarios* had shoulder-fired Redeye missiles to shoot down the Hinds with. The war had gone big-time.

About ninety miles east of El Espino, in the Río Bocay valley a couple of months ago, there was a battle, probably the biggest in the contra war, that showed what had come to pass since that Sunday in July when I left Nicaragua. The contras had established a forward base at Las Amatas, near Wina, where the Bocay and the Amaka join in Jinotega province. From there they were infiltrating into Nicaragua contra troops that were based in Honduras, which serves as a staging area for the contras just as Costa Rica did for the Sandinistas when they were the rebels. In the largest operation ever mounted by the Sandinista army, some three thousand Sandinista troops and thirty-six helicopters moved against as many as eight hundred contras at the base camp.

That was one battle in the war. Even so the numbers boggled my mind. At the end of the 1978–79 war, at the peak of their strength as a guerrilla army, the Sandinistas had a total of some seven thousand men and women under arms. And now this.

Even the tranquil stretch of border in front of us in El Espino, far from the fighting, has the feel of a war zone. The siege mentality has pushed the Nicaraguan customs and immigration installations back from the legal border. The offices are now housed in makeshift trailers and Quonset huts about ten kilometers back. All that's left at the border itself are a pair of Sandinista soldiers standing guard outside the tumbledown Somoza-era customshouse. The building's paint has almost all peeled off; its windows have been smashed like those of a junked auto.

Between the border and the new immigration facilities is a dead zone. Driving through it, you are tempted to think, It's too quiet. There is the rustle of a scrawny steer off to the left. You half expect the brush to erupt in a firefight. It doesn't. The lifeless stretch of Pan American Highway just stays dead quiet, a gangrenous limb waiting for the rest of the country to die.

At immigration, an officer sends us down the road another ten kilometers to Somoto, where customs inspectors turn the War Wagon and our luggage inside out. The whole process takes two hours—understandable in a country at war. Fully cognizant of what my own country is up to in Nicaragua, I feel funny knowing that as a citizen of the United States I still don't need a visa to get into Nicaragua. That will change as the contra war drags on, but even when U.S.–Nicaraguan relations hit their nadir, visitors from the States would rarely be made to feel unwelcome by the Nicaraguan people. Why? Nicaraguans are uncommonly warm and hospitable. That explains part of it. As in so many other Latin American nations, they also have learned from their own history to differentiate people from their government. That explains the rest of it.

My own feelings are much more jumbled. It is painful to be in Nicaragua. For the past month I've been reading that my country is awash in "Olliemania." For several days (between, as it happened, U.S. Independence Day and the July 19 celebration of the triumph of the Sandinista revolution) Col. Oliver North was busy testifying before House and Senate committees investigating the Iran-contra arms scandal. The arms-for-hostages-for-money-to-the-contras deal was "a neat idea," he testified. He testified that for over a month last year he shredded documents that might be used as evidence against him and Ronald Reagan. North was asked if any funds-diversion memos were approved by the president. He was asked this several times. Finally his attorney objected to the repetition. The objection was overruled. Then the attorney said he had forgotten the question. North said he had too: "My memory has been shredded." According to one report, he said this "jauntily." I can believe it, but it is appalling to contemplate such behavior as I begin to see some of the destruction that Ollie North's vile little plan unleashed in Nicaragua.

The sun is beginning to set as we leave the pushed-back border behind and head south toward Managua. Route 1, the Pan American Highway, is a disaster. Road repairs are not a top priority for a country that spends half of its total budget on defense. It seems every vehicle on the road, except the military ones, is crippled in some way by the lack of money and spare parts: taillights askew, headlight burnt out, wheels wobbling, frame bent so that the car sidles crablike down the road. Then every once in a while a big troop transport bequeathed by the Soviet bloc whooshes by in a puff of hot air.

Down south, Route 1 merges with the road down from Matagalpa. Nicaragua moves the celebration of the nineteenth to a different city each year. This year was Matagalpa's turn. So the road from here on in to Managua has been repaved. Now we are retracing the route of the big red fire truck. Through our wide-open windows we can hear the snapping salute of thousands of tiny red-and-black plastic Sandinista pennants. Tributes to that first, hopeful July 19, they have already begun to tear and split in the heat of the eighth summer of the Nicaraguan revolution.

Our trip went smoothly after we left Nebaj, on the Guatemalan mountain divide between the army and the guerrillas. We stopped off in Antigua to repack the Land Cruiser and then headed northeast toward Honduras. We were skipping the more direct route to Nicaragua, through El Salvador on the Pan American Highway. In April, as the civil war that had killed some fifty thousand Salvadorans ground through its seventh year, the leftist rebels had decreed their travel ban inside the country. It was designed as a protest against army recruiting policies and the rich. The children of the oligarchy were of course not touched by the dirty hand of army recruiting, which plucked from among the poor and near-poor the bodies to be thrown into the fray with the guerrillas. The rich were the most likely to be out and about in cars—their oligarchmobiles, as the press corps dubbed them—and over the next several days, rebel torches set fire to more than a dozen vehicles around the country.

We didn't need that kind of trouble, especially driving around in what looked suspiciously like a 'garchmobile even if we didn't have the telltale smoked windows. I had been to El Salvador on a number of occasions since the early days of the war. Enough of those visits had been steeped in tragedy to persuade me not to look for trouble in El Salvador if I didn't have to. One time I flew down on a medical-evacuation Lear jet from Miami to pick up Olivier Rebbot, a *Newsweek* photographer who had been shot through his bulletproof vest and would die not long afterward in a Florida hospital. Later John Hoagland, another friend and *Newsweek* photographer, was shot and killed there.

Had we gone to El Salvador we certainly would not have had to take anything like the risks that people like Rebbot and Hoagland routinely do, and I was fairly confident we would not be in any personal danger. But we couldn't even afford to run the risk of serious delays. So we had decided at the outset that we would bypass El Salvador. It's just as well we did: on July 24, the day we entered Honduras (and would have entered El Salvador), and on the following day, the Salvadoran guerrillas dynamited two bridges along the Pan American Highway.

We entered Honduras through the back door. A decent dirt road—Route 21 in Guatemala, which becomes Route 20 and paved across the border—led us to a wood-frame customshouse on the Honduran side. There on the front porch a customs agent hunted and pecked at an ancient gunmetal gray Royal typewriter with one of those extralong carriages favored by government bureaucracies not yet overrun by the computer. Alongside the Royal were a bottle of Guatemalan hot sauce and two apples—a kind of tithe the agent had extorted from a Honduran woman on her way back home from some border shopping. The process was repeated, without a fuss, for each shopper. Every once in a while the agent's left hand reached mechanically down, opened the big bottom drawer of his desk, and added some more booty to the accumulating cache. As tourists, we were exempted from this informal taxation system and not required to give him, say, a wheel or one trunk.

Honduras is the prototypical client state. Its governments have traditionally catered to constituencies outside its own boundaries—most notoriously, aside from its collaboration with Washington during the contra war, the United Fruit Company. In 1929, when the Cuyamel Fruit Company of Honduras merged with the Boston-based United Fruit, the legendary U.S. businessman Minor Cooper Keith forged another link in his monopolistic chain of cheap labor, railroads, cargo ships, and vast banana lands. By extending its reach beyond Costa Rica, where Keith had gotten his start, United Fruit was poised to become a formidable foreign power in Central America.

It did. When the United States temporarily quit its practice of direct intervention in regional affairs under the banner of President Franklin D. Roosevelt's Good Neighbor Policy, Honduras became a de facto subsidiary of United Fruit. The United States, distracted by the Great Depression and World War II, seemed content to let the company known as "El Pulpo" (The Octopus) assume Washington's old role as the plenipotentiary arbiter of Central American politics. Over the years, United Fruit's grip would be loosened, because of growing political resistance among its once so hospitable host countries and because the land, depleted by its awesome production and damaged by disease, could give no more.

The ebb and flow of U.S. involvement in the region followed a similar pattern. Washington's ability to impose U.S. authority directly in Central America would grow in the fifties and sixties, and begin to decline in the seventies. By the mid-1980s only Honduras and El Salvador could be counted on to respond unfailingly to Washington's beck and call. For the price of several hundred million dollars a year, Honduras turned itself into a boot camp and general headquarters command for the contras. The United States paved the countryside with runways, geared up a big CIA operation, and generally transformed the country into the USS *Honduras,* a North American aircraft carrier permanently anchored in Central America.

The Tegucigalpa government's behavior looked sordid and even silly: it wasn't until March of 1986 that the highest levels of Honduran government, with Sandinista troops crawling all over its southern border, officially acknowledged the presence of thousands of contra soldiers in Honduran territory; the rest of the world had forgotten the matter was ever a secret. When other Central American states attempted to hammer out peace accords, the good ship *Honduras,* acting as a blunt instrument of Ronald Reagan's foreign policy, dutifully used its vote as a Central American republic—in this case a putative democracy not only run by its military, like Guatemala, but also richly sponsored by the United States—to subvert and to slow the regional peace process for as long as possible.

Honduras's historical closeness with the United States has left an indelible mark on the country. Even pocket change has a gringo accent in Honduras: *daime* as in *dime,* *búfalo* as in the old buffalo nickel. The phrase *banana republic* was coined to describe Honduras's kowtowing to the United Fruit Company, but long after United Fruit declined as a proconsular force in the isthmus, the sorry label lives on in spirit as Tegucigalpa continues to serve its masters in Washington.

Given my sentiments about Honduras's recent history, it was a pleasant experience to cross the border and delve into the distant past before we confronted the squalid present in Tegucigalpa. The ruins at Copán, the southernmost of the great Maya cities to have been unearthed, are sensational. They are also remote enough not to have been trampled or scavenged to a second death. Excavations since the nineteenth century had laid bare a square kilometer of plazas, ballcourts, residences, and spectacular carved stelae. The most commented upon of the ruins is a friezelike monument known as Altar Q, which was once considered a pictorial who's who of Maya astronomers and is now thought to be a rogues' gallery of the Maya governors who ruled over the Copán Valley. Much of the valley has yet to be fully explored archaeologically. Outside the restored square kilometer, archaeologists have identified some 3,450 other structures buried beneath jungly mounds in a twenty-four-square-kilometer area.

I noted with displeasure that the U.S. archaeologist Sylvanus Griswold Morley had crowned Copán "the Athens of the New World." Why must we deracinate the cultures of people whose ancestors fall outside a direct line of Western civilization drawn from ancient Greece to MTV? In the case of Copán, the cultural comparison was particularly malapropos, verging on cultural imperialism. Here, after all, a great Maya civilization had declined and was gone four centuries before the Persian Wars were over and the Parthenon was built. Rather than crown a new Athens,

I would prefer to strike fear in the modern-day rulers of Honduras by pointing out one of the theories developed to explain the swift and mysterious decline of Copán: that the common people rose up against an increasingly distant oligarchy (to use a nice Grecoracinated word).

In Copán Ruinas, the town that has grown up at the edge of the ruins, we met, of all people, one of the original developers of the ski resort at Vail, Colorado (which one might think of as "the Copán of the Rockies"). He had bought land outside Copán Ruinas, started a self-help project for the locals, had seen the per capita income fall by two-thirds since the late 1970s (he was exaggerating a little), and now was convinced there would be a revolution in Honduras by the year 2000. There hasn't been any proper land reform, he said. A handful of families run the country. There've been palace coups here, but no revolution. The rich don't give a damn about their own country. They're protecting their interests; even not-so-rich shopkeepers in Copán Ruinas keep their money in the U.S. or in Panama. It's like Nicaragua. As soon as it became clear that the Sandinistas were going to win, Somoza's rich cronies bugged out; there must have been 117 Mercedeses with Nicaraguan license plates (he was exaggerating again) in the parking lot at the Honduras Maya Hotel in Tegucigalpa at one point.

Allowing for exaggeration and noblesse oblige, the Vail theory of Honduras's imminent decline was not a bad civics lesson. I could certainly imagine those Mercedeses with Nicaraguan plates in the parking lot at the Maya in Tegoose. I had met my first contra there. This was in the early eighties. The contras were then in their "open secret" period. You knew they were camped out down south along the border, but if you went down there, you would find people reluctant to say very much. So you went to the U.S. embassy and you got the phone number of a Tegucigalpa kitchen-appliances store. That was contra HQ at the time and run by the Bermúdez brothers, ex–National Guardsmen from Nicaragua. I set up an appointment with them at my room at the Maya. When I met them, they had just decided what to call themselves: the FDN, the Democratic Nicaraguan Force. They had just had their first uniform patches made. Proudly, but careful not to let go of it, they showed me one.

In the years since then, Tegucigalpa had changed dramatically. The contras were by now in their "definitely open for business" period. Even the see-no-evil, hear-no-evil, speak-no-evil Honduran government acknowledged the existence of the contras. The contras had real offices in Tegoose and Miami. They had press agents and lobbyists. (They had to maintain a presence in Washington—especially now that Ollie North was no longer employed in the White House basement and was on his way to becoming a convicted felon.) Out by the pool, we saw as we arrived, the Maya was chockablock with U.S. soldiers in town on R&R.

War had been good to the Maya Hotel (especially since all the fighting was taking place south of the border, in Nicaragua). We pulled into the parking lot at the Maya on a Saturday. The price of a room seemed to us like a small fortune: seventy-five dollars a night—a record we never broke on the road. I made up for it by using up vast quantities of water in the shower and steambath. Julith watched the Cubs and the Dodgers on satellite TV. I ordered up a hamburger. It was like being in the United States of America.

I certainly didn't feel that way the next morning, when we headed for Nicaragua. We left the Maya before eight in the morning. The whole purpose of this exercise was to arrive at the border with Nicaragua early, absorb any delays we might encounter there, and pull into Managua before dark. We got on Route 4 and headed for Danlí. I had been on the road before and knew it went to the border. We each thought the other person had checked the map. Before long we were south of Danlí and El Paraíso both, maybe eight miles or so from the border. We came upon a Honduran army checkpoint. The corporal said we couldn't go any further. We explained that we were journalists and just passing through on our way to Managua. He said that just yesterday the colonel had also refused to let some German journalists go through. The crossing, he said firmly, was closed.

By then it had dawned on me that we were headed for the wrong border crossing. We were well to the east of where we had meant to be. This border crossing was closed because there was a war going on just to the south of it. Then we realized—by this point looking at the map—that we had to go all the way back to Tegucigalpa to catch the right highway, Route 1, to the Pan Am Highway crossing at El Espino. In the process, we would lose four hours. So much for our rule about not driving at night.

The snapping Sandinista pennants are behind us now. We are driving into Managua along the airport road. It occurs to me that I had hardly ever been on this road in the dark. I've been up and down it dozens of times, but Managua was under a curfew during much of the time I was here in '78 and '79. It's a depressing road all the same, night or day, war or no war, *somocismo* or *sandinismo:* a potholed road, alternately muddy or dusty, through a grim corridor of light industry and heavy poverty. The Aeroflot billboards are new. The Diners Club billboards are not.

This is the way it was before: I'd fly into Managua and take a cab to the hotel. It's not quite the summer of 1979. Are there any trenches dug into the road? Are there any new barricades of paving stones and burning tires in the miserable barrios off to the left? Is the puny Somoza air force pushing any five-hundred-pound bombs out of cargo bays and down onto one of those miserable barrios? What about the *La Prensa* building? Has one of Somoza's tanks blown another hole through the wall of the opposition paper's offices?

This is the way it is now: I'm looking for a taxi driver—they are fixers the world over—to take me someplace where I can buy black-market gasoline. It will cost me five dollars (payable in U.S. currency, please) for ten gallons from a shanty in one of those miserable barrios off to the left. At the state-owned service stations the gas would come to a thousand cordobas a gallon (thirteen cents), but we haven't had time to buy any ration coupons yet. The lights are off at the *La Prensa* offices. *La Prensa* remains the opposition paper. It's been closed for thirteen months under government orders.

We settle into our temporary home—a house *Newsweek* shares with the *Washington Post* and the *Los Angeles Times,* a large two-story residence in a leafy, upper-middle-class neighborhood. We sit down to a late dinner. Julia Preston, a reporter for the *Post,* points to our plates. "You're eating the last meat in Nicaragua," she says. She's half-serious.

The last thing we do on our first night in Managua is

unscrew the side-view mirrors from the Land Cruiser and bring them inside for safekeeping.

In the daylight, Managua looks as it has for far too long: raggedy. When I first came to Managua, in August of 1978, my reaction was a common one: is the war already over? Buildings in what used to be the center of town were skeletons of cracked concrete. Vacant lots were strewn with the flotsam of disaster. Streets went nowhere. The city looked abandoned. But it didn't take a war to make Managua look war-torn.

Managua, like other Central American capitals, is built along a volcanic zone that runs down the isthmus, and is prone to earthquakes. Post-Columbian San Salvador has been destroyed or severely damaged fourteen times by quakes; Guatemala City, nine times. In the 1930s, first an earthquake and five years later a runaway fire left little of old Managua standing. The city was rebuilt. In 1972, two days before Christmas, another earthquake devastated Managua. In the center of the city only a few buildings, most of them modern, survived intact; five thousand to ten thousand people were killed and scores of thousands left homeless. In an extraordinary display of callousness and greed, Somoza abandoned downtown Managua and turned the reconstruction effort into a money tree for himself and his National Guard cronies.

It would later become clear that Somoza's handling of the earthquake's aftermath helped to set in motion his own demise. In the meantime, massive amounts of aid flowed into Nicaragua from foreign governments and private citizens overseas. These funds and the government's own money were diverted away from the debris of the center city and sluiced toward construction projects on suburban tracts owned by Somoza himself and by his inner circle. Building materials that might have sheltered the homeless found their way into the hands of Guard officers, who appropriated them for their own use or sold them. The new streets of the new Managua were paved with the distinctive cruciform paving stones manufactured by a Somoza-owned company. The dictator cut the private sector out of the dollar loop and began to earn even *their* enmity. The latticework sprawl of the new Managua around the abandoned core became a monument to Somoza's corruption.

Today, if you airbrush out the Sandinista motifs—the billboards and the banners and the martyrs-of-the-revolution statuary—the city doesn't look that different than it did before the fighting of '78–'79. The civil war just ground it further into the volcanic soil. The contra war, though its killing fields are way to the north, has since been a brutal drain on the economy and has limited any reconstruction or prettifying of Managua to feeble patching. The city, devoid of character other than the strength and resilience of its people, seems poisoned and listless, like the dull, khaki-colored, and ecologically dead lake at its edge.

It is easy to believe that Managua, so lacking in natural beauty, is an accidental capital bequeathed to the country by nineteenth-century politics—a compromise capital located halfway between the intellectual center of León, the heart of the Liberal Party, and hispanophile Granada, the heart of the Conservative Party. Managua is a disorienting place. Street signs are virtually nonexistent; so are addresses in the conventional sense. Landmarks are used instead of the cardinal points. North is *lago* (lake). South is *montaña* (mountain). East is *arriba* (up). West is *abajo* (down). As part of a street address, you might be given a landmark that no longer exists: a church destroyed in the earthquake, a movie house burned down in the civil war.

I'm sure that even now, eight years on, I see Managua—distorted—through the lens of my wartime experience there. My orientation in the city is based on my own personal landmarks: the house where the orange BECAT antiterrorist jeep came to arrest someone's son; the nameless street where the school bus bristling Sandinista rifles rounded the corner. I can't think of Lake Managua without recalling trips week after week to the lakeshore behind the Rubén Darío Theater to count the bodies of young people, hands tied behind their backs, shot through the head, that had been dumped there by the National Guard as the war careened fearsomely toward its close.

Rubén Darío had it half right. He was right about the United States, but wrong about Latin America. Darío was a great Nicaraguan poet at the turn of the century, and he remains one of Latin America's best-known and most widely acclaimed literary figures. The most powerful poem of his that I've read is called "A Roosevelt" ("To Roosevelt"), which should be required reading for any U.S. diplomat sent to Latin America. The poem, published in 1905, is an acid indictment of the United States' expansionist Manifest Destiny past and its economic imperialism to come.

The year before, Theodore Roosevelt had promulgated the "Roosevelt corollary" to the Monroe Doctrine of the previous century. The Monroe Doctrine, issued as a wave of independence swept through Spain's American colonies, proclaimed that no European nation should interfere in the affairs of American states nor increase its possessions on the

American continents. Teddy Roosevelt's corollary was brusquely simple: the Monroe Doctrine applied to Europe, but not to the United States. His meaning was clear: "These wretched republics cause me a great deal of trouble," he once complained. "I often think that a sort of protectorate over South and Central America is the only way out." The United States had already flexed its muscles in Cuba (during the Spanish-American War) and in Panama (by engineering Panama's independence from Colombia, clearing the way for the construction of the canal). Now it would police the rest of Latin America as it saw fit.

"To Roosevelt" is an epic condemnation of that policy. "It would take the voice of the Bible, or the verse of Walt Whitman, / to reach you, Hunter," Darío says in addressing Roosevelt. Darío then proceeds to find that voice and that verse. "You believe . . . / that where you place your bullet / there you place the future too." But, says Darío: "No." Latin Americans—"men with Saxon eyes and barbarian souls"—won't stand for it. Latin America—"the daughter of the Sun"—won't let it happen.

Latin Americans did let it happen. It turned out there were enough Latin Americans who were willing to let it happen, to help it happen, and to profit hugely by its happening. That's where Rubén Darío got it wrong. He didn't figure on there being so many people like Somoza's father, Anastasio Somoza García. By 1933, when Washington was shifting away from interventionism in the hemisphere once again, the U.S. Marines had been in Nicaragua for three decades and were managing the country's customs operations, its central bank, and its railroad. When they left that year, they put Somoza García in charge of a Marine Corps creation, the National Guard. Within three years

Somoza García had engineered his own election to the presidency, thus beginning what, with his sons Luis and Anastasio, would become the longest-lasting and probably the richest dynastic dictatorship in Latin American history—and certainly the only one that was started by a man who began his career as a toilet inspector and used-car salesman. "The Penguin"—sleek, round, soft—was what the rebel leader Augusto César Sandino used to call Anastasio Somoza García in ridicule before Sandino was detained by a National Guard patrol one night in 1934, taken into a field, and shot.

In the final days of the dynasty, the inheritors of the Penguin's legacy came slouching toward the Inter-Continental to seek refuge from the war. The fighting was closing in on Managua like a garrote. Out of shiny cars climbed the pashas of the embattled government of the last Somoza. Some of the hoods and windshields of the Mercedeses and Chevys had "TV" in big, adhesive-tape letters slapped onto them and flew white damask table napkins—their owners trying to camouflage them as the press vehicles that filed out of Managua in convoy each morning to cover the war. The lobby filled with women and their Louis Vuitton luggage, with children too big for their chrome strollers, with nursemaids and G.I. Joe dolls. Rumors—Somoza is leaving, U.S. troops are coming—caromed off the walls. Managua's *somocista* elite was breathing the thin air of panic.

At five in the evening the men assembled for cocktails on the top-floor terraces of the hotel. Below, small figures in uniform scurried about outside the office-apartment complex where Somoza spent his days and, increasingly, his nights. The low-slung building was called "el Bunker."

Some right-wing U.S. congressmen visited Managua on a humanitarian-aid mission, but mostly to drum up evidence for why the United States should not defend more forthrightly this beleaguered bastion of democracy that was being threatened not just by Communist insurgents but also by the news media. Sweltering in their polyesters, they stood outside the Inter-Con and asked why the press was always talking about Somoza being in his "bunker," as if under siege, when they had just seen him in his office and he seemed perfectly fine. The term was not an invention of the press; it was an old denomination and predated the current troubles. But now, ringed by trenches and sandbags, the Bunker was indeed looking more bunkerlike every day—a transformation that did not escape the notice of the men who looked down on it over their cocktails.

From the Inter-Con terraces the men gazed south toward the airport. Out there, a heat-wavy smudge of squat buildings and treetops, was one of those miserable barrios off the road in from the airport. Up above the horizon a plane droned in circles, out of reach of small-arms fire from below. You could not actually see them pushing the bombs out the cargo doors. But you knew it had happened by the faraway noise, and then a column of dust and fiery grit would rise into the cocktail-hour sky and join the other thin dirty coils, giving the barrio the oddly Dickensian aspect of an industrious smokestack city. On the terraces, the tinkling of iced gin and tonics mingled with the plangent thudding of the bombs.

Down on the ground, out in Barrio La Fuente, closer to the fight, panic had a sharper edge. Among the soldiers Somoza would soon leave behind, the panic had sapped strength and toppled even the pretense of victory. As I looked on, a weary Guard corporal cracked under the pressure as he did his job. He stopped a teenage boy and frisked him. The boy was not armed, but the soldier knew that the next night or the next day, the boy might be taking aim at him from ambush. Tears filled the corporal's eyes as he sent the teenager on his way. "I'm afraid," the soldier told the boy. "I'm scared of you and your kind of young people. I tell you frankly. Now go. Go."

Los muchachos. They were boys and girls with baseball caps and bandannas and popguns, improv revolutionaries who came to symbolize the early struggle against Somoza before the Frente Sandinista de Liberación Nacional sent its better-trained forces down from Honduras, up from Costa Rica, and out of the Nicaraguan hills. There's a monument to them in Matagalpa. Three kids in midfight: one with a pistol, one with a .22 rifle, and one with a baseball-size contact bomb he's about to hurl over a barricade. I can picture in my imagination where the bomb is going. In Matagalpa I first saw the *muchachos* at work. It was an August afternoon in 1978, and National Guard troops were bearing down on them from behind a giant shield: the blade of a moving road grader. The fighting, which would eventually take about fifty thousand lives, was just beginning. Already, the result of fighting the night before, just a few blocks away there was a pine-box wake for one of the early casualties of the war. There was still time, early in the war, for pine boxes and burials. Later the Red Cross would be dousing the dead with gasoline and setting them afire on the street to stave off disease.

Matagalpa is 2,224 feet above sea level. In Nicaragua that's positively alpine, and it's a pleasant change from the humid heat of low-lying Managua. When Julith and I arrive, Matagalpa is still dressed up from the eighth-anniversary hoopla ten days ago, and the rain-soaked hills around the city are a shimmering green from the coffee plants. If the name of the city seems at all familiar to you, it could well be that you bought packets of Nicaraguan coffee from organizations raising money in the United States and Europe for Nicaraguan relief efforts. If you didn't like the coffee, blame Ronald Reagan's "freedom fighters." The contras so disrupted coffee production that often the beans shipped outside Nicaragua for packaging had to be stretched by adding ground chicory roots.

Matagalpa is the northernmost of Nicaragua's larger cities, and the contra war is a palpable presence here. During the anniversary celebrations, troop reinforcements were shipped up here to beef up the Sixth Military Region regulars headquartered in Matagalpa. We decide to spend the night north of the city, on the road to Jinotega, at the Selva Negra, a cloud-shrouded mountain lodge that has gone to seed in the decade of fighting. From our cabin, which we apparently are sharing with a few rodents, we can hear the muffled pops of distant skirmishes in the night.

The saving grace of the contra war is that the fighting hasn't reached Nicaragua's cities. Were it not confined to the north, the death toll would be much higher than the fifteen thousand or so up to now. What we're seeing in the parts of Nicaragua that we're visiting is less bloody but nonetheless tragic, and proves that an unseen wound also kills: the slow economic death of Nicaragua. In the cities, it is as if the U.S.-sponsored contra warriors had dropped a reverse neutron bomb on Nicaragua: the people are left standing, the economy drops dead. It is calculated that by the summer of 1987, the total economic impact of the contra war has reached $1 billion to $1.5 billion, a devastation layered immediately on top of the devastation of the civil war and on top of the hundreds of millions of dollars Somoza had squirreled away.

The United States watches from a cool distance: some bureaucrats in Washington, teams in Tegucigalpa and San Salvador, an arms merchant here and there, some fundraisers appealing to deep pockets from Austin to Brunei, one marine lieutenant colonel. The United States pulls a lever now and then, and watches. It funds the contras and tosses onto the fire a credit boycott and a trade embargo, and watches. Its surrogate soldiers die surrogate deaths in out-of-the-way places. In Nicaragua, an omnivorous defense budget drains resources from education and health care. Economic austerity policies lower productivity and heighten public dissatisfaction. There is less fertilizer, fewer plows, a crisis in repair parts, no new industrial equipment. As family responsibilities begin to outweigh revolutionary commitment, scores of thousands of Nicaraguans leave the country, including too many from the key middle-income professional class, who were to be the bright hope in rebuilding post-Somoza Nicaragua. The inflation rate begins the decade at 25 percent and will end it at 36,000. And when it's all over, Nicaragua—never a prosperous land, only a promising one—will have been reduced to being the poorest of all Latin American nations.

When Anastasio Somoza Debayle fled to Miami, there were Nicaraguans who rejoiced not because the Sandinistas were taking over; they rejoiced because to them, Somoza's exodus brought down the curtain on a U.S. policy of intervention in their country. The U.S. Marines had left in

1933, but they had effectively turned over Nicaragua to the Penguin, who passed it along to his son Luis, who passed it along to his brother Anastasio. When the last Somoza left, there were Nicaraguans who thought they were getting their country back, and so they called him "the Last Marine." It seemed an elegant epitaph. But they hadn't figured on Marine Lt. Col. Oliver L. North. Semper fi.

This is one way the dynasty ended: the dictator was drunk. He too had sought refuge for this one evening at the Inter-Con. Upstairs at the cocktail party, one floor over the monster suite where Howard Hughes and then Robert Vesco used to live in this hotel for fugitives, he was drinking his usual "water" (read: vodka) on the rocks. Now he had gathered some aides together for a dinner that in restrospect would take on an eerie last-supper quality. A table full of reporters happened to be right outside the private dining room he had taken for the evening. Our table was in a nice open area. Hovering out over the lawn was the violet glow of bug zappers; you know the weird *eunnnNNGG!* sound they make as the poor moth flaps into the high-voltage lair: you half expect the room lights to dim as the electrocution takes place.

His door was shut, and we could only hear the rising voices. A stag affair. There were some women at our table, which was good, because it meant he would almost surely stop for a chat: he had a soft spot for women—even if they were journalists—in his dictator's heart. (He would soon be granting his farewell interview to Karen DeYoung of the *Washington Post,* telling her that "I am like a tied donkey fighting with a tiger.") Right now, as the door swung open and the boisterous claque of *somocistas* came toward us, he was just "a Latin from Manhattan," as he once put it in the Technicolor English he'd picked up in the States in the thirties and forties.

He was on something of a tear. He rambled on about the sad state of his presidency, about being abandoned by Washington, and about being badly portrayed in the press. All in that English. He was just a regular guy. We were just regular guys. We were all of us, apparently, just regular guys up against the Communist menace. "You guys"—now he was getting personal—"you bastards are just a bunch of sons of bitches, just like me." His security people were starting to get a little nervous, especially when he got on Jimmy Carter's case: "That fucking asshole."

The security men were trying to coax him away from the table and out of there, which was like turning a supertanker around. They had noticed the bulbous broadcast-quality microphone set on top of the table with insufficient discretion. Under the table, unseen, a cassette recorder was recording every obscenity, every syllable of slurred speech. The security men had obviously figured this out. They were circling the table, leaning over, peering under. We were onto them, so by now the cassette itself was being passed from one lap to another under the table.

Just as the whole affair was coming unraveled, things seemed to slip into slow motion. A reporter tucked away the cassette, walked away from the table, went up to a room with enough TV technology in it to start up a major-market station, dubbed a copy of the cassette at high speed, and returned to the table. Nice: just a trip to the bathroom. The dictator, now in his tied-donkey mode, was being led away from the table. A couple of his security people stayed behind to demand the tape. They got what they thought was all the incriminating evidence. We adjourned upstairs to listen.

When you talk to Nicaraguans about their leaders, they respond with respect and admiration about one: Dionisio Herrera. The problem is that Dionisio Herrera governed Nicaragua from 1829 to 1833, when it was part of a federation of newly independent Central American states, not even a separate republic yet. And yet his tenure seems to be the one unambiguous exception to a history of greedy caudillos, instability, and bloodshed that stretches all the way back to the arrival of the Spanish in 1522.

And the Sandinistas? They've given Nicaraguans self-respect.

They may not have given Nicaraguans much else. Certainly neither democratic self-governance nor economic self-reliance. The Sandinista revolution was always going to be fundamentally socialist, though even that fact was largely overlooked in the euphoria of Somoza's ouster, both inside and outside Nicaragua. It would have to be a socialist revolution in order to bring even minimal fairness to the obscenely out-of-kilter Somoza-era economy and repay the Nicaraguan poor, who had fought hardest and suffered the most during the civil war. But with the economy mired in a decade of war, not much has been brought into balance and very few have been paid back.

Up in Las Colinas, a residential neighborhood in suburban Managua, there is the Dollar Store. The Dollar Store is a shabby shrine to Nicaraguan communism, just as the ones in Havana are to communism in Cuba. You need two things to get into the Dollar Store: a non-Nicaraguan passport and U.S. dollars. Once inside, you've walked into a different Nicaragua. This is not the Mercado Oriental, where reporters show up at dawn to see if there's any chicken today and where the government inspectors will haul off any merchant so capitalist as to sell her goods for free-market prices.

Technically, it's the Tienda Diplomática, but everybody calls it the Dollar Store, since dollars are what count and the lack of a foreign passport doesn't keep out government officials or party members of sufficient rank. The air-conditioning, this being Managua, is enough to start a dull throbbing pain in your gums. That's the first thing you notice. The second thing are hot dogs and popcorn for sale just inside the door. People in Managua have been complaining to us that they can't get eggs this week; there are eggs here. *Sandinismo*'s enemy states are well represented here. A carton of U.S.-made Marlboro cigarettes, probably obtained via Panama, is $8, which in this crazy-quilt economy will buy you several months' worth of gasoline ration coupons or less than a week's worth of penicillin. A made-in-Taiwan Rex one-speed bike: $160, or two months of a doctor's income. No G.I. Joe dolls, but Barbie and Ken are $10 apiece.

The sad reliance on dollars at the Dollar Store is one thing. There is also a creepy quality to some of the items for sale. Skin-fade creams. Hair straighteners.

The revolution didn't start in Las Colinas. But a piece of it may die there. This used to be a *colonia* for the rich. Now it's a *colonia* for the privileged. Tomás Borge, the minister of the interior who emerged as the most powerful of the Sandinista leaders in 1979, has a well-guarded house in the neighborhood. (Some post–civil war weirdness: the last time I saw Borge was at a *Newsweek*-sponsored dinner for high-ranking members of the then-new revolutionary government in September 1979; he had removed his machine pistol from his lap so that Bianca Jagger could sit down and say hi.) In the early eighties I once visited a house in this neighborhood that served as a propaganda headquarters for the Salvadoran guerrillas. The Guatemalan guerrillas had a place nearby. The contradictions engendered by places like the Dollar Store and Las Colinas can be deadly to Communist regimes. It took three decades for the contradictions to start causing real damage to Fidel Castro. Unless things change, it won't take anywhere near that long in Nicaragua.

Down the road from Las Colinas is where the revolution did in fact begin: in Monimbó, a tough Indian barrio in Masaya. On January 10, 1978, Pedro Joaquín Chamorro, the editor of *La Prensa,* was driving to work in Managua when his Saab was forced off the road and into a lamppost by a pickup truck. Three shotgun blasts finished the job. At a memorial mass in Monimbó the next month, National Guard troops lobbed tear gas canisters into the congregation. Overnight the Indians of Monimbó threw up barricades and dug trenches against overwhelming odds. The Sandinistas had for years staged isolated assaults and kidnappings. But the uprising in Monimbó was the first popular uprising against Somoza.

Of all the towns I went to in Nicaragua in 1978 and 1979, no place took more of a pounding from the National Guard than Masaya. On some streets there were no roofs left from the bombing, anything wooden had been incinerated, and flames that had leapt out of windows and doors left their fan-shaped imprint on walls singed black. Even now, after the physical damage from one war and the economic damage from another, the spirit of defiance and endurance is strong in Masaya and symptomatic of the reservoir of goodwill and trust that the Sandinistas can draw from. "Eight years means more dignity, more sacrifice, more victories," says the neatly hand-lettered vow on a Masaya housefront. It's a pledge of allegiance to the revolution. But for how many more years will Nicaraguans have to say it in such baleful language?

Somoza left yesterday. Tomorrow the big red fire truck will take this town. Earlier tonight I turned on the radio. They were playing a song by one of the Godoy brothers; I think it's called "La Tumba del Guerrillero"—"The Guerrilla's Tomb." A revolutionary folk song. Of course: they would have taken the radio station by now. There was a nearby crackle of automatic-weapons fire, drowning out the music. It took a second to realize it was a celebratory noise. That was a first.

The Inter-Con was strangely quiet. A college dorm between semesters. Something like that. I walked down the hall to Alon Reininger's room. Reininger, a photographer, seemed to be writing a letter home, a fittingly peaceful way to pass the time. Then I saw that he was holding a bloody towel to his head. The Last Mercenary, a blond German hired by Somoza, had pistol-whipped Reininger, taken what cash he could find and a credit card, and set about getting himself out of the country. Reininger's letter was to American Express.

This morning Reininger and I went over to Somoza's Bunker. The Guard had deserted it. Later in the day some guerrillas would come by. In the office, they would pocket some souvenirs and with their rifle butts and bayonets they would smash and cut up Somoza family portraits: there was one of the Penguin, saluting, next to one of the pope. In the bedroom, for the photographers, a woman would throw herself onto Somoza's unmade king-size bed and wrap herself in an enormous red-and-black Sandinista flag. In the bathroom, also for pictures, a man would playfully bathe in the tub.

Right now the Bunker was empty. In the outer offices where Somoza's staff worked, a room that faced outside was knee deep in shredded documents. The paper crunched and squeaked under our feet; it sounded like popcorn. In the panicky exodus of the Guard that quickly followed the flight of Somoza himself, like the back-to-back shock waves of an atomic explosion, weapons had been left behind on desks and filing cabinets. Somoza's staff apparently shared his taste for vodka: empty Stolichnaya bottles were strewn about.

Off of Somoza's office there was the War Room. Maps were tacked and taped to the walls; pins and concentric circles tracked with disconcerting impersonality the steady retreat and collapse of the National Guard. On a table at the back of the room there was a radio receiver and transmitter. It was on; from Somoza's office, I had heard its electronic sputter. Suddenly it came to life. A National Guard driver was calling in from somewhere on the outskirts of the capital. The officer next to him in the jeep had been shot, badly shot, and he needed some help. Help, I heard. Is anybody there? Over and out. Help. Is anybody there? Over and out.

Julith and I leave Managua on a Sunday in August in the eighth summer of the Nicaraguan revolution. We pass the streets with no names where Somoza's BECAT prowled, and the khaki lake on whose shores the bodies of young people no longer show up dumped. We pass Masaya, walls singed black in the shapes of wings of angels and pledging: "Eight years means more dignity, more sacrifice, more victories."

We pass Diriamba's church bells; they are silent. The roads seem filled with military vehicles, and nothing else. The fighting that won't end has turned the whole country into that school bus I saw rounding the corner eight years ago, bristling with rifles, into a fortified bunker from sea to shining sea. I can't remember seeing a single tractor.

Rivas, and then a stamp in my passport. "República de Nicaragua. Peñas Blancas. 04." Green ink the color of the Sandinista army uniform. No more poetry. No sun.

CHAPTER FOUR
Costa Rica: Something Wild

THE COSTA RICAN agriculture official has finished fumigating the underside and tires of the Land Cruiser at the Peñas Blancas crossing. He wields the nozzled wand of his sprayer with determination and precision. It's a weapon in his hands. No microbe that might have hitched a ride with us across the Nicaraguan border is going to survive his inspection. He holsters his sprayer, slaps his hands clean on his pant legs, and hands me a receipt for the fee I owe him. I jokingly offer to pay in Nicaraguan cordobas.

"My children play with cordobas," he says.

A couple of minutes later we are processing our passports and the car's carnet through Costa Rican immigration. There are a couple of cheesecake calendars on the walls; the girls are blond. One of the immigration officers asks us where we've come from and where we are headed. We tell him, and he gives a sideways glance to the north.

"Well, you're through the ugly part," he says.

Despite the sneers on parade on the south side of the

Peñas Blancas border crossing, Costa Ricans aren't blow-hards who look down on their Nicaraguan neighbors. And yet the gap between the two countries has grown so much wider over the past decade—Costa Rica enjoys the highest standard of living in Central America, Nicaragua the low-est—that pride if not quite braggadocio increasingly salts the conversation of Costa Ricans when they're on the subject of Nicaraguans.

The two countries are radically, sadly different. At few borders in the Americas are the contrasts so striking: the United States and Mexico, of course; Peru-Chile is another.

Nicaragua looks like a boot camp, a nation swathed in khaki. Costa Rica is essentially demilitarized, a country policed by a lightly armed Civil Guard. During a month in Costa Rica we will not see a single troop transport or any weapon more sophisticated than an M-16 rifle. Though the constitution that was designed after the Costa Rican civil war of 1948 abolished the army, the tradition of peaceable-ness in Costa Rica has roots that extend deep into its past. Among the first known settlers of pre-Columbian Costa Rica were the Chorotegas, who migrated from southern Mexico to escape enemies who wanted to enslave them; their name means "fleeing people."

The indigenous population was not very large when the Spanish arrived, and it immediately began to diminish drastically because of diseases against which it had no immunity. The Spaniards who shortly thereafter came to colonize Costa Rica found no gold or silver to mine and too few Indians to support plantation farming. So contrary to the experience in almost all the other Spanish colonies, the European settlers here, like those in England's colonies to the north, had to till the soil themselves and come to terms with the land that was their sustenance. They came, according to one theory, not so much from the hard, southern Spanish provinces like Extremadura or Andalucía that yielded many of the conquistadores, but from the more progressive farming communities of northern Spain. According to this theory, among the Spanish settlers were many Sephardic Jews who sought to make a land that was more tolerant than the Spain of the Inquisition.

There was no bloody struggle for independence from Spain. The fighting was way to the north in Guatemala and Mexico, and the grand day—September 15, 1821—had come and gone by the time Costa Ricans even heard of their liberation: official notification arrived by post from Guatemala City the following month. Even the not-always-democratic "coffee presidents" who were installed by the agricultural oligarchs of the nineteenth century were notably progressive, and their regimes were remarkably free of the tumult that raged in the republics around them.

By the turn of the century Costa Ricans had outlawed the death penalty and guaranteed with their taxes a free, obligatory education for their children. After the civil war of 1948, which put to rest an incipient mini-dynasty at the cost of several thousand lives, Costa Rica did not celebrate any combatants as heroes.

The country that emerges from this tradition stands apart from its neighbors. It has poverty and it has wealth, but not to the deformed extent of a country like El Salvador, where a large impoverished population has traditionally been under the thumb of a few oligarchic families. Costa Rica's large middle class—there are seven times as many private autos per capita as in Nicaragua—softens the edge of contrast that so starkly identifies other Latin American countries. Of the sixteen Latin American capitals I've been to, only San José and Havana, for very different historical reasons, are not ringed to any great extent by squalid slums.

With a democratic tradition that goes back to the late 1800s, the country in choosing its president switches back and forth between two mainstream political parties with quartz-movement regularity every four years. On election day, towns are filled with the honking of horns, and people proudly display their index fingers dipped in indelible purple ink to show that they have voted. At dusk on the eve of each Independence Day, Costa Ricans stop what they are doing and, like three million fans at a giant ballpark, sing their national anthem (which strikes only one martial note: if invaded, Costa Rica will turn its plowshares into swords).

Whereas Nicaragua spends massively on defense, Costa Rica can afford to spend 27 percent of its federal budget on education and culture. Whereas El Salvador couldn't manage across a full decade to bring the known killers of Archbishop Oscar Arnulfo Romero to justice or Guatemala deign to solve the puzzle of its disappeared, Costa Rica has a judicial system that is notably impartial. This kind of evidence has inspired some commentators to conclude that Costa Ricans are more patriotic than their neighbors, that they care more for their fellow man and woman. These commentators then tiptoe self-consciously across explanations that boil down to racialism: Costa Rica is 80 percent white, 1 percent Indian, 2 percent black, and 17 percent mestizo, whereas its northern neighbors are mostly mestizo or Indian. All of which misses the point.

Nations are forged not by genetics but in the crucible of history. Costa Rica was not conquered. It was settled less brusingly than most Latin American countries. Because its cordilleras hid no thick veins of precious minerals, because it was not a prospective site for a canal, because it escaped for the most part the grasping geopolitics of superpowers past and present, its political system developed with far less outside interference. The chief difference between Costa Rica and its neighbors is the circular cause-and-effect of its history: it has had more than its share of good government; the others have had more than their share of bad government.

When you drive south through the battered states of Central America and come out of that tunnel into the daylight of Costa Rica, this country seems sweetly endearing almost to the point of boredom. Its homogeneity and equilibrium are appealing and a tad dull at the same time: Connecticut with volcanoes.

That was fine by me in '78–'79. I would come down here every so often during Nicaragua's civil war in search of a little placidity. Costa Rica's roads were not plowed with trenches or blocked by boulders or policed at checkpoints by one side or the other; they seemed like silken ribbons through a promised land. Nobody was shooting at cars; you felt a bit silly in your car extravagantly outfitted to show you were a noncombatant, with white flags flying and the taped-on letters blaring out "TV," for press. Here you could interview a future minister of Managua's revolutionary government at his villa outside San José. On the streets of the capital, perambulating fund-raisers for the revolution sold red-and-black Sandinista key chains.

It got worse for Costa Rica toward the end. The Sandinistas knew that unarmed Costa Rica was a sanctuary safe from Somoza's troops. But then it was as if the back of the church had started filling with war wounded. In La Cruz, the first town in the Costa Rican interior, a Peace Corps nurse treated shot-up guerrillas. In Liberia, forty-nine miles from Peñas Blancas, the public hospital was doing little other than treating rebels shipped back from the front of another country's war.

Costa Ricans had made it easy for the Sandinistas to use the province of Guanacaste as a springboard for its offensives. They were frankly glad to see Somoza under fire, and didn't mind lending the Sandinistas a corner of their backyard. The war never seemed to come close enough for long enough to give the people or the government second thoughts. But it wasn't just a matter of the wounded winding up in Costa Rican hospitals. The fighting itself, in fact, dipped across the border more often than most Costa Ricans realized. The press in San José, with the exception of the English-language *Tico Times,* pliantly and dutifully camouflaged those incidents by talking about the "southern front" of the war and avoiding any mention of the fact that Costa Rican territory was involved.

The war in Nicaragua ended soon enough, but Costa Rica's harboring of the Sandinistas had set a dangerous precedent. Soon the contras were camping out in Guanacaste. With its moral authority dented by its earlier hospitality to Sandinista fighters, Costa Rica looked particularly vulnerable for a while. The Costa Rican people were in a double bind. This time around they didn't want anything to do with insurgents seeking to overthrow a neighbor's government. And they were alarmed by the ferocious military buildup being undertaken by the Sandinistas. Suddenly all the saber rattling had the saberless Costa Ricans worried.

The country's antimilitarism faltered most critically under President Luis Alberto Monge Alvarez. Worried chiefly about his country's shaky economy, he gobbled up U.S. aid. The money was a poorly disguised bribe proffered by Washington to build a nest for the contras, whom Ronald Reagan had by then come to admire so that he praised them as the moral equivalent of the Founding Fathers. San José banked the aid and, catching Honduras's facial tic, took up winking and nodding at the contra camps: Camps? What camps?

Monge's country was getting sucked deeper and deeper into the contra war. Border skirmishes pitted members of Costa Rica's Civil Guard against Sandinistas in hot pursuit of contra bands. In self-defense, San José had invited the U.S. Green Berets to train its guardsmen and there was talk of the United States helping the Costa Ricans upgrade their armaments. Fortunately, Monge's term—and the contras' as well—was running out.

Today there's little danger of Costa Rica becoming Honduras South. As we drive through the contra's southern front, it is calm once again, and the country's equilibrium is being restored. Earlier this year, disclosures of secret CIA aid to the contras, against the intent of the Congress, had embarrassed the intelligence agency and its Costa Rican beneficiaries. The CIA's control has been slipping; it recently had to dump its San José station chief. The new administration in San José, of Oscar Arias Sánchez, has been rounding up contras for violating Costa Rica's neutrality laws. And the contras' southern front is fast disintegrating in a welter of internecine fighting.

President Arias is edging his country back from the brink. He has reversed the Monge contra policy, has shown that a small country can maintain its independence from the United States, and has used Costa Rica's regained moral authority to jump-start the stalled Central American peace process. Later this year, when we are in Lima, I'll walk by a news kiosk and see that Osar Arias has won the Nobel Peace Prize for his efforts.

In Alajuela, a bougainvillea-draped town outside the capital where San Josefinos summer, there's a monument to the closest thing Costa Rica has to a military hero. It commemorates Juan Santamaría, a drummer boy who died in an effort to rid Central America of the political pirate William Walker.

For a man who would become the great nemesis of nineteenth-century Central America, Walker was an unprepossessing sort. Having failed as a doctor, lawyer, journalist, and gold miner, he became a soldier of fortune. At five feet three inches tall, and weighing in at one hundred pounds, Walker surely was one of the shortest and lightest of the species. And yet some kernel of genius lurked within his bantam frame, for soon he would be much more than a hired gun; he would be the president of Nicaragua.

Walker started out in government as the self-proclaimed "President of Sonora and Baja California" until the Mexican army, having just lost two-fifths of its territory to the United States in the Mexican War, booted him out of the country. The filibuster turned his attention to smaller fry. A consortium of Americans dispatched him to Nicaragua to check it out as the site for a transisthmus canal. The idea was that ships would sail up the San Juan River that formed part of the Nicaragua–Costa Rica border, cross Lake Nicaragua, and then pass through an eighteen-mile canal that would be constructed through the slender neck of land north of Peñas Blancas.

Such a canal plan was very much in vogue at the time. Cornelius Vanderbilt, who after the U.S. Civil War would go on to build his railroad empire, was already a shipping magnate. During the California gold rush he opened up a freight and passenger route from the East Coast to California via Nicaragua to avoid the long and hazardous trek overland across the United States. Vanderbilt's ships, having sailed down from New Orleans, would deposit their wares and travelers on Nicaragua's Atlantic Coast. Stagecoaches took them to the eastern shore of Lake Nicaragua, a riverboat to the western shore, and then another stagecoach to the Pacific, where they resumed their journey by ship to San Francisco. The idea of facilitating the passage of a single ship along the whole route was an attractive one, if feasible. (It would be—through Panama. To clear the way for it, the United States got the eagerly complicitous Panamanians to secede from Colombia in 1903 and over Colombian objections declare themselves an independent republic. The canal, fifty-one miles long from deep water to deep water, was completed eleven years later.)

In June 1855 Walker landed in Nicaragua with some fifty-six men. Like a latter-day Hernán Cortés, the American conquistador came with newfangled weaponry and set warring internal factions against one another to serve his purposes. He and his mercenaries, through their backers in the United States, had already arranged to sign on as troops with the Liberal Party. For three decades the Liberals had been fighting with the Conservatives over which party would control Nicaragua and whether, among other things, the nation's capital would be in León or Granada. Walker lost his first encounter with the Conservatives. But he finally emerged victorious after several hundred freebooting reinforcements arrived from California with additional late-model carbines and six-shooters. Walker was made commander in chief of the Nicaraguan army, and after a sham election won the presidency in June 1856. To gain support in the United States from what would soon be known as the Confederacy, Walker suspended Nicaraguan laws against slavery.

In February 1856 Costa Rica, hearing that an invading army of filibusters was headed its way, formally declared war—not on Nicaragua, but on Walker personally. President Juan Rafael Mora raised an army and personally led his motley troops north into Guanacaste. The Costa Ricans were poorly armed with farm tools and old rifles, but they greatly outnumbered the filibusters and drove them back into Nicaragua after a battle that lasted fourteen minutes. The Costa Ricans pursued the filibusters to Rivas, where Walker had holed up with his men inside a sturdy wooden building known as La Casona. Juan Santamaría volunteered to set fire to Walker's redoubt. He did so and, though he died in the process, forced Walker's retreat. That was the beginning of the end for Walker.

All across Central America, Nicaragua's neighbors had begun mounting an effort to rid the isthmus of the *filibusteros*. They were encouraged and aided financially by Vanderbilt. Walker, in his rise to power in Nicaragua, had seized one of Vanderbilt's steamers on Lake Nicaragua. Walker fought with Vanderbilt's agents over taxes to be paid Nicaragua by the transport company and generally threatened to undo the Vanderbilt transisthmus shipping monopoly. Walker ended up fleeing Nicaragua in 1857 to escape capture by the Vanderbilt-backed forces. He returned later that year, and was arrested and sent back to the United States. At the beginning of the Civil War in the United States, the pesky filibuster returned to Central America once again, this time to Honduras, where after claiming to be its president he was tried and executed by a firing squad.

The role of the United States government during this period was an interesting and precursory one. It shied away from direct involvement in Central America and urged the British to follow suit in keeping with the Monroe Doctrine. But from the sidelines Washington cheered on both Walker's imperial fantasies and Vanderbilt's commercial incursions as valid expressions of Manifest Destiny. The control of Central America was in that historical moment seen as a crucial step in the development of the American West, and if private individuals could arrange for these young and malleable nations to serve U.S. interests, then so be it. Washington recognized Walker's Nicaraguan government with no qualms in 1856. If Vanderbilt was the first in a long line of United Fruit–like commercial powers seeking a foothold in Central America, then Walker was a kind of founding father in his own right: the first contra.

The Quakers from Alabama came to Monteverde in peace. Now we've come to the mountaintop they chose. We had turned east off the Pan American Highway at a town called Lagarto, and taken what was supposed to be a gravel road—it was under repair and was in parts a heavy, laterite-red mud that would have been impassable in most cars—up to a cloud forest in the Cordillera de Tilarán. From a distance, we can see mountains draped in thick, moist carpets of green with puffs of clouds stuck Velcro-like to them. Warmer air wafting in from the Pacific meets the colder air of the cordillera, and their collision sends sheets of clouds shooting straight up and down sharp valleys. Up close, along trails cut into the cloud forest, trees lushly ornamented with orchids and air plants and moss capes resound with a cacophony of birdcalls, frog talk, and monkey chatter. On the days we're here, the fauna, suddenly and very briefly silent, joins the rest of us in a reverent break at six in the evening: cloudy curtains part and the sun bows over the azure Golfo de Nicoya, reminding me that, although it took us two and a half hours to drive from the Pan Am Highway turnoff, the coast is only about fifteen miles to the west of us and one mile below us.

When the Quakers came, Costa Rica had recently abolished its army. The United States had dropped the first atomic bombs on Hiroshima and Nagasaki, after which the Soviet Union parlayed Klaus Fuchs's spying into its own "Joe I" version, Harry Truman countered by bankrolling Edward Teller's development of "the Super," a hydrogen bomb, and Washington dusted off the Selective Service provisions to draft Americans into a new war: Korea. So a group of Quakers left Alabama and came to Costa Rica to look for a new way of life.

The Quakers started a farming community here, and they still produce good cheeses and home-baked bread. Much of their energy now seems directed toward incorporating more uncleared land into their growing private nature preserve. To do so, they've had to encourage tourism, which while providing funds has also taken a small toll on the wildlife and the once-pristine beauty of the mountain village. The consolation is that part of what little it costs to traipse through the cloud forest goes toward buying additional land.

Most of the tourists who come here are of the sort who understand the delicacy of their surroundings. Certainly the birders who flock to this place wouldn't hurt a fly—or anything else with wings—though I'd be wary, as a human being, of getting between them and a three-wattled bellbird. For the birders, Monteverde is Mecca, Machu Picchu, Lourdes, and Dodger Stadium all wrapped up into one. This is the avian capital of what must be, acre for acre, the most bird-ridden country in the world: nine hundred species in a country smaller than West Virginia. (There are only six hundred species in all of the United States.)

If I were a birder, I'd file a claim with the Internal Revenue Service for tax-exempt status: birding is clearly a religion. How else do you explain that spacey, just-inducted-Moonie look on the birder's face while waiting for his turn at the binoculars when someone's got a prize species in their sights? Then over dinner, when the birds themselves are gone: the rapturous attention paid to the day's taped birdcalls, which when played back on an expensive Sony at every imaginable speed sound like the TV cartoons on Saturday morning. Then after dinner: No birds? No problem. Just walk out onto the porch at the woody Pensión Quetzal, forget that it looks out over some of the most gorgeous moonlit acreage in all of Central America, and stare into the electric porch lights. Moths. They have wings.

Then one morning I get religion. Now I understand.

It was very high up in a cool, peaceful grove of trees, which seem particularly tall and elegant in the early-morning shadows they cast on each other. We had followed some birders here. A man held the binoculars to his eyes and scanned the pointillist canvas of leaves and branches and sunlight. His right arm shot out and pointed stiffly. I followed with my eyes. And there it was. A flash of iridescent blue and green and black and red etching an arc between two branches. A quetzal. It stopped moving. A superb male quetzal trailing glorious ribbons of tail feathers three times his body length.

That was the first of many we would see in the grove. It's Guatemala's national bird, but we never did manage to find one there, though we looked. Wouldn't you know that Costa Rica, which has so much of what its neighbors lack, would even have Guatemala's bird.

The last time I drove into San José was in the heady aftermath of July 19, 1979, in Nicaragua, with the sun of freedom stamped in my passport. My rental car—which looked as if it had been through a war, as they say—died just outside the tollgate north of the Costa Rican capital.

So there we were, on the asphalt apron approaching the tollbooths, Mark Starr and I and a couple of other journalist refugees from Nicaragua. Stranded. Stranded in Costa Rica. Not to worry: in Latin America, everything always works out, especially in lucky Costa Rica. We deposited the car off to one side of the road, unpacked it, locked it carefully, and made arrangements for the reporter from Ireland who was with us to deal with Avis de Costa Rica on Monday; in return, the rest of us would pay his share of the car rental.

In a matter of minutes—we were politely accosting drivers as they paid their tolls—we secured a ride. With a tennis pro, this being Costa Rica and not Nicaragua. It had been a while since any of us had seen a tennis pro. We climbed into the back of his pickup and drove toward the distant flickering lights of San José while listening to Starr's Jefferson Airplane tape.

It was a good thing we had all saved various major news organizations the money it would have cost us to pay that toll back there. The tennis pro dropped us off on the plaza by the Gran Hotel Costa Rica. There were no rooms available. Well, just one. The Presidential Suite. We took it. All of us. We walked over to a nice restaurant. Anything on the menu that had a French word in its description, we ordered.

Now, eight years later, my visit to San José would be similarly serendipitous. We had planned only where we would stay—with friends, Dick Dyer and his daughter, Dery Dyer, who edit and publish the *Tico Times*. (*Tico* is universal shorthand for "Costa Rican"—*costarricence*. The word is derived from the fact that Ticos, like Cubans and Chileans, use the suffix *-tico* in forming the diminutive of nouns.) Other than that, we would basically wander.

There's a precision and logic to the country that allows visitors accustomed to order to feel comfortable wandering. Sometimes the orderliness seems excessive. I kind of like the idea that in the *Guía Roji* street guide to Mexico City there are 157 listings for streets, avenues, and alleys named after Benito Juárez. In Managua, the streets have no names. That's true in Costa Rica too; here they have numbers. In every single city the streets and avenues are numbered with the exception of the two that establish the grid pattern: Avenida Central and Calle Central. To their credit, Ticos, as if asserting their Latin Americanness, of course never actually use the numbers. Like Managuans, they use landmarks; at least here the landmarks haven't been demolished. And Costa Ricans use the landmarks with Tico precision: go up this street one hundred meters (one block) to Pollos Kentucky (Kentucky Fried Chicken, red and white, just like home), take a left, go fifty meters (half a block).

To its credit and detriment both, the country feels a little like home. That's why the second largest U.S. expatriate community (after Mexico) has settled here. Their dollars go a long way, they don't have to worry about guerrilla kidnappings, and the golf courses aren't mined. And yet part of the excitement of serious travel is the mildly threatening feeling of losing your bearings, of every once in a while having to ask yourself, Am I lost? Part, too, is the awakening slap of something, someplace, somebody totally new and different.

There's some of that in Costa Rica's wild geology, and in its abundant and startling plant and animal life. But overall Costa Rica can feel too easy to take, too smooth to the touch. Stolichnaya as opposed to aguardiente. There is an earnestness about this country that verges on preciousness. Once you're here for a while you can lose sight of the hard work and good fortune that made Costa Rica the regional exception, and example, that it is today.

One rainy afternoon in San José, after our usual stop at the handsome café off the lobby of the National Theater, we hop over to a cinema to see *Something Wild,* a movie that starts out sexy and takes on an increasingly hard edge. At one point in the movie one of the characters lets loose a fiery, protracted barrage of insult, vituperation, and obscenity. I glance at the subtitles to see how this cauldron of foul verbiage will be handled. There is one word on the screen: "*Maldito!*" Damn!

Obviously subtitles are crafted with the universal Spanish-language audience in mind—not just Costa Rica. Nonetheless, the distillation of so much anger and violence into a single, simple *damn!* strikes me as perfectly Costa Rican.

On a Tuesday in March 1963, the day John F. Kennedy landed in San José for a state visit, the Irazú Volcano erupted. A shower of gritty ash fell on the Meseta Central. It left fields looking charred and, piling up like black snow, caved in rooftops. So gringo-friendly is Costa Rica that I like to think of Irazú's angry eruption as a protest, an expression of some latent, seething anti-*yanqui* sentiment secretly harbored by the placid Ticos.

We are headed to Volcán Irazú up a rain-slick road. The mountain has been dormant for more than a generation now. There's a tidy symmetry to its sleek slopes: squared-off fields of wheat and barley, neat walls of volcanic rock. This is *invierno* in Costa Rica—"winter," or the rainy season, even though we're into August—so all the vegetation is dripping wet, the soil jet black. Amid vines high above feathery beds of ferns so big they seem magnified by a glass, parasitic plants climb trees, looking like children dressed in brightly colored clothes. We are east of San José, in the exact middle of the country. From the top of Irazú, if it weren't for the omnipresent barriers of clouds, you could see both the Atlantic and the Pacific.

Irazú is one of Costa Rica's two dozen national parks and biological reserves. The park system is impressive; it and Chile's are probably Latin America's finest. The parks are emblematic not only of the Ticos' concern for the environment but also of their relative wealth, which enables the government to practice the kind of minimal protection that would be an unaffordable luxury in most other Latin American countries. It would be wrong, however, to conclude on the basis of Costa Rica's pretty parks that the country is immune to the ecological devastation that has plagued its neighbors. Costa Rica is among the most severely deforested countries of Latin America. In Guatemala, where farmers and villagers hauling firewood on their backs or atop rickety handcarts down from the hills are routine roadside sights, it is easy to blame household use of wood for the scarred mountain flanks. Costa Rica is a reminder that here and in Guatemala and elsewhere the grand deforesters are in fact commercial enterprises, the big land clearers and woodcutters and ranchers.

Here cooking and heating fuels other than wood are much more common and you see very few people carrying firewood from one place to another. And yet, while forty years ago almost three-quarters of Costa Rica was forested, today only about one-quarter is. Landowners with five hundred acres or more own half the arable land in the country. They have made steep profits by turning forested land into erosion-prone pastureland for cattle, much of the livestock destined to show up nestled in Styrofoam boxes with side orders of fries at American fast-food restaurants. According to one estimate, Costa Rica loses to erosion a ton of topsoil for every pound of beef produced from Tico cattle—a quarter ton for each Quarter Pounder if the All Beef Patty comes from Tico cattle.

Irazú's cratered summit looks like a lunar beach. When we arrive, there are none of the usual junco birds darting through the mist. We can't even see the fumaroles on the northwestern slope, or their ventings of steam and gas. We seem to be crossing a chilly 11,000-foot-high desert. What a sight we must have been from a distance: two grainy figures under umbrellas marching along in a fine drizzle, the sky above a dingy backdrop, the gray sand below. It restores one's faith in Costa Rica's capacity for hazard to know that a blinding cloak of rain clouds can sneak up on walkers. Suddenly, all the landmarks—the horizon, what's up, what's down, Julith a short distance ahead of me—disappear. For a brief moment, I'm stranded again in Costa Rica.

One morning we are driving with Dick and Dery Dyer along the San José–Cartago highway. I'm at the wheel. Having forgotten by this point in the trip what a speed-limit sign is, I'm going a bit fast. A police squad car pulls me over. (A police car! It's been ages since I've even seen one. Flashing lights. Siren. Decals. It might as well have been a flying saucer.)

At this juncture, in any other Latin American country I've driven in except Chile, you begin a kind of pas de deux that always ends with the same step: a certain amount of your money becomes somebody else's. In Mexico it's the *mordida* dance:

"Morning."

"Morning."

"Where you headed?"

"Puebla."

"Puebla? Nice. In a bit of a hurry, I guess?"

"Well, you know . . ."

"Think you should come down to the station with me so . . ."

"That'll take up quite a bit of time."

"A while."

"Maybe I could just leave the fine with you?"

"Might do it that way."

"How much might the fine be?"

"Twenty thousand pesos."

"Five."

"Ten."

"Okay. Ten."

"Hey, you need any directions? Know the way?"

"No problem."

"Later."

"Later. Bye."

Not in Costa Rica.

In this democracy they take rules and regulations very seriously. It is a police state run by school crossing guards. Where else in Latin America are you required, by a law that somebody actually enforces, to wear seat belts? Where else do they have a park in the capital with a scaled-down village where kids go to tool around in battery-powered cars to learn good driving habits? Here values not only count but are enforced: Mother's Day is a national holiday.

So forget trying to pull out six hundred colones to grease the skids with this space cadet from the flying saucer who's pulled over the Land Cruiser. We shall be fined. Not only that, but he shall remove one of our license plates. With a screwdriver and a pair of pliers that these guys carry around with them for this very purpose, he will take our license plate and keep it. We get it back after we pay our fine, which, no, we can't pay to him, but which we will have to do next week since it's the weekend, and appear before the appropriate authorities to do so.

Wait. We're from Massachusetts. . . . It's a state. It's some kind of Indian name. . . . Anyway, we have only one license plate. I don't know. They're stingy, I guess; just trying to save the taxpayers money. So we can't give you our only license plate. What if some other policeman stops us? We don't want to go home and park. We're on a trip. We'll be stranded here.

(Stranded in Costa Rica. Again?)

At this point the Dyers intervene, summoning up at least three decades apiece of experience in the fine art of Costa Rican diplomacy. Dick is looking particularly wise; he has lighted his meerschaum. Dery mentions offhandedly her association with a certain major metropolitan weekly newspaper; she drops the name gently, like a rose petal.

They explain. Our North American friends, you see, don't live here. (That is to say, they are not used to refined Costa Rican ways. They should be forgiven their speeding and their boorishness.) They are on a very long trip through many countries. (Time is important to them, and it's important that they take away a good impression of Costa Rica compared to the other countries they are visiting.) They're used to driving in Mexico. (That is the clincher: they are accustomed to dealing with crooked cops.) They will be returning to Mexico to live. (Poor souls.)

We get off scot-free.

The train has settled into a rollicking gait. Paul Theroux, who wrote about this train trip, would have been sitting at this end of the car too, I imagine. The latrine is at the other end, an outhouse trapped inside this box of wood and steel. Theroux would have had his copy of Poe's *The Narrative of Arthur Gordon Pym* at the ready. He carried his books as other people carry umbrellas and would pull one out to fend off threatening clouds: an intrusive foreigner, dismal scenery.

The dismal scenery is behind us now. The train from

San José to Puerto Limón passes through the seediest part of the capital, where one of the city's few slums presses up tight against the tracks. Through the train window, the motion picture of tin shacks, clapboard bungalows, and drying laundry is a reminder that while Costa Rica's per capita income ($1,352 a year) is 40 percent higher than Honduras's, it is still half of Venezuela's. The government is careful not to let such reminders proliferate. Clusters of *tugurios*—huts—pop up every so often on the airport road as squatters gravitate to the capital, only to be scraped away by government bulldozers as an offense to tourists' eyes.

At the train station in San José it was easy to spot the crowd going to Limón. Travel destinations among people at train stations or bus terminals are easier to discern than at airports, where the money it costs to fly lends a sameness to the passengers. In a country so uniformly either white or mestizo, the blacks waiting for the 11:00 A.M. train to Limón stood out. The sounds in the waiting area were an especially pleasant change, for we had not yet ventured to the eastern parts of Central America during our trip. The metallic jounce of tape-deck reggae. The syncopated lilt of Caribbean English in which the jive greeting "What's happenin', man?" becomes one and a half beats on a verbal drum, da-dum: "Whoppen?" Then the slap of hands meeting in salutation.

Costa Rica's Atlantic Coast, as in Honduras and Nicaragua, was from the earliest days only thinly populated by indigenous peoples. In all three countries, the coast was settled by the British and later the Americans, who imported—not as slaves, but as cheap labor—blacks from Africa and the Caribbean to work the cacao and banana plantations and the hardwood trees like mahogany and black walnut. The coast is a low, steamy land spiderwebbed by rivers and the banana companies' man-made canals. Away from the cities and where the roads are few, the principal mode of transportation is the riverboat. Before the British navy was around to protect English settlements, pirates skulked about the ports. There is still an Amazonian remoteness and mystery to some of the more isolated zones of the Atlantic Coast (so called because the Caribbean is part of the Atlantic). As a rule, these littorals—largely ignored by the Spaniards because of the heat, heavy rainfall, and unhealthiness—were settled relatively late in the countries' development process, and the people of the coast have historically been treated as second-class citizens by the central governments.

Because of their remoteness from the capitals, the people of the coast have also been spared some of the internecine battles that have raged further inland. The Miskito Indians of Nicaragua's Atlantic Coast escaped all but the occasional stray skirmish in the civil war. The Sandinistas met no resistance when they took the National Guard post at Bluefields; the cost to them was the boat fuel they burned to get there.

In the case of the contra war, however, the U.S.-backed rebels have capitalized on the alienation of the coastal population, drawing the Miskitos in Nicaragua and Honduras into the thick of the conflict. So news of the war occasionally brings with it wonderfully eclectic Atlantic Coast names like Brooklyn Rivera, the leader of the Misurata Miskito Indian anti-Sandinista group; Steadman Fagoth Muller, the leader of the Misura Indian rebels; and Wycliffe Diego Blandón, the leader of the Kisan Indians.

Costa Rica's Atlantic Coast is not nearly as remote as

Nicaragua's. A century of big-business agriculture has turned Limón into an important port. We are headed there because it is our gateway to South America. We will be shipping the Land Cruiser and our gear, safely locked inside a sturdy red container, by freighter from Limón, through the Panama Canal, and on to Ecuador's chief Pacific port, Guayaquil. We need to go to Limón to check on the shipping arrangements and to see what chance, if any, we have of booking passage for ourselves on the same ship. (The answer will be: no chance. We will end up flying to Quito and then on to Guayaquil to get the car.)

We could have driven to Limón—a trip that takes two hours and fifteen minutes. But we wanted to take the train. We had been forewarned that it takes longer (it did) and that we would have second thoughts (we did).

The Costa Rica Tourism Institute and the national railroads are refurbishing vintage railcars and embellishing the trip with such frills as bar and restaurant service. They are available for group tours.

It's pretty obvious we are not part of a group tour. The only refurbishing that's been done to our train was performed gratis by countless decades of monsoonlike rains: a car wash. The wood-slatted seats are very vintage and definitely made of hardwood, very hard wood. Bar and restaurant? The service personnel were with us at the station in San José, mingling with the purveyors of "gold" chains and equally bogus "Ray Ban" sunglasses: vendors hawking fried plantains, Cokes, and *mamón chino,* an exotic fruit that resembles a thorny dingleberry enlarged by proximity to a nuclear power plant.

This is not a famously life-threatening rail voyage as far as I have heard, so it was with some apprehension that I noted a shrine to the Virgin Mary at one end of the station platform. The inscription was not reassuring: it said that in 1956 the manager of one of Costa Rica's railroads "contributed generously" to the construction of the shrine. Considering that all the shrines I've been seeing recently memorialized victims of highway wrecks, three questions: Why did C. W. Averre of the Northern Railroad contribute to a shrine? What exactly happened in 1956? And what has the safety record of the railroad been in the intervening three decades?

One thing I am not worried about is speeding. If safety and speed were inversely proportional, we would be really safe. San José–Limón. 103 miles. 7.5 hours. 13.73 MPH. Slow.

The train climbs up and over the continental divide near Cartago, which was the Costa Rican capital until 1823, a city hit so often by earthquakes that nothing looks old. The truly scenic part of the trip begins as the train works its way down the narrow, still-heavily wooded valley of the aptly named Río Reventazón, "the bursting river."

At Turrialba, the train tracks cling to a narrow ledge. Ahead of us and behind us are what look like small piles of discarded Popsicle sticks: rail bridges too delicate-looking to be bridges. Hugging cliffs on the left, the train rides high above the Reventazón, which is threading its own way down to the coast through cool-looking forests and that special green sheen of the coffee farms. After about five hours, after having gone from high-mountain pine down through an ecological whirl of highland and lowland tropical foliage, the train spills out onto the banana coast at Siquirres.

When I first read that four thousand workers died in

the construction of the San José–Puerto Limón rail line in the second half of the nineteenth century, I assumed they had perished while blasting, cutting, and carving their way through the Reventazón Valley. Some did, but most died from diseases like yellow fever as they laid the track across the flat stretch from Siquirres straight east to the coastline and down to Limón. Building this railroad was a formidable task. It took nineteen years, from 1871 to 1890. For nearly a century, until the San José–Limón highway was completed in 1970, it was the only direct and practical land route between the capital and the Atlantic Coast.

The work began under the "coffee presidents." Costa Rica was the first Central American country to cultivate coffee, and the first major exporter, beginning in about 1825. By the mid-1800s, it became clear that the country's coffee industry, in order to expand, needed a port on the Atlantic Coast to ship more efficiently to the European market. The country turned to Henry Meiggs, a U.S. engineer who had masterminded several railroad projects in South America. Meiggs had laid track from the foggy coastal deserts of Peru and Chile to the snowy reaches of the Andes. Now it was as if Costa Rica were asking him to go down the backside of the Andes and into the Amazon.

To launch the project, Costa Rica incurred its first foreign debt—to English banks, the big lenders of the period. Meiggs had to recruit thousands of Jamaican, Italian, and Chinese workers. Years passed. The project was taking longer and costing more than expected. A stopgap solution was devised by one of the on-scene project overseers, Minor Cooper Keith. Keith had gotten into the banana business down on the coast, and began using banana exports to fund railway construction. In 1884 he made what would prove to be a very lucrative deal with the Costa Rican government. He would complete the money-snarled, long-delayed project on his own. In return, he wanted eight hundred thousand acres of untilled land along the tracks—tax-free for twenty years—and a long-term lease on the railroad. He got his deal, and Costa Rica got its railroad.

The railroad was a boon all around. The coffee-president period ended with the advent of mostly permanent democracy in 1889. But the coffee industry got its port, and for a few years early in the new century, Costa Rica was the biggest coffee exporter in the world.

Costa Rica also became the world's biggest banana exporter. As for Minor Keith, the end result of his banana investments and his farsighted railroad deal was the company he founded with a partner in 1899, the United Fruit Company of Boston. "La United," they call it here in the banana lands—"La Yunai," as rendered in the soft, elided Spanish of the Atlantic Coast. Keith, who married the daughter of a Costa Rican president, and La Yunai both would move on to other countries, ever expanding the reach of the legendary El Pulpo. The Octopus would fade as a power in Costa Rica and elsewhere. Today the most pervasive vestige of La Yunai may be linguistic. I had for years wondered why the people of Honduras and Costa Rica call a corner store *la pulpería*. Then it dawned on me that the word *pulpería* may well be a throwback to the days when almost everybody had to shop at the ubiquitous Yunai company store.

Keith's railroad too has, like a French weave, become an indistinguishable, integral part of the Atlantic Coast. You can see that best if you ride the train through the lowlands. You could get off the train when it comes to

Siquirres, when the train comes out of the mountains and onto the old La Yunai banana lands where yellow fever once killed so many and where the towns have imported names: Waldeck, Liverpool, and, of course, Boston. It's only thirty-five more miles to Limón, and you could switch to a fast bus.

We stay on the extra couple of hours. It's not so bad. The sun is setting, dulling the edge of the afternoon heat. The train is definitely a local at this point. Students—boys in blue pants and white shirts, girls in purple smocks and white shirts—pile on and pile off. Seats fill and seats empty. The kids chatter away in a vaguely English patois we can hardly understand. The train stops often—in town, between towns, almost everywhere the heavy, flapping banana leaves yawn open to a road. The land, like the train, is worn down, though not quite used up. The train is a part of the coast. Today it's a school bus. Some days it's an ambulance, carrying the sick to the hospital. And some days it's a hearse, carrying the dead to their graves.

CHAPTER FIVE
Ecuador: The Color of Money

THE FIRST TIME you saw them, you would smile involuntarily because they looked like tiny, raggedy businessmen swinging attaché cases. They introduced themselves with surprising formality. A small hand reaching out, a name, and an age. Always the age at the next birthday, because they were young men on the move, rushing headlong into the future. The future being after lunch, or tonight, or maybe as distant as that next birthday. They were brightly young, and they shunned the sadness of the drab streets around them. They wouldn't let it near them.

You knew what Juan Carlos would say if you had gotten so serious as to ask him what he would do if something not fun, like sadness, started coming around and making a pest out of itself. "I'd punch it all the way from here to Chimborazo," he'd say. He'd make a tiny fist and dip his right shoulder into an uppercut. He was always threatening, in an eight-years-old-going-on-nine kind of way, to send unwanted things or people to Chimborazo.

He liked the sound of it: Chim-bo-razo, really rolling the *r*. He knew the great volcano was far away and very tall. He hadn't been there. But he knew that to punch somebody or something unwanted all the way there would be a sign of strength and determination.

No, Juan Carlos and his friends on Avenida Pichincha today wouldn't let sadness near them. They paid no attention whatsoever to the revival tent hawking doom right across the street: "Revelations of the Apocalypse. Enter Free. Minors, 18:00 hrs. Adults, 19:00." They didn't know any better.

There they were in the distance, swinging their shoeshine boxes. When you came up to them, they sat on their shoeshine boxes, crouched over them, or slouched against the wall with the boxes tucked between arm and waist. That was one of the first things they had learned as shoeshine boys: watch that box; it's your life.

They stood up straight for the handshake. Their hands were still almost baby-soft, despite their work, and a little waxy, because of it.

Cristián Alvear, ten in December. Cristián lives in a two-room walk-up across from the main post office at Benalcázar and Santiago de Chile streets. Do you know where the president lives? he asks. Sure: that was where the ceremonial guards in blue waistcoats, tight white pants, and tall plumed hats stood guard by well-waxed wooden doors that open onto the patio greensward of the official presidential residence; where, less ceremoniously, discreetly posted at the street corners, soldiers also stood watch, in camouflage with their Uzis, on heightened alert since the president was kidnapped by his own air force eight months ago. Cristián lives right around the corner from the president with his six brothers and three sisters and his parents.

Jorge Núñez, nine in January. Washington Rodríguez, eleven (perhaps because of his advanced age, he doesn't feel obliged to say when he'll turn twelve). Juan Tierra, seven going on eight; a good, solid name: John Earth. Wellington, just turned seven, the youngest of the lot, and with such a fine first name that he leaves it at that.

Víctor Añasco, ten in December, is Juan Carlos's brother. When he's around all his friends, he stands away from his younger brother: Juan Carlos, who stands about three and a half feet tall, is growing too fast for Víctor's liking. Every once in a while, if they're walking down the street with the other boys, Víctor will sneak up behind Juan Carlos and give him a tricky little soccer kick, a tap on the heel that sends him reeling.

And as for Juan Carlos, he'll be nine in "eleven months," he says, as if his last birthday took place during some remote geologic period.

Víctor and Juan Carlos live in a part of Quito called Chillo Gallo, on land where the old Hacienda Ibarra once was. The hacienda lands were broken up by Ecuador's land-reform laws. If you've traveled through Latin America, you've probably stayed at ex-haciendas that have been turned into post-land-reform tourist hotels. If so, you can be forgiven for thinking that land reform did more for tourism than for the sometimes primitive, little-mechanized agricultural societies they were supposed to benefit. But in the case of the Hacienda Ibarra anyway, the land is actually being homesteaded by the poor.

Víctor and Juan Carlos come in to old Quito, to the Plaza San Martín up the street, on the bus six days a week. It takes them two hours, so they get up before five-thirty in the morning. The fare is five cents if you're over ten, half that if you're under ten, and fifteen cents if you want a seat.

The shoeshine business is very competitive. Even at only a dime a shine—the price of a soft drink—the boys still aren't doing more than four to seven pairs of shoes a day.

Their lives revolve around their shoeshine boxes. The box itself costs sixty cents. Each tin of polishing wax is thirty cents. Empty bottles for the "ink," or coloring agent, are fifteen cents. To fill them costs fifteen cents. The polishing cloths the boys buy by weight, ten cents an ounce. The two brushes, one for light colors and one for dark, are twenty-five cents apiece.

The shoeshine boys start out in the morning with their tins and bottles carefully wrapped in synthetic chamois cloth that muffles the sound of metal and glass on wood. By the end of the day their boxes clunk loudly, wearily.

Juan Carlos is something of a scatterbrain, and an easy target for the bad luck that seems to await him around every street corner. In his two years and one month as a shoeshine boy, he has had five of his boxes snatched from him, always by older shoeshine boys who can use his materials and are always looking for a way to eliminate competition. He's made twenty cents today, spent half of it, and it is noontime.

Cristián, Juan Carlos's best friend, has better luck. His days are more orderly; they look less like overturned trash bins than Juan Carlos's. He's more aggressive, and being smaller, he gets more sympathy shines. He's made thirty-five cents, spent none of it, and this morning when he went out to buy his mother some matches, he found a hundred-sucre bill (worth fifty cents) on the street. Cristián has never had his shoeshine box taken from him. He got it when he graduated from kindergarten. It would be his life for a while. He painted it green.

* * *

Cristián got his colors wrong.

Perhaps in no other Latin American capital is the physical divide between rich and poor so plain to see as it is in Quito. Avenida Patria (meaning "homeland," as in *patriotic*) is the line of demarcation, an equator that divides Quito into hemispheres: new and rich Quito to the north, old and poor Quito to the south. City maps are color coded. The *residenciales burgueses* (as in *bourgeoisie*) are green. The *residenciales populares* are pale yellow.

Beyond a buffer zone of parkland, a green wedge of wealth is a dagger pointed at the heart of old Quito. It extends north from Avenida Patria and rises into the hills, coming to an abrupt halt on the sharp edges of dramatic canyons. Here a long, snaking phalanx of high-rise condominiums with names like Bello Horizonte and Vista del Valle stands guard, glistening sentries of steel and glass themselves guarded by uniformed rent-a-cops.

New Quito differs from other Latin American bastions of the rich only in that it grew extraordinarily fast and confined itself to one part of the metropolis. The burst began in 1972 upon the completion of the 330-mile-long trans-Andean pipeline, which opened up the rich Amazonian oil fields of Ecuador's Oriente region. Ecuador is a relatively small and, for South America, densely populated country; the size of Colorado, it has about ten million inhabitants. In 1972, virtually overnight, Ecuador became the third largest oil producer and exporter in Latin America (after Mexico and Venezuela). And overnight, oil replaced bananas as Ecuador's chief earner of foreign exchange (Ecuador having supplanted the Central American countries as the world's No. 1 banana republic).

The Amazon oil boom triggered a decade of fabulous prosperity. Oil money generated rapid industrial growth in such areas as food products, textiles, pharmaceuticals, and cement. In the 1970s manufacturing growth in Ecuador was far and away the highest in Latin America (11.9 percent between 1973 and 1978). Ecuador doubled the size of its shipping fleet. Not surprisingly, the benefits from this Amazonian El Dorado, as they would have in any of the other grotesquely top-heavy economic cultures of Latin America, accrued chiefly to an Ecuadoran elite.

Fittingly, one of the principal avenues of new Quito is Amazonas, an urban arroyo of money-exchange houses, sidewalk cafés, hamburger and pizza joints, jeans shops, haute-couture boutiques, pastry shops, and travel agencies. It's a typically disorienting, acultural mix: Miami and Maracaibo, nowhere and anywhere. Between here and the hilltop high-rises is La Carolina, a broad, green park where well-to-do children can dress up in jodhpurs and riding boots to exercise their sleek ponies or, in Reeboks and designer jeans, do wheelies on a special track made for BMX-type trick bicycles that here are manufactured under the signal brand name Mister.

Around La Carolina, up and down the side streets and into the scantily forested hills, are the houses of the rich. They are the typical minifortresses of the Latin American upper crust. Villas large and small are concealed behind high walls iced along the top with a layer of glittery glass shards. Water, like blood from some unseen bludgeoning, seeps onto the sidewalk from under a driveway gate, puddling in the street: a servant is washing the Mercedes. For protection, wealth is only hinted at to the passerby: a TV satellite dish peeking over the wall. As you walk along—

only servants and cops walk these streets—snarling dogs, also unseen, lunge noisily against the sheet metal of the gates.

On Calle Juan León Mera, a block off Avenida Amazonas, there's a trendy Spanish tapa bar called La Rana Verde, whose name (The Green Frog) is vaguely suggestive of the Amazon. One afternoon at La Rana Verde a richly made-up middle-aged woman is expounding on the wonders and perils of travels abroad to two younger women. It seems one of the younger women is about to go off on a trip—twenty days in Italy, and another twenty split between Paris and London. The older woman is advising her to think not in sucres, but always in dollars, when she's traveling. The older woman dispenses her advice in a typically upper-class mix of both Spanish and English, like Tolstoy's Russians speaking their French so the maids won't understand. In so doing, she employs a phrase in English that has its roots somewhere between the game of baseball, which is not played in Ecuador, and the colloquial expression "you're out of it." She says: "*Cuando se viaja, si piensas en sucres,* you're out." When you travel, if you think in sucres, you're out.

Think dollars.

Think green.

On the other side of Avenida Patria is old Quito, the part of the city that is pale yellow on the maps. Here, south of the Ralph Lauren store and the leather shop and the chic *peña* (folk-music bar) where the rich can listen to songs about the poor, the real Quito begins. The English, who in their accounts of journeys abroad seem to be struck first by ethnic and racial contrasts, would quickly notice a predominance of Indians and mestizos on this side of town. Americans, who seem to be struck first by economic contrasts, would feel the poverty. Latin Americans from outside Ecuador, whether they cared or didn't, would not be at all surprised.

Political slogans begin to appear on the walls. "The Left and the People Together." "Yanqui Troops Go Home." That last one is relatively fresh still—sparked by the arrival in March of U.S. Army helicopters and engineers down from the Panama Canal Zone to survey earthquake damage to the road system paralleling the trans-Andean pipeline. It's the end of August now and the issue is still fermenting in the left-wing press, which suspects the worst. The cover of the magazine *Nueva* has toy U.S. soldiers encamped on a map of Ecuador. The Vietnam War movie *Platoon* has just hit town, so the coverline is, OUR OWN "PLATOON"? Inside, one of the five articles devoted to the subject is a dissertation ("Two Centuries of Aggression") on the Monroe Doctrine, Manifest Destiny, and the prescience of Simón Bolívar, who after liberating northern South America from the Spaniards, says the article, warned of another imperialist threat: "The United States seems destined by Providence to plague the Americas with misery in the name of liberty."

La Alameda Park, with its quaint old observatory set among the cottonwoods, forms an unobtrusive DMZ between the two Quitos. Overlooking the northern end is a sleekly modern hotel, the Colón Internacional, with its unending marble floors and a gallery of expensive shops, the last island of haute consumerism before you cross the border. On the southern edge of the park is an impressive statue of Bolívar of recent vintage. A policeman is posted at the forehooves of the Liberator's hard-charging steed to keep the graffiti artists at bay.

Quito is nearly three kilometers above sea level, so with dusk, the warmth of the city's sun-drenched days turns quickly to the cool of its starry nights. The nights, somebody said, are the winter of the tropics. As downtown empties, the narrow, cobbled one-way streets of old Quito fill quickly with the smell of cooking pork from streetside stands and with the choking fumes from innumerable buses, whose sidewalk-to-sidewalk girth turns a stroll into a defensive sport.

It has often been said—too often—that Quito is a city of a hundred churches and one bathroom. And there are indeed in old Quito eighty-six churches that bear witness to the religious stamp left by the Spanish here and across Latin America. Most are well preserved, along with government palaces and at least the facades of colonial homes, if only because urban and economic growth has struck elsewhere. The grace of the architecture stands in stark contrast to the overwrought, sanguinary religious painting churned out by the School of Quito. That production is aptly summed up by a story they tell about Miguel de Santiago, one of three artists comprising the so-called "glorious trinity" of colonial Ecuadoran painting. Intent on re-creating the agony of Christ on the cross, the painter worked with a number of male models, dissatisfied with each, until in desperation he chucked a spear at one and used that dying man's face as the image he was seeking.

On the now shadowless plaza in front of the National Theater, two street actors have drawn an after-work crowd. One plays a cop or a soldier, some authority figure in uniform; he's wearing a camouflage shirt and a web belt. The other plays a drunk; he's lying on the ground. The cop barks out questions to the drunk. After each question he yells—"*Silencio!*"—not giving the drunk time to answer. He starts to haul the drunk off to jail. The drunk kicks the cop in the balls. The cop points his right hand at the drunk, squeezes his trigger finger, and repeatedly shoots the drunk. The cop speaks into his hand, radioing his superior: "Came across a drunk. . . . An accident. . . . Somebody shot him. . . . Wounded. . . . Send an ambulance."

The final skit of the evening is about a topic that's been in the Quito papers all week: Ecuador's foreign debt. The actor who played the authority figure has changed roles. Now he tells the audience he's figured out that the national debt of about nine billion dollars comes out to 180,000 sucres for each and every Ecuadoran. So he picks out kids in the crowd and asks each one, "Did you ever borrow a hundred and eighty thousand sucres from a foreign bank?" He asks several giggling boys and girls the same question. Then he turns, wheeling, to a tall gringo standing at the edge of the crowd:

"Did you ever lend a hundred and eighty thousand sucres to one of these children?"

For a second it's no longer theater, and it seems cold all of a sudden. Then an explosion of laughter from the crowd breaks the silence. To the tall gringo, shaken, the burst of laughter is painfully sharp, the sound of a desert rock cracking under the heat of the morning sun.

Every once in a while, Juan Carlos Añasco, eight going on nine, keen observer of the ways of the world, issues a pronouncement that lends some order to the unpredictable world of the shoeshine boys of Quito. He utters each decree with almost sacred authority: a small pope in sneakers. This morning's papal bull: "Gringos all write with their left hand, don't they? We all write with our right hand."

The boys are making their early rounds. Because of their proximity to Plaza San Martín, unofficial headquarters for Quito's swarms of shoeshine boys, the shopkeepers along Avenida Pichincha probably have the shiniest shoes this side—which is now the south side—of the equator. Pichincha is named after the grand, snow-etched volcano that towers over the capital. The avenue drops down into one of the many ravines that slice up old Quito. The main streets, like Pichincha, are grimly urban, overrun by commercial businesses, crowded and noisy with traffic, the curbsides filling with a city's debris. The side streets are pleasantly antique: cobbles set in place long ago, rail-thin sidewalks, whitewashed colonial buildings, balconies dripping with the morning's laundry.

You can look down on this part of Quito from the top of a nearby hill, the Cerro Panecillo, the one with a new statue of the Virgen de las Américas at the crest. You cross over the Río Manchángara on the García Moreno Street bridge and head up half a mile of steps and footpaths. The neighborhood women used to do their wash in the Manchángara and then take their clothes home to hang them out to dry. The river's gotten too polluted for that. Before you get very far, the women at the public laundry near the foot of the hill—a roof over concrete sinks and a water tap—stop you to say that it is too dangerous to walk up there anymore. That's life in a city closing in on a million people.

Along Pichincha the small troop of shoeshine boys weaves in and out of shops like a Chinese dragon in a parade. It would be better business if they split up, but not as much fun. It would be better business on the other side of the city, cruising the tourist haunts and the rich businessmen's sidewalk coffee klatches along Avenida Amazonas, but the police over there shoo the ragamuffin kids away. So in and out of a small grocery: one shine for one ice cream cone. Past the aproned woman boiling chicken feet at her soup stand.

At a crummy bar with wood stools and scratchy music from an old transistor radio, Juan Carlos shines the owner's shoes. The owner refuses to pay. He tells Juan Carlos he did a bad job the last time. The tiny pope retreats.

Juan Carlos's day has started off badly. He sulks. He picks a bone with Jorge Núñez, nine in January. Jorge stole his wax the other day, he says. He threatens to punch Jorge all the way to Chimborazo, but Jorge espies a client and runs off in that direction. Juan Carlos has got Jorge figured out: *"Es ambicioso."* Jorge's too ambitious for his own good.

"You see?" says Juan Carlos a minute later. Jorge has just charged his client five cents, half the going rate, undercutting the competition. "Didn't I tell you how ambitious he is?" Meanwhile, little Cristián has spotted a customer and scurries over there. "Jeeeeezzz," says Juan Carlos. He's disgusted.

Víctor—almost ten, and his brother Juan Carlos better not forget it—is shining the shoes of a man named Alfonso. Alfonso owns a small store on Pichincha that sells gold necklaces and bracelets. The jewelry is the booty of the returnee, the undocumented worker back from the United States. Alfonso went to New York City, and with the money he made there, he has set himself up in business back home. Even this far south in Latin America it's a common occurrence. Alfonso was in New York for ten years. He lived in Queens and worked as a short-order cook at Nathan's and at Brewburger. He met and married a Colombian woman there, and they came to Quito to settle down.

Hearing all this has Juan Carlos wondering a little about life. He has a question:

"When do children start working in the United States?"

By now the whole crew of shoeshine boys is heading down Pichincha toward the ravine. Ah, the ravine. That reminds one of the boys: somebody he knows told him that he had heard they found the head of a man down by the river. Pandemonium. The kids race past a soccer field, where sometimes they stop to buy roasted corn kernels, and down to the bridge: five pairs of sneakers and pants are all that's visible as they lean over the bridge railing and stare down at the banks of the Manchángara, looking for heads. There's just a lot of trash; Víctor, being older, spots a vagrant condom, which makes his day. Uncharacteristically, all the boys have carelessly left their shoeshine boxes unattended at their feet.

One rumor leads to another. AIDS is a favorite topic of conversation among the boys. "There's AIDS down there," says one. He points to a house in a row of houses.

Feeding the rumor mill quickly becomes a game.

Whenever possible the rumor should be attributed to a newspaper. The newspapers say such outrageous things that nobody will challenge you, lie or no lie. For that matter, in Ecuador a lot of the truth is outrageous.

The newspaper said Cotopaxi—one of Ecuador's several active volcanoes—was going "to explode." The radio said it was a lie. This self-negating rumor is Juan Carlos's contribution. He's big on volcanoes.

The newspaper said they assassinated "León." The kids all refer to the president as "León." León Febres Cordero encourages it. All over the country there are signs hailing his public-works projects: *"Otra Obra de León."* Another project for the people from León.

The news of his assassination comes from Víctor. The newspaper reported it. Víctor is considered a reliable source when it comes to newspapers. He's older after all—almost ten—and in the late afternoon he peddles papers on the streets of old Quito. Víctor is a bit of a con artist, and you can almost imagine him trying to boost his paper sales by yelling over the din of the fat buses in his newsboy's voice: *"ASESINARON AL PRESIDENTE!!"*

The president is alive and well and still living around the corner from Cristián. Actually, "well" is a relative term. It's been a tough year for León.

• January. Renegade air force troops opened fire on the president and his entourage during a military review at Tauro Air Force Base near Guayaquil, down on the coast. Two presidential bodyguards were killed. The disgruntled paratroopers seized the president, the defense minister, the air force chief of staff, and a couple of other members of Febres Cordero's military staff. They were held for twelve hours. To negotiate his own release, the president had to agree to free an air force general, Frank Vargas Passos, who had been jailed in Quito for a mutiny and attempted rebellion in 1986. This ruined the president's reputation as an uncompromising, tough leader who wore a pistol in his belt, swore he'd never negotiate with terrorists, and was the only South American head of state who supported Ronald Reagan's contra policy.

• March. The president was still nursing his wounded pride. The opposition-controlled Congress had formally petitioned his resignation for having "disgraced" the "national honor" by negotiating with his captors; the president rejected the request. Frank Vargas, the mutinous general turned professional self-promoter, would pop up from "hiding" every so often to say he was going to run for president in 1988. Then on two successive days a series of earthquakes shook the jungles of the Oriente. Only a small fraction of Ecuador's population lives there, but the quake killed three hundred people and left four thousand missing and twenty thousand homeless. The earthquake and attendant mudslides and flooding destroyed part of the trans-Andean pipeline and the road alongside it. The president had to halt oil exports, ration domestic gasoline supplies, and suspend interest payments on the foreign debt. Practically begging his left-wing opponents to give him grief, he invited the U.S. Army in to lend a hand with the roadwork. Enter the choppers.

• April. When is the truth outrageous? The president's own Social Christian Party put up Frank Vargas's bail money—five million sucres—on a still-pending charge of corruption stemming from the air force's curious purchase of a passenger jetliner. The president's party got tired of Vargas's using his seemingly embattled position as someone "in hiding" (a taxi driver could have taken you to him) as a political weapon.

• May. When is the truth outrageous? One of Ecuador's Communist parties backed the presidential bid of the military coupmaster General Vargas. The Communist party joined nine other left-wing parties in a coalition to run candidates in the 1988 elections. Vargas announced he was a nationalist, not a leftist. The leftist coalition began to disintegrate. The Communist party withdrew when other coalition members proposed a pro-Albanian Maoist as a unity candidate. Some parties stuck with Vargas. Other parties were adamantly against him. The whole thing fell apart. Meanwhile, the radical Ecuadoran guerrilla organization with the most bizarre name known to world rebeldom—Alfaro Vive, ¡Carajo!, or Alfaro Lives, Goddammit!, named after a turn-of-the-century president—was urging the people of Ecuador not to vote for anybody under any circumstances.

• July. Along the Río Aguarico deep in the Amazonian oil lands, the bodies of two Catholic missionaries were found. The missionaries—a bishop and a nun—had apparently been killed by members of a primitive Indian tribe known as the Red Feet. The official version of the story was that the pair had sought to contact the tribe and convert the Indians as part of an effort to prevent the killing of oil company employees working the petroleum fields in the area.

However, the liberal archbishop of Cuenca, in southern Ecuador, was promoting a different version. He didn't necessarily deny that the Red Feet murdered the missionaries. But he said the bishop and the nun were not in cahoots with the government or the oil companies. He said the missionaries had gotten wind that somebody—the government, the oil companies, or both—was about to initiate a "sanitizing operation" in the jungle outback to remove any and all obstacles to further oil exploration and development, including the Red Feet. Whoever killed the missionaries, said the archbishop, their deaths served to lay bare what was going on in the jungle.

Over the past decade, the Red Feet had attacked and

sometimes killed a number of intruders—lumbermen, people who worked for the palm-oil companies, and now petroleum workers. During the Febres Cordero administration and at its invitation, some fifteen foreign oil companies had begun exploring the Amazon. The state oil company had sent explorers into the wilds to make peace with the Red Feet. Clearly they were having limited success.

• August. On the fourteenth, the trans-Andean pipeline resumed pumping oil to the nation's largest refinery. On the twenty-first, oil exports resumed. Within a month, however, the president's planning minister would announce the tally in lost oil export revenues—over one billion dollars—and his government would announce a temporary halt in exploration in the land of the Red Feet. By now all of Ecuador's ills, whatever the cause, were being blamed on the feckless president. A bridge washed out? A dog-eared housing project dying for a paint job? Some smart aleck would come along with a can of spray paint: OTRA OBRA DE LEÓN.

Juan Carlos Añasco, shoeshine boy on his day off, is right where he said he would be: under "the horse." He'd only said it about a thousand times: *bajo el caballo en Chillo Gallo*. He liked the singsong rhyme of it. He also didn't want you to forget to meet him. The horse in question is part of a statue to José de San Martín, the liberation figure from Argentina and the third most memorialized hero in Quito after the homegrown liberator Antonio José de Sucre and the Great Liberator himself, Bolívar, who was from Venezuela. The bus stop at the horse in Chillo Gallo is an important landmark for Juan Carlos; it is as close as you can get by public transportation to his house.

It's a Sunday morning, and in terms of his personal grooming, Juan Carlos is more together than usual. His light brown hair is brushed more or less to one side, but pointy sprongs have begun to break loose—indicating certain victory in the struggle for liberation against a greasy cream that surely could not have been applied to his head without the assistance of several neighbors to hold him down. Pale yellow pullover; it looks good against his skin, lightly freckled and the color of honey. Gray flannels rolled up at the cuffs and a lighter gray at the knees; probably hand-me-downs from a brother. Sneakers that at one point in their no doubt colorful history—looking for severed heads, chasing after shoeshine box thieves, sending people all the way to Chimborazo—were white.

To get to Juan Carlos's house you walk down a pretty lane shaded and fragrantly scented by eucalyptus trees. On the left is a sports complex that looks like a public park but is actually privately owned and charges admission. It has electricity for its cash register and water for its pool. On the right is the old Hacienda Ibarra, a grassy expanse crisscrossed by dirt roads and dotted by small homes that all look as if they're under construction even though many have been lived in for some time now. There is no electricity. The water is brought in in tankers.

Juan Carlos's first stop is the cinder-block house where his half brother Franklin Rey lives. A small Sunday gathering—seven people—is in progress. You wouldn't call it a brunch. Some fresh cheese. Some bread. One bottle of orange soda and two bottles of Coca-Cola, all in those big family-size plastic bottles with black, opaque bottoms. Juan Carlos, experienced bartender, hefts a container of Coke over the mouth of a plastic drinking cup. He cradles the container as one would lift a small but heavy child. "Gringos like Coke," intones Juan Carlos with his customary infallibility.

Franklin Rey, a twenty-seven-year-old bachelor, works as a jack-of-all-trades at the Centro del Muchacho Trabajador (Center for the Working Boy). The CMT was founded and is still run by Father John Halligan, a chain-smoking Jesuit from the South Bronx. If you happen to catch him at work in his black Jack Daniel's T-shirt, he can look—and talk—like an aging Hell's Angel, a biker in service to God and Man. Halligan started out working with Quito street kids out of the attic at the Church of La Compañía in the mid-1960s. He eventually limited his project to families only, his rationale being that the family is society's basic building block. The Center offers food, medicine, and schooling. In return, the participating families, like Franklin Rey's, must comply with a strict code of behavior and such rules as regular attendance at Center meals. On the children, now girls as well as boys, the Center's self-help programs impose a discipline of the tough-love sort: a swift kick might work if a friendly shoulder to lean on proves insufficient.

In quiet gratitude to "Padre Juan," Franklin Rey one day etched the letters *CMT* into some wet cement at the entrance to the old Hacienda Ibarra. Franklin paid a little less than a thousand dollars for a plot of land (ten meters by eighteen meters) seven years ago. Ever since he's been saving and building, block by block, occasionally paying a helper three dollars a day. He's put in a cement floor, a bedroom, a living area, and a kitchen. The bathroom will be out of doors but with plumbing, if the city and the developer ever get around to the sewer lines. He hopes to build an apartment for his mother on what is now his roof; for the time being, that project is a promise embodied in the tentacles of reinforcing wire he has left sticking out of the top of his house.

At the moment Franklin's mother lives across a field with her sister. Melba Rey, fifty-two years old, shares a room with three of her children by a second marriage: Juan Carlos, Víctor, and twelve-year-old Italo. Juan Carlos's father, like Franklin's before him, left home years ago. In the room there is a hot plate, a dresser with some toys Víctor got from his godfather on top of it, and two bunk beds. The sister's house, like Franklin's, is a work in progress. On the edge of a dusty patio, there's a hopeful-looking pile of cinder blocks and bags of cement.

The old Hacienda Ibarra was all pastureland not long ago. It would have been a grassy blond at this time of the year, having been waiting since May for the mountain rains to begin falling again in November. Between the eucalyptus-spiced lane and the beckoning, gentle slope of the nearby foothills, the land is still sparsely populated and only moderately built up as cities go. It has yet to succumb to the vicissitudes of urban overcrowding, the sights and sounds and unsanitary smells of too many people amidst too much poverty and too little hope. For now, in fact, like the wire spaghetti protruding from Franklin's roof, it seems to hold promise of more and better things to come. Sunday has brought whole families out from the central city or in from the country to hammer and spackle their new little houses into shape.

Franklin and his family came to Quito the way many Ecuadorans still do, climbing a ladder of small cities and medium-size cities to get here. He grew up in Arenillas, a town near the Peruvian border in the bone-dry, knife-edged badlands of southwest Ecuador that are so shocking to anyone who has seen the tropical wetlands further up the Pacific coast. The family made its money by trafficking in medicines and other goods bought in Peru, living off the fluctuating exchange rate. Later the family made its way up the coast and inland to Santo Domingo de los Colorados, a bedraggled crossroads city from which a lowland highway climbs dizzyingly through the western ridge of the Andes, past 10,000 feet and down again slightly to the Pan American Highway. Melba Rey—who by this time had had nine children—followed that route with the kids who were still at home, including the infant Juan Carlos, and arrived in Quito only to have Ecuador's oil boom end shortly thereafter.

Over lunch in the sister's dining room—sugared coffee made from the ubiquitous Ecuadoran liquid concentrate, tamales, rice, and because it's Sunday, a fried egg on top of the rice—Franklin sinks into a depressing diatribe. His mind is on a meeting of Hacienda Ibarra landowners next Sunday to take legal action against the board of directors of the cooperative corporation that is supposed to represent the property owners.

Over the years, the neighborhood's fifty-two hundred property owners have paid thirty million sucres into the co-op's utility fund. By 1984 there should have been electricity, sewers, and drinking water. There's nothing—just some sidewalks. Now it turns out that two-thirds of the utility fund is missing and unaccounted for. At the same time, a search has turned up landownership titles for only fifteen hundred of the fifty-two hundred tracts, meaning that the rest of the property owners cannot borrow money using their land as collateral. Franklin suspects collusion among the co-op directors, the developers, and the government. "That's the way it works here," he says. "Where there's money, there's a way. Where there's no money, there's no way."

Halfway through lunch, Juan Carlos excuses himself. He was a bit taken aback by Franklin's sharp tone—shaken just enough to keep him quiet and staring down at the tabletop, abnormally interested in the backs of his hands as they rested there impatiently. Politely, he leaves the room to go outside and play with three ratty dogs out on the patio. Most of the family did not come to the lunch table, just "the men." Nobody talked about this, but it seems there wasn't enough food to go around.

At the time of the Conquest, Quito was, along with Cuzco in Peru, one of two capitals of the fractious and doomed Inca Empire. In 1533, one of the Spanish crown's conquistador juggernauts came up from Peru to Ecuador, snuffled and poked around and found none of the mineral riches it was after, laid claim to the land, and moved on into what is now Colombia. In time, however, Quito, as it had for the Incas, would emerge as an important seat of government for the Spanish, the capital of the audiencia of Quito under the viceregal seat at Lima. At the time of its independence from Spain, in 1830, Quito would retain its administrative importance over a territory four times the size of today's Ecuador and with a population of just half a million.

But already a crucial rivalry was developing between Quito and what has since become Ecuador's largest city, a sprawling metropolis twice Quito's size: Guayaquil. Quito would remain the seat of government and the headquarters of the conservative landowning oligarchy. But the exports would in the main be produced in and launched from coastal Ecuador, and its de facto capital, Guayaquil, would establish itself as the country's commercial and banking center, a font of entrepreneurship and mercantilism. The tension between the two cities would create and define the most durable political conflict in Ecuador, the struggle between the sierra conservatives and the liberals of the coast. And when the politicians of the two factions bogged down in their struggle for control, the military was pleased to fill the vacuum.

The country's most popular leaders have had to transcend the sierra-coast strife. The first to do so was Gabriel García Moreno. He was born in Guayaquil but was steeped in the conservatism of the sierra and would become the mayor of Quito before being elected president, in 1861. His personal and political hallmark was a zealous Catholicism that would turn Ecuador into a theocracy unlike anything else in the history of Latin America—fulfilling Bolívar's admonition that Ecuador was destined to become "a convent" among nations. Even as Juárez in Mexico was hanging the church out to dry, García Moreno was dedicating his state to the Sacred Heart of Jesus and drawing up his remarkable "Catholic Constitution," which required citizens to be Catholics and subordinated civil authority to ecclesiastical authority.

He ruled until his assassination in 1875. His followers did then and still do now consider his death a martyrdom, and indeed it was, in its gruesomeness, reminiscent of a School of Quito painting. Outside the cathedral in Quito, an ex–government official came up to García Moreno and swung a machete into his neck. Three more assailants approached and fired gunshots into the president, who fell off the gray stone portico to the street below. There the machete wielder once again fell upon him and finished him off.

The next truly popular leader was another dictator, Gen. Eloy Alfaro, whose name and bellicose idealism, if not much else, live on in the eponymous guerrilla group of today's Ecuador. He came to power on the heels of a period of fragile compromise worked out between sierra and coastal interests. He shattered that compromise with his radical coastal liberalism, carried out extensive anticlerical reforms that curtailed church power, and groomed Ecuador for the Pacific Coast agricultural export boom that would characterize much of its twentieth century. He was lynched by a Quito mob in 1912.

Ever since then the sierra-coast tension has been tempered politically by compromise. The balance of political power has teetered unsteadily and sometimes chaotically, though less so since 1979, when Ecuador became the first of a dozen Latin American countries that were then ruled by their military to return to civilian government. Economically, despite the Amazon oil trove and some industrial expansion around Quito, the shift has been almost entirely to the coast—in particular to Guayaquil and the adjacent, thirty-year-old Maritime Port, gateway for 90 percent of Ecuador's imports and 50 percent of its exports (oil is shipped out of another Pacific port, Puerto Balao, hard by the old slave port of Esmeraldas).

The population has shifted in similar fashion as sierrans have gravitated to where the jobs are. The highlanders who once predominated almost to the exclusion of all others are now outnumbered by the *costeños*. Between the bank towers and black markets of Guayaquil and the praying-mantis cranes and derricks of the Maritime Port there is an impromptu city in the making. This is Guasmo. It is made up of *invasores;* the word means "invaders," but to call this a squatter city distorts the extent to which various strata of development are evident here as a result of ad hoc immigration. There are the brand-new arrivals, crammed into lamplit makeshift homes of scrap wood and metal. There are the residents who have shot roots into the Guasmo soil and begged, borrowed, or stolen electricity for permanent dwellings with concrete floors and glass windows. Then there are the veteran squatters who've struck it more or less rich, living in scruffy two- and three-story Guasmo palaces with balconies overlooking the rutted dirt streets.

The coastal reality belies the efforts of Ecuador to pass itself off as an "Amazonian country." True, it has developed and populated, if only meagerly, the rich oil fields of the Oriente, which in its entirety comprises more than a third of the Ecuadoran land mass. But treaties have handed to Brazil, Colombia, and Peru more of Ecuador's Amazon than what remains. Ecuador lost the latest chunk—an area the size of the whole of Oriente—after Peruvian forces invaded the province of El Oro in 1941, bombing defenseless villages and swiftly capturing the provincial capital. The issue was adjudicated by a conference of Western Hemisphere foreign ministers in Rio de Janeiro at the time. Ecuador claims now that it was cheated in the bargain arranged by the ministers, who were preoccupied to distraction with events in Europe. (As a result, the otherwise excellent maps put out by the Military Geographic Institute are part cartographic fiction, and Amazon travelers use them at their peril.)

For all its sidelong glances at the Amazon, Ecuador remains, like virtually all of South America, what Spain trained all of its colonies to be: nonintrospective, outward-looking states whose eyes are set on the watery horizon, whose inland frontiers have almost always been afterthoughts in the minds of blindered planners, and whose economies are made or broken by foreign interests.

"Do you know the History of Year One?"

Juan Carlos again. The child philosopher. Ortega y Gasset in sneakers, boggling the minds of those around him.

He doesn't wait for an answer.

"That was when cars didn't have brakes and they would fall into the river. There was one accident a day."

Great timing. Why does he have to talk about accidents? He's riding in a car with his best friend and León's neighbor, Cristián. They're on their way to the hot springs at Papallacta, the best hot springs in Ecuador. You want to say to Juan Carlos: Hey, Juan Carlos, cool it. You'll scare the daylights out of your best friend Cristián.

Sure enough, there comes a bridge up ahead. A bridge spanning a gorge so deep you can't even see if there's a river at the bottom of it.

Juan Carlos and Cristián both start making this breathing-out noise with their mouths, a tremorous hum that begins deep in the chests: *eee-EEE-hhh*. It's a noise that means: we're scared. With their hands on their knees, they rock back and forth in their seats and make this strange noise. What are they pretending to be? Catatonic?

Halfway across the bridge, they can't stand it any longer. Each one pops his head out a side window to see if he can see a river at the bottom of the gorge.

Get back in the car, guys. Please.

Juan Carlos again.

"Good thing we didn't eat yet." Brief pause. "I might've thrown up back there."

Jeeezzz.

It's touch and go as it is. Bad enough without Juan Carlos's clowning around. Neither one of the boys is used to being in a car. A bus is one thing. A long car trip is another. These are real city kids. On the outskirts of Quito, they were wondering if they were there yet, if that was Papallacta over there, how many minutes it would take, would it be sunny when they got there, or dark.

This is a picnic. It'll be daylight. It won't be dark yet.

Cristián is even more of a city kid than Juan Carlos is. He wants to know how far it is to Papallacta.

It's eighty kilometers from Quito to Papallacta.

There's silence from Cristián's corner. Then he asks, in all seriousness: "How many blocks is that?"

More and more, Cristián is saying things that sound as if they should be coming out of Juan Carlos's mouth. At the Center the other day, everybody was having lunch. Rice. Corn in a strange, milky broth. A kind of stew made with potatoes and cabbage. Even the juice was off-white. Only the rice didn't look like some sort of surprise. Then Cristián, who doesn't ever say very much, pipes up. "Gringos always like the rice," he said matter-of-factly.

Isabel was at lunch too. She's twelve or thirteen. She's got eleven brothers and sisters, a mother, and an absent father. Isabel's got a theory about gringos too. Quite a number of them have dropped by the Center, passed through, visited, stayed for a while to work, and moved on. This is her theory:

"All the gringos, they always leave."

But Father Halligan stayed.

"That's different."

Climbing toward Papallacta on the last stretch of paved road, between Tumbaco and Pifo, the car passes a bus groaning up a steep incline. Like just about every single bus north of Chile, this one's got a slogan on its tail end. *"No Soy Dólar, Pero Subo."* I Might Not Be A Dollar, But I Go Up.

The kids love it. You try to explain to them that in some countries, the dollar is weak, that the currencies of some other nations in the world are in better shape than the dollar, that because of trading back and forth between the United States and these other nations . . . Even if you could make some sense out of this subject, the kids wouldn't believe it. They give you this blank look. Like you're crazy.

After it turns to dirt at Pifo, the road climbs steadily to over 13,000 feet. At one point, just over the highest rise, the road and the trans-Andean pipeline cross each other, like swords joined in a common purpose. From here on out the road and the pipeline travel side by side, watching over each other.

On the Military Geographic Institute map, you can see the road and the pipeline meeting up with the Río Papallacta and sliding down the lesser-known backside of the Andes. Down from the beige contour rings—10,000 feet— to the dirty-sand color—5,000 feet—at Baeza. There the road splits. One fork goes northeast with the pipeline, which is purple, a heartline rushing back over the Andes toward Puerto Balao and the refinery tanks waiting impatiently on the Pacific Coast, 250 miles away. The Sardinas Grande, the Oyacachi, the Cascabel (the Rattlesnake), and unnamed thin blue veins. These rivers—who knows how big or small they are?—join the road and the pipeline in the valley of the Río Quijos: 3,000 feet.

The road and the pipeline leave the Quijos in their wake. The Quijos turns into the Coca, which is so big the map shows islands breaking the blue of the river. Then comes the town of Puerto Francisco de Orellana, named after the Spanish explorer who helped conquer the Peru of the Incas with the conquistador Francisco Pizarro, who discovered the Amazon with Francisco's brother Gonzalo, and who followed the Amazon, followed it for four thousand miles, until it emptied into the Atlantic. The Coca does the same. Downstream a thousand miles or so, it meets up with the giant Río Napo. Downstream on the Amazon from Iquitos, which the map says is in disputed territory but the world says is in Peru, the Napo finally runs into the Amazon, which is so enormous that it looks like an inland sea.

The road and the pipeline cut across an ivory-colored plain on the map—2,000 feet. Then the map turns green: the Amazon Basin. As on the Quito city map, here too green means money. The road and the pipeline, dropping down from 1,000 feet and down further, travel for a while with the Río Aguarico, the river along which the bodies of the bishop and the nun were found. On the map the bustle of business is evident across the green flatness. The pipeline splinters, looking for oil. Roads scamper off in all directions, going to what looks like nowhere but isn't. Towns—or are they just places?—towns without roads have airstrips. There are airstrips where there are no towns. The Aguarico leaves the bustle behind, moves silently through the land of the Red Feet, then joins the Napo for the long journey to the Atlantic.

Fortunately, from where the road and the pipeline cross like swords, Juan Carlos and Cristián have only ten miles to go on their day trip. Everybody takes a break while Juan Carlos, who's terribly embarrassed about it, runs across the spongy grass to a boulder and gets sick.

It's quiet out here. There have been a few cars, also headed for Papallacta. And a few military vehicles, including a hulking old Caterpillar DC-9 bulldozer, its tracks thick with mud, riding piggyback on an army trailer that barely made it over the last bridge, a skinny affair lodged in a mountain's elbow. They're not through working on the earthquake damage from last March. You can still see raw, dark, wet wounds in the hillsides where big chunks of dirt slithered down onto the road and the pipeline. The pipeline looks particularly vulnerable to earthquake and to the mud that could also be dislodged by torrents of rain: a thin-skinned steel drinking straw wouldn't seem to have a prayer against the volcanic threats lodged deep below or the mountains of clouds in the skies above.

There's a special stillness to a mountain road when there's nothing above you. When there is no more mountain, there is no more windswept whistle for you to hear. What you hear is the quiet. Or at least that's the way it is today. There's a big, snow-covered volcano twenty-five miles to the north: Cayambe, 19,000 feet, above where the Río Cascabel begins. And another one thirteen miles to the south: unnamed on the map, over 16,000 feet, above where the Río Quijos begins. But you can't see either one of the volcanoes. It's a bright, not dreary, day, but the light is filtered through a canopy of clouds of solid pewter.

The ground is dull and not quite green at this altitude. Where it's flat it collects water like globs of costume jewelry on an old olive-colored shawl. You're not sure where the water is headed. Then you look at the gathering streams— now you can discern some faraway noise, a compressed tinkling sound—and you realize that you've in fact already turned the corner and that now the water is all flowing east. It's a small, but exhilarating, thing. This is where it begins: water's incredibly long voyage across an entire continent, through languages, rocks, jungles, history, geography, geology, and who knows what else to an ocean that is not the one this pipeline goes to.

Juan Carlos is now slinking back into the car. On to Papallacta. Even if you're not a kid from Quito, Papallacta is a special place. Not idyllic, but a special place. A valley whose puffs of mist off the hot water seem to feed the close clouds. This stream runs hot: steam. That one runs cold: nothing. The hot comes up from the scary deep in its most benevolent form. The cold comes down from unseen, iced volcanoes, just hinting of snowy cliffs, avalanches, pitons stabbed into a frozen crust. You wonder about the restaurant (that's why you brought a picnic) and you're careful about the dressing rooms, but you still relish the water. Streams and pools that are warm, hot, and almost unbearably hot—all alongside a rushing, tumbling rivulet of ice water.

And if you are a kid from Quito, a shoeshine boy on his day off?

Juan Carlos invades the private cubicle he's been assigned in the dressing area. The cubicle has a pair of swinging doors, like a saloon in a cowboy Western. You can see him hopping on one foot, then the other—right foot, left foot—as he tears off his pants and pulls on the bathing suit that he was so proud to have even had. He secures his valuables: he insists on carrying around this old wallet he found on the street with a parking receipt in it.

He rushes to the lime green edge of a warm pool, drops his towel, does this interminable dance of indecision, toward the edge, away from the edge, and then finally—too many people already in the pool are watching this absurd performance—backs off with this really sheepish look. A sigh, the collected disappointment of the onlookers, joins the mist and floats toward the clouds. Juan Carlos turns, runs, holds his nose with his right hand ("Gringos all write with their left hand, don't they?"), and jumps. Splash. Cheers.

It's about a foot deep.

This goes on for hours. Warm, hot, very hot pools. Punishing, slow trips, like walks up Calvary, to the iced stream. Lightning trips back to the warm pool. A break for lunch: Juan Carlos, no more than three feet from the pool, a towel draped over his bony, eight-going-on-nine shoulders, shivering, arms flapping, hands shaking so they threaten to cast his sandwich to the winds.

A final scene. The memory is gray-blue. Juan Carlos by the side of his pool. Cristián, his best friend, beside him. Their white towels iridescent in the neon light of the late afternoon. Two shoeshine boys on their day off. Juan Carlos is shivering. Covered now by a white bandage, also iridescent, there's an ugly, open gash on his leg, which he's forgotten about today, even though he's already gotten three shots at the Center for it because his leg got infected. Why didn't his mother notice it sooner? How could it take four days for her to notice it if all four of them have to share the same room? Dammit! The memory settles down again. Then it's just Juan Carlos standing out there. Alone, shivering terribly, smiling a lot.

* * *

Back in Quito, a small hand reaches out. I take Juan Carlos's hand in mine. It was always surprisingly soft for a working boy's hand. Now it's mostly just wrinkly from the green pools at Papallacta. And we say good-bye.

CHAPTER SIX
Peru: The Night the Dead Danced

THE GREAT AND RICH land of the Incas had fallen. Someone asked a sixteenth-century Spanish sailor how to get to
there. *Cuando ya no veáis ningún árbol,* he replied, *querrá
decir que habéis llegado al Peru.* When you no longer see a
single tree, that means you have reached Peru.

And there it is: not a tree in sight. South of the border
with Ecuador there's a hubbub of fixers and money changers and yammering guides to thread you through the
bureaucratic intricacies of Peru, each prepared to rip you
off at the slightest opportunity. And beyond, a desert
bazaar, street stands and tents, cars and trucks running a
gauntlet of hawkers and brightly colored gimcrackery. And
beyond the border town of Tumbes, an expanse of sand
beneath a hazy sky that will turn to mist, a thick mist rolling
in off the Pacific and over the surprisingly cool sand.

Peru?

It's one thing to find yourself at Machu Picchu early in
the morning before the caravans of tourists climb off the

bright orange train down from Cuzco and are bused up the thirty-six switchbacks to the ticket booth. To stand amid the mastery over mountain rock and the mystery of why here, why a city-fortress-temple carved into an impossibly remote tangle of rocks and wind and water, and not really believe what you're seeing, to feel the full weight of somebody else's religion and history upon your soul: that is Peru.

This sand is Peru?

Francisco Pizarro must have wondered too about what he had come upon. The conquistador had sailed down the west coast of South America in search of a landfall not buried in the steaming green, mosquito-infested vegetation that promised his men only disease and misery. He passed the Colombian lowlands that have been known to suffer as much as 275 inches of rain in a year. He passed the coast of what is now Ecuador, beyond the mosquito-ridden mangrove islands north of the Santa Elena Peninsula, and beyond where the lush foliage turns to arid, brittle stone. He entered the suddenly cold waters of what three centuries later would be called the Humboldt Current. Now, as his one-ship armada stood off the coast at Tumbes, Pizarro awaited a report from the scouts he had sent into town. When he heard of the temple sheathed in silver and in gold, he knew he would be back. The year was 1528, and in four years, all Peru would be his.

This whole enterprise—the Conquest of the Americas—had once been about spices. Spain and Portugal both, the lands of the great navigators and explorers of the era, had set out to find a way to the East Indies, the "spice islands" that had become so valuable to the European economy. Exotic spices—pepper, ginger root, cinnamon bark, nutmeg—had inspired a kind of nouvelle cuisine de rigueur among the aristocracy. In Tudor England, still sorting through the debris and depression of the Hundred Years War and the Wars of the Roses, a single pound of cloves had come to be worth two cows.

To control the spice trade was to be a world economic power. At the time, the Italians were such a power because of their commercial ties in Alexandria, Egypt, with Moham-medan traders who dealt in luxury items brought by sea and then overland from India. Indeed, the great wealth that the spice trade had brought to Italy helped to finance the Renaissance in its infancy. So when word came that the Portuguese Vasco da Gama had discovered the sea route to India in 1498, the bad news swept through Genoa and Venice and Milan like a Black Monday thunderstorm.

The enterprise was infused too with the manifest destiny of a last great religious crusade. When one of da Gama's men was asked what had brought him to the Indian port of Calicut (now Kozhikode), he answered, "Christian-ity and spices." Spain's fervor was all the greater, having just crystallized in the final triumph over the Muslim king-dom of Granada after nearly eight centuries of Moorish occupation on the Iberian Peninsula. So long in coming was this victory—and so expensive, for Spain had run up enormous war debts with Flemish bankers—that it could not be contained at the water's edge. The fanaticism of the Moors against the Visigoths in the eighth century would now be repaid by the fanaticism of the Spaniards, and the Americas would be caught in the awful symmetry of it all.

The year Granada fell, an Italian explorer in service to a Spain united at last under Ferdinand the Catholic of Aragon and Isabella the Catholic of Castile rigged his sails and anchored off an island called Guanahani, which would come to be known to others as San Salvador or Watling Island. Christopher Columbus hadn't the faintest idea where he was, but he knew very well why he was there. Fray Bartolomé de Las Casas, the missionary who would become an eager if quixotic defender of the indigenous peoples of this soon-to-be-called New World against the depredations of his fellow Spaniards, passed along to history Columbus's diary entries for October 12, 1492:

> [The Indians] do not carry weapons nor do they have knowledge of them, for I showed them our swords, and they took hold of them by the blade and cut themselves out of ignorance. . . .
> And I was alert, and I labored to learn if they had gold, and I saw that some of them wore a [gold] fragment. . . .

Let the Portuguese have their spices. Gold, and silver after it, would drive Spain's conquest. Spain kicked open the door to the greatest land grab that history had known. On the eve of the revolution in its American colonies, England had only a strip of land the size of Central America, and Portugal had no more than the continental bulge of Brazil. All the rest, from San Francisco to Tierra del Fuego, all but what little had not yet been taken from the Indian—all the rest belonged to Spain. Within a half century, Spain would lose title to everything save its Caribbean islands, but no matter. For better and for worse as well, the cross and the sword of the Spanish crown had transformed the face of America's two continents as surely and as permanently as any tectonic movement in the earth's crust.

* * *

It's Ember Day, late in September, a day of fasting and prayer in some Christian religions. As if in sympathy, the desert sky under which we are journeying is raining the black ash of bagasse from the smokestacks of a distant sugarcane mill. We need the windshield wipers again. We also needed them early this morning to feel our way through the *garúa,* the eerie heavy mist that rolls on and off the coast like a tide but never turns to rain. This strange Peruvian coast, looking so bleak and forlorn, stretches from Tumbes to the Chilean border: fourteen hundred miles of desert sand, never more than a hundred miles wide.

The Humboldt Current is the deus ex machina of Peru's weather. It air-conditions the desert, blankets it with the garua, and chills the coastal waters to a temperature that most swimmers would find uncomfortable, leaving Peru with fourteen hundred miles of rarely used beaches. Halfway down the coast sits Lima, where bus travelers coming down from the north on the old highway sometimes have to bide their time while graders and front-end loaders, like snowplows, clear sand drifts from the roadway. Bundled up from June through October in the cool, gray garua of its antipodal winter, Lima may look as wet as London to visitors. And yet among major world capitals only Cairo gets less rain than Lima: not even two inches a year.

In the north, the dilapidated Pan American Highway is evidence of what can go wrong when the Humboldt shifts a bit in its watery lair. The resulting climatological phenomenon is known as El Niño, or "The Child," because it often starts up at Christmastime. The waters off the coast warm so much as to create a different, more typically tropical climate. Fish migrate south and with them go the seabirds. Fierce rains and winds lash the unaccustomed coast. Well up into Ecuador, as we traveled down from Quito over the past ten days, we saw the damage wrought by El Niño's last big tantrum, in 1983. The Ecuadoran sierra, though inured to moderate annual rainfall, caught El Niño's wet backlash. Even four years later, we found whole sections of the Pan American Highway in Ecuador covered or wiped out by mudslides, necessitating sweeping detours down into the lowlands and back up into the mountains again. Today, as we make our way from Tumbes to Chiclayo, a distance of roughly three hundred miles, virtually every bridge we come across is under repair after having been washed out in '83. At each crossing, we veer off into the desert and back onto the threadbare highway, kicking up dust through a dry creek or riverbed: Rain did this? What rain?

The desert is deceptive in its starkness. It has stored riches, and still does. All around Talara the desert is a buff-colored pincushion stuck with black oil pumps. Many are idle and sit there at loose ends, the desert around them stained a greasy, sticky black. Others are pumping away. Up close you can hear the putt-putt of the motor, the creaking of the cable, and the moneymaking sucking sound of the hydraulics. From a distance you hear nothing but can see the slightly humorous, odd-looking head of the pump nodding up and down. Oil people insist the pump heads bob in a rhythmic expression of profound gratitude: thank-you-very-much, thank-you-very-much. Out on the water, amid wheeling sea gulls, and presumably even more grateful for the earth's bounty, are the filigreed rigs of big offshore wells.

Talara itself is sometimes described as a desert oasis. If

water—which Talara has only because it is pumped in across twenty-five miles from the Chira River—is what makes an oasis an oasis, then Talara is an oasis. Otherwise it is merely a pleasant, if faded, town with the good fortune to be near some nice beaches and the misfortune to be the site of a malodorous fishmeal plant. Talara pops up as a curious footnote to the history of World War II. The town is the westernmost point on the South American mainland; the United States built a U.S. Army air base at Talara in something of a panic after the Japanese bombed Pearl Harbor. Talara, and in particular the La Brea oil field to the southeast, are most famous, however, for something that happened three decades later, when they became a giant blot on Washington's foreign policy copybook.

The Talara–La Brea fields are among the oldest working fields in South America. At their peak, their annual production was six times Peru's total annual consumption. The owners of the La Brea field were first a British firm and later, after 1924, the International Petroleum Company, a subsidiary of Standard Oil of New Jersey. The La Brea field turned a hefty profit for IPC. For decades Peru, which from the outset had disputed the legality of the sale to IPC, attempted to get a piece of the La Brea pie. In 1963, by which time the Talara–La Brea fields were producing at less than one-half their peak levels and Peru had ceased to be self-sufficient in oil, the Lima government put pressure on IPC to settle the old La Brea claims in exchange for concessions in the exploration and drilling getting under way in new Amazonian fields.

IPC balked. Moreover, IPC persuaded the United States to bring pressure to bear on the Peruvian government to quit pestering the oil company. This was the dawn of the

Alliance for Progress, but still Washington did IPC's bidding rather than remain neutral or try to encourage a compromise solution. It halted practically all economic aid to Peru and so enflamed Peruvian sentiments against the United States that events cascaded in such a way as to not please anybody at all anywhere: a settlement, in 1968, was seen by Peruvians as a sellout; a coup toppled the government that had made the deal; the new military government expropriated La Brea; IPC demanded compensation; Lima demanded its share of IPC's La Brea profits over the years, which it said totaled $690 million; Peru began seizing U.S. fishing boats off its coast; the United States cut off what remained of U.S. aid to Peru; the rest of Latin America leapt to Peru's defense; Peru leapt at least partway into the arms of the Soviet Union; and U.S.-Peruvian relations have never quite recovered.

Stories about Peru's wealth are almost always old stories about exhausted potential, or they are stories about its unfulfilled potential. Present-day Peru is the saddest of South American economies: Nicaragua without direct outside military interference. The wildly swinging pendulum of civilian government to military government and back again, a now-fading plutocracy of the so-called Forty Families (a term no more nor less accurate than El Salvador's Thirteen Families) that impeded orderly economic development and built up a perilously deep reservoir of resentment among the lower classes, a stupefyingly cynical guerrilla movement that seems determined to scorch the earth in order to inherit it, the crippling repercussions of three centuries of Spanish rule, the usual ill-timed blows or poorly conceived assistance from the United States—these factors have reduced Peru to the pauper of South America.

Under the circumstances, it is perhaps an inappropriately romantic fillip to note that the Peruvian tragedy of the past five centuries followed the demise of the Incas, the greatest civilization South America has known.

The desert sands cannot hide the tatters of today's Peru. Piura is an old city—founded in 1532, before Lima—on the northern edge of the Sechura Desert, which is the blankest stretch along the coast—so low and flat that it became an inland sea for a while after El Niño struck. To the south of the city is a sight common to Peru's coastal communities and epidemic in Lima. Hundreds of squatter huts made of sticks and straw and nothing else spread across the sand, creeping deeper and deeper into the shifting desert. The only hints of permanence, of the fact that this is not some queer overnight encampment, are a few gawky antennas for television sets that run off generators or car batteries. Some of the houses fly white flags in seeming surrender to the forces that have brought these people to this place. Actually, the flags indicate *chicha,* a maize beer, for sale.

The Pan American Highway takes us straight through the Sechura and inland from the coast. Despite the rising heat, the change is not unwelcome, for in Peru the coastline is dotted by factories that grind anchovies into fishmeal for animal fodder and fertilizer, and the stench of decaying fish is everywhere. Like grain, the coarse flour from the factories is piled up in mountain after mountain of fishmeal. Along much of the north coast, these fishmeal cordilleras are the highest points. We notice that wherever there is a fishmeal factory there is often an array of open-air sheds—long, low-slung, and narrow. After eating chicken for a while in Peru and detecting a slight fishy taste, it occurs to us what the chickens were fed and where they were fed it.

The anchovy shoals off the Peruvian coast—schools of fish the size of provinces—are legendary. The cool waters teem with fish large and small. The world's largest fish ever taken on a rod (other than a shark) was a 1,560-pound black marlin caught off Cabo Blanco, north of Talara, in 1953. In some years Peru has had the largest overall fish catch in the world. The 1983 El Niño badly hurt the industry. The Humboldt Current moved south and took Peru's fish with it. (This was a boon to Chile, which on more occasions than Peruvians would like to think about has benefited at the expense of Peru). Peruvian catches since then have been disappointing, and the fishing industry is concerned that the pattern of fish schooling further south is permanent and not just a temporary aftershock of a particularly intense El Niño.

With the fish come seabirds and with the birds comes guano, which made for one of the more freakish episodes in the history of Peru's roller-coaster economy. The treeless, sunburnt islands off the Peruvian coast, especially down south, look like batteries that have leaked their acid into the corroding air: they are Reddi-Whipped with thick, crusty toppings of chalk-colored bird dung. *Guano* is one of the very few words in Quechua, the Inca language that is still spoken in the Andes, that have been absorbed into English. The Incas knew the value of bird dung, which they used to fertilize their famous terraced farms in the Andean highlands: under Inca law, to kill a guano-producing bird was a capital offense.

There was big money in guano, and nineteenth-century Peru became the Saudi Arabia of bird dung, enriched by but at the same time dangerously dependent upon this one resource. Because of its high nitrogen content, guano was an invaluable fertilizer for exhausted European agricultural land. Peru began to exploit its guano reserves as a major export commodity in about 1840. By the 1860s the country was exporting nearly half a million tons a year. By then guano was worth eighty dollars a ton, and the government derived three-quarters of its total income from guano exports.

Soon other fertilizers, natural and synthetic, came along to replace guano. Even as demand from abroad dropped, the supplies of guano were themselves tapering off. Peru would continue to mine the guano islands for its own use, and it would combine guano from the sea with water from the mountains to make its desert bloom. But as a source of fabled wealth, guano went the way of silver, which had gone the way of gold. And in time, the oil— from the desert, from the offshore fields, and even from the Amazon—will go the way of the others.

The odds are stacked badly against Peru. Its twenty million inhabitants are miserably distributed. A third of the people live in or around the urban mire of Lima. Almost all the rest live in the sierra—a tough place to live. These highlanders live on miserly soil at an average altitude of 10,000 feet. Imagine the impoverished land around Denver, and add another 4,000-plus feet in altitude. In being unkind to Peru, history has not had to make much of an effort.

Still, the country's natural riches are far from exhausted. Peru as a whole may not be overpopulated; it is, after all, twice the size of France. Virtually unpopulated and undeveloped, more than six-tenths of Peruvian territory lies on the far side of the Andes. The eastern slope is so heavily forested that aerial photography has been unable to discern much about the ancient Inca presence, or absence, there. The far side of the mountains, the rich forests and plains beyond, the deep, well-watered valleys, and the dense jungle have immense potential. There are vast timberlands. The land is well suited for plantations of coffee and tropical fruit, and for jute and rice and rubber. And there is oil; over 80 percent of the country's reserves are believed to be in the Amazonian fields. For Peru, as for Peru's neighbors Ecuador and Bolivia, the Amazon is where the future lies—if its muddled leadership and the traumatizing burden of internal chaos ever give the country a chance.

Were it not for the faint glow of hope emanating from the far side of the mountains it would be tempting to conclude—another romantic notion—that history has already passed Peru by, that its golden age was during the reigns of Pachacútec and Huayna Capac in the fifteenth century. With a population of six to twelve million, the great Inca Empire stretched from southern Colombia to northern Argentina. It was an orderly, if regimented, society of *ayllus,* or village communities, bound together by a common unwritten language and a common religion—worship of the sun. The Incas were not so much creators of Peruvian culture as they were great organizers of what already existed. They took the best that disparate existing societies had to offer—language, religion, building skills—and then organized them into a single, synergistic whole. Economically, this benefited the whole society. Politically, it strengthened the central government and fueled the empire's expansion.

In the somewhat idealized version of the Incas that has filtered down through the ages, crime was negligible, virtually no one wanted for food since state storehouses provided sustenance when the land did not, and there was peace except on the rough edges of the empire's frontiers. Commerce sped across rope footbridges spanning deep gorges, up footpaths etched into sheer cliffs, and along a network of stone-paved roads that included two broad north-south highways, a fifteen-hundred-mile coast route, and a remarkable two-thousand-mile highland route that ran practically the length of the empire. In the urban aerie of Cuzco, 11,500 feet high in the Andes, where metalworkers had crafted a life-size garden of solid-gold flora, the Sapa Inca himself dined on sea bass still fresh after its swift delivery by *chasquis,* or messengers, up several hundred miles from the Pacific. Inca weavings are beautifully intricate. The Incas were remarkable farmers who managed to till more highland acreage six hundred years ago than their descendants do today.

The end came swiftly. Toward the end of the fifteenth century, just before his death, Huayna Capac decided to divide the empire between two sons. Huáscar would rule the south from the traditional power center of Cuzco. Atahualpa would rule the north from Quito, which was already becoming a rival capital. Huáscar was to be *primus inter pares* in this twin-kingdom arrangement, but Atahualpa challenged his authority soon after the death of their father. It was a fateful moment in Inca history, for it coincided with Francisco Pizarro's return to Peru to check out the rulers of a society that could afford to sheath in gold and silver a temple so remote and relatively unimportant as the one the conquistador had been told existed in the desert outpost of Tumbes.

Atahualpa had just emerged victorious from the ensu-
ing civil war. He was encamped outside the mountain town
of Cajamarca, his billowing royal travel pavilions staked to
the ground not far from the curative waters of a sulfurous
warm springs, when Pizarro, his men, his horses, and his
new portable guns, the harquebuses, came into the Cajamarca Valley.

The Spaniards said mass in the morning. "Arise, O
Lord, in thy wrath. . . ." They prayed for strength in battle
against this corrupt land, where "the Devil stands upon
their altars and with his evil light, hides the true God."
They sang a song to the new Jerusalem, "its palaces of
shining gold, its streets paved with precious stones and its
gates of pearl." They were ready for their appointment with
Atahualpa.

The priest, Vicente de Valverde, met Atahualpa as the
Inca and his retinue entered the main square. The Sapa
Inca, like those with him, was unarmed. The priest carried
a crucifix in one hand, a Bible in the other. He explained
their mission: to convert the Indians to the true faith of the
Holy Trinity, the crucifixion, the resurrection, in the name
of the Incas' new master, Charles V of Spain, who was in
this New World the representative of the pope, who was
God's representative on earth.

Who told you this? Atahualpa wanted to know. The
Bible, said the priest. Atahualpa took the book in his hands.
He turned it over, he shook it. It said nothing. He let it fall
to the ground.

Furious, the priest went over to Francisco Pizarro and
told him to go ahead with his plan: "I absolve you."

They fell upon Atahualpa, and held him hostage for a
ransom of one room filled with gold and two with silver.

Atahualpa did not die at the stake, the chroniclers tell us; he was spared that torturous indignity because he renounced his faith and took his new masters'. When he was baptized, they tell us, he took the name Francisco. He was garroted.

We approached Cajamarca as Pizarro had—up from the coast. Modern Cajamarca would be an ordinary enough city except for one thing: it is filled with unfinished bell towers. They say the bell towers were left ragged and incomplete as a way of protesting the imperiousness of the Spanish crown, which imposed a tax upon the completion of each church. But to me, the bell towers reaching in vain for the heavens looked like a penance for Pizarro's villainy.

We left Cajamarca behind us—the San Francisco Hotel, the Hostal Atahualpa, the Rescate (Ransom) restaurant— and headed back to the coast. We continued our zigzag south, heading into the mountains when we could, retreating to the coast when bad roads forced us back down to the desert.

Considering the history of Peru, there is something disconcerting about the homage that Peruvians continue to pay to their Spanish conquistadores. Trujillo, Peru's second city, is named after Pizarro's birthplace in Spanish Extremadura, the tough cattle-ranching land that also yielded other conquistadores, including Hernán Cortés (Mexico) and Pedro de Alvarado (Guatemala). Pizarro himself continues to be honored. In many Peruvian cities, his statue occupies a hallowed spot on the main square, called the Plaza de Armas since colonial days, when the crown's troops mustered there.

It is especially disconcerting for anybody accustomed

to the staunch proindigenous, even anti-Spanish attitudes one encounters in Mexico. Peru and Mexico are in some ways markedly similar: when Columbus bumped into the New World, the Incas and the Aztecs were important, developed societies with sophisticated agricultural and social systems administered by a central government. And yet the way Peru and Mexico treat the Spanish Conquest opens a window on a stunning difference in the cultural identities of these two countries.

In Peru, the homage to the conquistadores hardly begins or ends with statues. The presidential residence is popularly called the Pizarro Palace. Members of Lima's aristocracy proudly trace their bloodlines and fair skin to the original Spanish families that came to Peru. In Peruvian schoolbooks the Conquest and the colonial period continue to be portrayed as the benign introduction of Western civilization and Christianity.

Peru's virtually uncritical veneration of Spanish rule is unthinkable in Mexico. Each year on October 12 a small group of people lay wreaths at the foot of the Columbus statue on Avenida de la Reforma in Mexico City. And each year, *indigenista,* or pro-Indian, activists march on the monument, chanting, *"Colón, ¡al paredón!"* ("Up against the wall, Columbus!"). There are regularly physical clashes between the two groups or between the protestors and police.

There would probably be more incidents like the one at Columbus's statue if there were more statues in Mexico related to the Spanish Conquest. In a country replete with monuments—Mexico has memorialized highway-construction crews—hardly any tributes to the colonial period exist. The statue of Columbus survives probably because he never set foot on Mexican soil and because he was an Italian on the Spanish payroll. Anyone so reckless as to commemorate a Spaniard in Mexico had better put the statue in a spot inaccessible to hammer or crowbar. Cortés's Mexican legacy consists of one bust, in a dark passageway at Mexico City's Hospital de Jesús, which he founded in 1524, and one man-on-horseback statue with no plaque to identify it, at a rundown hotel-casino in Cuernavaca. There is a handsome statue of Charles IV of Spain in front of the National Museum of Art. El Caballito (The Little Horse), as it is known, has been moved twice and is lucky to have survived, protected in part by an apologetic notice: "Mexico preserves it as a work of art."

Why the contrast? The colonization process itself was different in the two countries. In Mexico, the Spaniards placed their capital where the Aztecs' had been. They overpowered the existing elite but never could they eradicate the existing culture. Thus began a syncretism that today characterizes not just the religion in Mexico but other parts of the culture as well. In Mexico, furthermore, *mestizaje,* the mixing of the races, was a relatively rapid process. In Peru, there was and still is a much clearer line between the conquerors and the conquered. *Mestizaje* has come much more slowly. Spain concentrated its people and its power on the coast, controlling the Indian population in the mountains from the viceregal seat in Lima.

The two countries also took very different roads to independence. The independence movement in Mexico began in 1810, at the dawn of the rebellion in the Americas that sought to take advantage of Spain's weakness following its invasion by Napoleon. In Peru, the independence movement was not so much born as it was imposed from the outside. And when independence finally came—Peru was one of the last of the American states to achieve it—Peru inherited an independence it neither sought nor won itself.

Lima's upper class was a center of reactionary opposition to the struggle for independence. The fervor for independence that burned within the literate classes in Venezuela and Argentina was not evident in Peru. The white minority, basking in Spanish rule, feared the black slaves and the Indians, whom they treated as serfs. As Spain's grip on its colonies loosened, the people of Lima were increasingly panic-stricken. When the Spanish viceroy decided to abandon the capital in July 1821, Lima's elite worried that the slave population would rise up against the whites and that the Indians and proindependence guerrillas in the hinterlands would invade the city once the viceregal troops had gone. When the city's leading citizens invited San Martín, the Argentine liberator, to enter Lima and occupy it, they were really seeking protection—not liberation.

Unlike Mexico, whose 1910 revolution was in part a class struggle and had overtones of *anti-hispanidad* (anti-Spanishness), Peru has never really resolved the classist and racial tensions that were planted by the Conquest. In Mexico, the Indian was sanctified in the revolution-era constitution. In the aftermath of the revolution, anticlericalism, itself a strain of anti-Spanishness, was cemented even more firmly in Mexican culture. So too was *indigenismo*, which became linked in the popular consciousness with the sacred right to till the land.

Peru has not passed through such a bloody but cleansing catharsis, except to the extent that today's fierce rebellions by the Sendero Luminoso and Tupac Amaru guerrilla movements are part of that process. Quite to the contrary,

Indian rebellions in Peru have historically been beaten back swiftly with a ferociousness that has only helped to intensify the class tensions, however latent. Such was the case of the most famous Indian rebel leader, Tupac Amaru II, whose eighteenth-century revolt mirrored one in the sixteenth century by the original Tupac Amaru. When Tupac Amaru II was captured, the Spanish authorities decided to make a lesson of his punishment. He was forced to witness the death of his wife, one of his sons, an uncle, a brother-in-law, and his captains. His executioner then cut out his tongue. His arms and legs were tethered to horses. When his body resisted being drawn and quartered, he was decapitated. His torso was immolated on the heights of Machu Picchu, his head and various extremities impaled upon poles and set up in villages that had been loyal to him. Across the land, the Quechua language was banned, along with Indian dress and ceremonies. Mourning the death of Tupac Amaru II was prohibited.

Indigenismo never took hold in Peru the way it did in Mexico. Its foremost manifestation has been the American Popular Revolutionary Alliance, the political party known as APRA. APRA was founded by Víctor Raúl Haya de la Torre in the 1920s while he was in exile in Mexico during the heady aftermath of Mexico's revolution. APRA was heavily influenced by the Mexican revolution, as well as by bolshevism and by socialism. Pro-Indian and antielitist, the party did not achieve lasting political success until its presidential candidate Alan García won office in the mid-1980s, by which time the spirit of *indigenismo* was all but lost in the chaos of an imploding economy and the terror of an emerging civil war that, as usual, caught the indigenous population in the middle.

The Mexican Nobel laureate Octavio Paz has written that his country's "plural past" is "a jungle of roots and branches that suffocate us. How to live with all of them without being their prisoner? This is a question we ask ourselves endlessly." The fact that Peruvians spend less energy agonizing over their past may not mean that they have the answer—but rather that they have put off asking the question. Julith and I are in Peru at a time when the country seems to be coming to grips with long-repressed anger and deep-seated resentment. In another three years, determined not to elect the writer Mario Vargas Llosa, who is firmly identified with Lima's white elite, the not-so-white majority of voters of Peru will elect as their president Alberto Fujimori, a Peruvian of Japanese descent; it would take a while to test his mettle and his uncertain credentials, but Fujimori's election had all the look of a desperate move to do something, anything, to stave off disaster. It's scary to contemplate that if Fujimori fails, it could take a Mexican-style revolution to sort out the tangled Peruvian past.

Outside of Trujillo is Chan Chan, the famed eleven-square-mile capital of the pre-Inca Chimu Indians. The remains, a sprawling sand castle in the mist within earshot of the Pacific surf, are the largest adobe city in the world, a sturdy brickwork of mud, cactus juice, and pebbles. It was badly damaged in even the relatively little rain that fell this far south during the '83 El Niño, though the original walls, some of them thirty feet high and a thousand feet long, fared far better than the ones rebuilt in recent years.

No corner of this land is free of the forces of disintegration that are eating away at Peru, not even here on the Trujillo coast, far from the urban collapse of Lima and the rural mayhem in the ever-widening sierra regions that have fallen to the guerrillas. At Chan Chan, *huaqueros,* the robbers of Indian graves (*huacas*), have been gnawing away at the site; the state does not have the money to protect its patrimony. Our guide at Chan Chan asks us if we are German. He's seen very few Americans this year; Germans have a reputation as hardy travelers, but many tourists are being scared off by rising street crime and rebel terror. The litany of Peru's woes seems never-ending.

Two hours south of Trujillo, we cut east into the valley of the Santa River and onto a road that our map describes as a *carretera afirmada*—a "highway" of packed dirt. It could be worse; the next road into the mountains is a *carretera no afirmada.* Or could it? By the time we've gone fifteen miles, we have gotten stuck in a mudhole and then punctured a tire and bent its rim, leaving us with no spare tire and 140 miles to go before reaching our planned destination.

It soon becomes clear why this road is so troublesome. It's not a road. Not all of it. Most of it is the old track bed of the old Santa Corporation Railway to and from the rich Andean coal mines to the east. The railroad was destroyed in Peru's big 1970 earthquake. Destroyed railroad? No problem. Turn it into a road. Stomp on it a bit and call it a *carretera afirmada.*

Away from the air-conditioned coastline, the land is hot and dry. Only along the banks of the slender river are there irrigated islands of green—rice and cana brava, a low-yielding sugarcane. Otherwise the land is bleached white or baked burnt orange until the old railroad bed begins its steep ascent into Peru's Cordillera Negra.

The approach to Huallanca, a village at the near, northern end of the Cañón del Pato, takes us through twelve old railroad tunnels and around one more that is still buried in rock from the earthquake. In spots the road is dusted with soot, and gashes in the mountain reveal a few shiny coal veins. Outside of Colombia, Brazil, and most recently Venezuela, coal is not plentiful in South America. Here the mines have played out, but a few free-lancers still work the deposits for the leftovers. Between tunnels we pass some miners. It is an eerie sight: they are black as night with coal dust, and look like the dead out for a stroll. Some women and children appear in the doorways of huts of sticks and straw; by now we have seen so many of these meager homes that they have lost their power to shock.

A thrumming hydroelectric project sits in the Cañón del Pato (Duck Canyon), leeching energy from the cascading Santa. You cannot see it from the road, and all access to it is heavily guarded. Power plants are prime guerrilla targets. In Peru, hydro plants are especially important because the country depends on them for two-thirds of its electrical power. To the south, Lima is held hostage to the hydroelectricity from the Mantaro Valley, where there has already been extensive confrontation between the government and the guerrillas. This project in the Cañón del Pato, though well to the north, is particularly vulnerable because the labyrinth of rock that surrounds it is hard to patrol.

We passed through one military checkpoint at the northern end of the canyon. The road is dirt, one lane. Over the next half hour, we will drive through another forty old railroad tunnels. The canyon is a thin slice in the mountain—so narrow that you can throw a stone and hit the other side. Far below, the Santa sparkles in the sunlight, a mere strand of fishing line lying at the bottom of the canyon.

At the other end of the canyon is a second checkpoint. The antiterrorist squad rummages through our personal documents and car papers. They keep a list of everybody leaving the Cañón del Pato. With great care, an officer logs my name in on an official form: "Smith Road," my street address in Massachusetts.

We are now in the Callejón de Huaylas, an alley at 10,000 feet between rocky peaks on the right and the snow up high on the left, dominated by Nevado Huascarán, a majestic peak and Peru's highest, at 22,205 feet. The air is dry and thin and getting cold in the late afternoon. Then suddenly on the left there is a huge cemetery.

It used to be a town.

This is Old Yungay. The 1970 earthquake broke a piece of mountain off Huascarán. The first thing the people of Yungay noticed was the roar of the wind. Then they felt the wind. Then came an eight-foot wall of mud, rock, and ice. It was moving so fast—as fast as an airplane—that it climbed partway up the far side of the valley. Then there was silence.

The 1970 earthquake is the worst disaster on record in the Americas, killing as many as seventy-five thousand people, injuring fifty thousand, and destroying 186,000 buildings up and down this valley. Debris avalanches in the snow-capped Cordillera Blanca are notorious scourges. In 1941 one killed six thousand in the valley's central town, Huaraz, capital of Ancash department, which was also struck by the 1970 quake. In 1962 an avalanche demolished several small settlements and partly obliterated the village of Ranrahirca, killing at least thirty-five hundred. The same sharp angles and towering heights that give the valley its spectacular beauty are also mighty instruments of destruction.

In Yungay alone in 1970, twenty thousand people were buried alive. The *aluvión*—part landslide, part avalanche—left only bits and pieces of the town sticking up as in some sick pop-art sculpture: the tops of four palm trees at the Plaza de Armas, front and rear ends of somersaulted automobiles. There wasn't much that could be done. The authorities turned Viejo Yungay into a *camposanto*. On a concrete arch, they erected a sign designating the town a "holy field," and started building Nuevo Yungay just up the road to the north. At the old town, there's a small hill. It is the old cemetery. The only people in Yungay who survived the wall of mud stood on that hill and witnessed the instant transformation of their town into a necropolis.

As vantage points go, there must be few flat surfaces on the face of the earth that can match the Plaza de Armas in Huaraz. Before us stretch the Cordillera Blanca and the Cordillera Negra. It's an impressive sight. Where we are in the tropics, snow does not build up below 16,000 feet. From the plaza we can see twenty-three snow-capped mountains.

Huaraz, like Riobamba in Ecuador, is one of the principal mountaineering centers in Latin America. Climbers are attracted by the price of accommodations and guides—no more than ten dollars a day for a good hotel room, forty a day for the best guides—and by the fact that because the high mountains are packed together so closely, you can come to Huaraz for ten days, get acclimated, and squeeze in climbs on two, maybe even three, mountains. Climbers also like the idea of getting away from the popular climbing venues that are not only pricier but more crowded. Because Peru is off the main circuit, paraphernalia that has disappeared or is too expensive elsewhere can still be found and afforded in Peru, including such Holy Grail collector's items as hand-forged Gravel ice picks from France.

Mountain climbing has fallen on hard times here. We had dinner one evening with two climbers from Virginia at our hotel, the state-run Turistas in Monterrey, outside Huaraz. The hotel has the slightly faded, rumpled quality of a Catskills resort. The climbers, Nancy White and Glenn Carlson, talked fondly of their guide, Lucio, who was in his mid-fifties and had never done his mountain lungs the disservice of stepping one inch below Huaraz's 10,000 feet ("The young guides," he told them, "they know how to tie a lot of fancy knots, but they get tired"). Lucio and the handful of other highly experienced guides are not getting much business nowadays. So White and Carlson will leave behind not just a tip, but also one of their down sleeping bags.

Climbers see the same danger flags that other would-be tourists see in Peru. The warning flag of a collapsing economy: the inti, which was brought in not long ago to replace the battered sol (the words are Quechua and Spanish, respectively, for "sun"), was worth 6.5 cents in March, 2.5 cents when we got to Peru, and will fall to 1.4 cents by the time we leave the country. The warning flag of rampant street crime: warned of bag-slashing thieves on buses and in the streets, backpackers line their packs with wire mesh. And scariest of all, the warning flag of uncontainable guerrilla activity.

As in Guatemala, there is in Peru a moving border between safe and unsafe areas. We knew to steer clear of the highlands in Ayacucho department and of the Huallaga Valley, where the largest rebel group, the Sendero Luminoso (Shining Path), is in league with the cocaine traffickers. The difference is that in Peru, the border is moving fast and in the guerrillas' favor.

We got a sense of the moving edge. One day we drove up Huascarán, past the twin turquoise glacial lakes of Llanganuco, at 12,000 feet, and up into the tundralike *puna*. We came upon a truckload of army troops moving up the mist-shrouded road. They were heavily armed and looked as if they were heading for a confrontation with Sendero rebels on the other side of the mountain. We didn't follow them for long. Two years later, the line had moved much closer to Huaraz: I read that the Hotel Turistas in Monterrey was blown up by rebel explosives.

The drive down from Huaraz doesn't prepare you for Lima. The two cordilleras, the Blanca and the Negra, veer apart, leaving a valley so broad it becomes a high plain. In the crisp light of early October, almost-springtime fields of ocher and gold stretch right up to the dark rock of the cordilleras. Then the road cuts sharply down from the mountains, through the valley of the Río Fortaleza, and down onto the cool desert coast.

Lima's profound poverty announces itself brusquely. As plain as billboards, the telltales flutter on the sandscape as far as twenty-five miles north of the faded colonial buildings of downtown Lima: the straw huts of Piura grossly magnified. In the middle of what just a month or two ago was vacant desert sand, migrant cities proliferate. They are called *pueblos jóvenes*—young towns—which is accurate if a bit too euphemistic for what's happening here. They are huge de facto refugee camps. The poor have come in from the hopeless countryside to the microscopically less hopeless capital. And here in the desert, in houses of sticks and straw mats with floors of sand, they wait.

It's a waiting line gone berserk. You come in from the countryside with your family. You stop at the hut where they sell straw mats (for walls, floor, and ceiling) and poles (for support). You buy your house. You strike camp in the sand, and you get in line for work and food. Every so often, the purveyors of straw mats and poles move to the new edge of the spreading stain of city. They set out their wares again, and they too wait. The buses from the provinces empty; "The Fugitive" is the nickname of one just down from Cajamarca. And the strange, cool desert around Lima thickens with people, doubling, tripling, quadrupling in size over the past decade.

This is not the jumbled impromptu city of Guasmo, outside Guayaquil in Ecuador. Here there is a clear progression: from new to old, in concentric circles and, like the growth rings on a fresh-cut tree trunk, plainly visible. The camps farthest from the city are too new to be squalid yet. With no city services in the camps farthest out, squalor will come soon enough, however. The older the *pueblo jóven* is, the more numerous the signs of permanence: stores, shaded bus stops, spiderwebs of electricity lines, boldly lettered announcements by the government of what it is doing for the people.

The *pueblos jóvenes* signal back with signs of their own, creating a kind of semiotic Babel as the country and its capital disintegrate. Some nights, when Sendero explosives have blacked out chunks of Lima, people have seen torchlit hammer-and-sickle symbols dance mockingly on the hillsides above such squatter settlements as Villa El Salvador and Ciudad de Dios. The *pueblos jóvenes* are focal points of the government's anti-guerrilla activity. Migration patterns in from the countryside—patterns determined by word of mouth—take the new waves of squatters to settlements where their family members and townspeople from the same Andean village have already begun new lives. Certain *pueblos jóvenes,* like El Salvador and Ciudad de Dios, are particularly suspect in the eyes of the authorities because they have been settled in large numbers by Indians from regions where the Sendero holds great sway. On occasion police set up blockades along the transportation routes into El Salvador and Ciudad de Dios to run checks on people's identity cards and packages.

Lima is a city at the brink. Just as 70 percent of the country's industry is in or around the capital, all of Peru's ills seem concentrated here. A sense of impending trouble envelops the place, like the *garúa* in winter. It is not panic, not yet. It is more like the unrelenting throb of depression. Time is running out in some way; you can read it on the faces of people and hear it in their conversations, which turn confessional with surprising speed. A man I meet casually is, after a few minutes, telling me his life story, grousing about his work, explaining why he's unfaithful to his wife. He is like a man whose life is coming to a close— soon.

What we're seeing is Lima in the middle stages of its depression. Lima will get much, much worse. For the time being incidents of violence and terror are isolated, some- times close by, sometimes far away. They pop like small explosions against the constant background noise of pover- ty's death rattle.

October 6. In the well-to-do Lima neighborhood of San Isidro, a child is kidnapped. October 7. In Ica, down the Pan American Highway, three policemen are executed on a bus. October 8. In the neighborhood of Miraflores, which is adjacent to San Isidro, a man in a jogging outfit hurls a stick of dynamite at the offices of the U.S. consulate, knocking out some windows.

We're keeping our car in the multitiered lot at a swank shopping center in San Isidro, the Centro Comercial Camino Real. Everybody's worried about car bombs. There is as much security at the parking garage here as there is at the underground lot at Los Pinos, the Mexican White House. Crime has everyone fretting. In the yellow pages of the Lima phone book there are nine pages of listings for security-guard services. The notion that one's personal security is always under threat has been totally absorbed into the lifestyle of the capital. While we're in Lima a supermarket chain is raffling away a "dream house." The chain is running big ads in the daily papers, including a color photo that's meant to conjure up life in suburbia for the contestants. There is the Dream House itself, a new car in the driveway—and a German shepherd standing guard on the green lawn.

I am standing in a window on the second floor of the National Museum of Art in Lima. On the broad Lima avenue named after one of the few Inca chroniclers of Spanish rule, Garcilaso de la Vega, striking penitentiary workers are setting tires afire. I can hear chants, but the words are muffled, broken by the wind, the distance, and the mist off the Pacific. As if pricked by some unseen needle, the balloon of this demonstration deflates, skitters spasmodically, and dies. People simply walk, or at most trot, away.

I hear a siren's wail and screeching tires, and then I can see some big olive-drab buses. Members of the Civil Guard pour out of them and onto the street. Any young person is a target. The guardsmen start collaring young people.

There was one young man. I had seen him walking down the street for a couple of blocks. As far as I could tell from my museum window, he had nothing to do with the demonstration. He seemed to be just walking down the street. You can tell he sees a paddy wagon coming up behind him out of the corner of his eye. He looks over his left shoulder and begins to run down the street. The driver of the paddy wagon guns his engine. The young man trips, falls to the ground, the soldiers grab him, and he's dragged into the van.

Seemingly far from the mad collapse of Lima, in the most beautiful valley I've ever seen, where the cold waters of the Colca River polish the pewter stone of one of the world's deepest canyons, Erasmo Guanaco Vilca, a four-teen-year-old farmboy, tells us about the night he saw the dead dance:

"I was here by the old church once when the moon died. When the sun dies, everything will cease to exist, and we will all be joined together, we and those from here, the ancient ones. But when the moon dies, this place looks like a pretty town. Music is heard. There is a great big dance. They are making a fiesta. The old town is reborn. It happened that I was here once when the moon died. It was harvest time. I was staying overnight with my father in our shepherd's hut. We were up on the hillside. The town looked pretty, as it was in the old times. And I saw them dance. I saw the ancient ones dance."

On the night of a new moon, when it has died and left the sky, it would be so dark you would squint at the relative brightness when you looked up at the stars. You would hear the roar of the river. The towering dark forms of the twin mountains that give the tight valley its shape would frame the sky. The light from just the stars would cast soft shadows. Erasmo's hut, of straw and stone, would be up there on the hillock, overlooking the vestigial stone piles of Yanque Viejo, Old Yanque. The remaining stone walls of the pre-Hispanic settlement would vaguely suggest the old town before the Spaniards moved the people to the other side of the valley, to Yanque Neuvo, New Yanque. More of the old church remains than any other building because it was so solidly built. If you were a boy steeped in the oral history of this place and inclined to believe in magic, would that sound you hear be music, would those dancing shapes be your ancestors?

We had met Erasmo down on the road that skirts the north side of the valley. We drove up from Arequipa, the whitewashed capital of Peruvian intellectualism. Few people ever make the trip, even though it is less than a day's drive on a passable dirt road over the mountains and across a high plain. The trip affords a swift transition from Peru's most pleasant big city—an unhurried city of bookstores and coffee shops—to a place of surprising remoteness. Before its descent into the valley, the road reaches 15,600 feet. When you climb to that altitude as fast as we did, in a car, the beauty of the scenery is magnified by light-headedness, and the views seem psychedelic: colors pop and sizzle, vicuñas flee approaching vehicles with exaggerated grace.

For the most part, the Colca Valley itself seems suspended in time, much like Erasmo himself. A boy with dark, shiny hair and caramel-colored skin, he was walking a pair of burros loaded down with sacks of *guano de corral,* cow manure. He told us a little about his family—a mother, father, and ten children who farm some corn and potatoes on this side of the valley. The cadence and vocabulary of Erasmo's language is archaic, like the American English of Appalachian valleys before the leveling effect of radio and television. Listen to Erasmo. *"Hartos somos,"* he says of his family. "Many are we." *"Se veía lindo el pueblo, como antes era,"* he says of what he saw on the night of the new moon. "Pretty looked the town, as before it was." Even his name spans centuries and civilizations: Erasmo, after the Dutch humanist and loyal Catholic who challenged Martin Luther's reforms and who so profoundly affected Spanish thought at the time of the Conquest; Guanaco, after the untamed relative of the llama and the camel.

Except for a few modern trappings—electricity in most of the valley towns, a few automobiles—the Colca is as it was left by the Spanish. They herded the Indians from their farms and small settlements into organized communities called *reducciones.* They did it here for the same reason they did it in Guatemala: to control and to tax. The Indians who lived in the Colca were driven down from their ranches and into compact little towns that make the Colca Valley today seem so orderly: there's a town every ten kilometers or so— a church, a plaza, and a grid of streets.

The valley's greatest distinction is the magnificent staircase terraces that have been built into the hillsides. It's an incredible sight—unlike anything I've ever seen, vastly more impressive than the much better known terracing we had visited at Pisac, north of Cuzco in the "sacred" valley of the

Urubamba River. At the east end of the valley the terracing opens wide like a fan and curves gracefully up the hillsides. Towering over it all are snow-covered mountains. Terraced throughout—from the banks of the river as high up the mountains as climate and soil will allow—the valley narrows into a funnel pointed west as it approaches the Colca Canyon, which at its deepest is a spectacular gash in the rock, 10,500 feet from river to mountain snow.

The entire valley was once a huge garden. It was the Incas' breadbasket and the main granary for their army. To the stone-enclosed terraces the Indians brought rich soil from the river bottom, gravel and rocks for drainage, guano and fish heads from the coast for fertilizer. What first attracted modern-day outsiders to the Colca was the terracing. It was as if someone had stumbled upon Kansas after centuries of oblivion. The photographic expeditions of George R. Johnson and Robert Shippee, whose works were published in the early 1930s, documented what was here and kindled scientific interest in the spectacular terracing. Since then, researchers, many of them from the United States, have come to the Colca Valley in small investigatory waves. What has kept them coming is a small mystery that surrounds the Colca Valley: the mystery of its decline.

The middle, thirty-seven-mile section of the Colca Valley, between Tuti and Cabanaconde, at elevations from 10,781 feet to 12,431 feet, is dotted by twelve small villages with about twenty-one thousand people and has a semiarid climate. The middle section contains almost continuous terracing. It is one of the densest zones of bench terraces in the Andes. But like the rest of the Andes, much of the farmland has been abandoned.

And like the rest of the Andes, the reasons why so

much terraced land was abandoned is not clear. In the
fifteenth century probably more than ten thousand hectares
were terraced along this section of the Colca. Now only
forty-six hundred hectares are in cultivation. Most of the
land that is now worked consists of irrigated terraces devoted to maize, potatoes, beans, quinoa, wheat, barley, and
alfalfa. The abandonment is primarily on the higher slopes,
far from the river and from the towns the Spanish penned
the Indians up in. William M. Denevan, a geographer from
the University of Wisconsin who has done extensive re-
search in the Colca Valley, has written that what happened
here was an "agrarian collapse."

The population of the middle section has been reduced
from about 67,000 in 1530 to 33,000 by 1972. The
sixteenth-century Indian population was reduced from
somewhere between 62,500 and 71,000 in 1530 to 35,000
in 1570, primarily by epidemic disease. This would lead to
abandonment of terraces. Another theory is that there is
less rainfall now than in the past and hence less water for
irrigation, but this thesis, according to Denevan, has yet to
be satisfactorily demonstrated. Most likely, what has happened here is the confluence of several possible causes:
tectonic uplift may have disrupted terrace irrigation systems; the *reducciones* may have contributed to abandonment
of the higher slopes; the rising labor costs of building and
maintaining terraces may have pushed people into other
livelihoods; the introduction of European crops, which are
more water demanding than the indigenous ones, and
cattle, which trample the terraces and waterways, may have
caused a breakdown of the fragile agroecology.

Denevan compresses what has happened here since the
fifteenth century into four historical stages. There was the

late prehistory period, when the Inca social system fostered extensive terrace agriculture in the valley coupled with herding of llamas and other camelids. On the heels of the Spanish Conquest, battle and disease winnowed the population down, and the Indians who remained over time congregated in the *reducciones* away from the higher terraces, or, as renegades eluding Spanish control, they clambered to the highest elevations, where little can be grown, with their small llama herds. Over the centuries, for a variety of still-murky reasons, farming was deemphasized. Most recently, the Indians of the Colca Valley have intensified their cultivation of irrigated alfalfa for cattle production, giving short shrift to subsistence crops.

The decline of terrace farming, in the Colca Valley and elsewhere on the old Inca lands in the Andes, is a metaphor for Peru's historical decline. In all of Peru today there are 2.6 million hectares of land under cultivation. Before the Spanish Conquest there were in Peru 1 million hectares of terracing alone—of which 75 percent are abandoned today.

Places such as the Colca can manage to stand outside of time for only so long. The timeless quality of the valley was most seriously challenged in the 1970s. The government decided to burrow long tunnels through the mountains and scoop out canals in order to deliver water from the Colca across more than sixty miles to the dry coastal valley of the Majes River east of Camaná, where some fifty-seven thousand hectares of new irrigated agricultural land were being planned. The system cost several billion dollars and took ten years to build. It brought roadwork and electricity, and for a time the valley's population ballooned by several thousand people. Upon completion of the tunneling, the tide of Project Majes receded, leaving behind its modern infrastructure like permanent footprints in the sand: a broad gravel road on the south side of the valley, humming high-tension power lines ricocheting off jagged peaks, tunnels heavy with the sound of swift water disappearing into the rockface.

We drove down the Project Majes road one day, covering the thirty-eight-kilometer stretch from Achoma to Cabanaconde. Achoma is the site of the housing built by the Peruvians for the European engineers who came to tunnel through the mountains. Now it serves as a motel for visitors like us. With the giant earth-moving and rock-boring equipment gone, along with the bustle of truck traffic that accompanied Project Majes, the gravel road they left behind seems incongruously broad and smooth.

Past Cruz del Cóndor—where we could look straight down 4,000 feet at the minuscule river and straight up at four condors wheeling past in the sky, close enough so that we could hear the whoosh of their nine-foot wingspans slicing through the air—we came upon Cabanaconde, feeling we had escaped the imported modernity of Achoma. Cabanaconde is the last village on the road and has no electricity. Then we stopped in a small general store to pick up some lunch, and were brusquely brought back to reality.

Into the general store walked a twelve-year-old girl, her jet black hair braided long down her back. She wanted to buy some gasoline from us. I surmised there was a taxi in her parents' backyard and that they needed to drive to the gas station in Chivay, fifty-eight kilometers back down the road, past Achoma. The girl's father came by, sucked expertly on a hose, spit out a bit of gasoline, and then siphoned off a gallon or so. They paid me seventy-five cents.

I followed them next door. The father and the daughter uncovered a shiny Honda electrical generator and poured gasoline into it. There was a Betamax VCR, a Sony color TV, and a sign on the wall. This Saturday. *Exterminador II*. *Moonraker*. Admission: twenty cents.

The next day we drove along the road on the other side of the canyon to the mining town of Madrigal. You can see signs of Madrigal from Cabanaconde—filmy veils of dust rising above the cliffs. The Madrigal mine—a source of zinc, copper, and lead—used to be owned by the Homestake Mining Company of San Francisco. From the canyon walls downstream you can look out over the mine's detritus. A growing sea of chalky dust spills out from the rusting mine buildings and spreads inexorably down the hillside. On even the most beautiful of days, the swirling canyon winds scoop up the dust in billowing clouds and scatter it on thousands of nearby terraces, scarring the soil.

On the way back we picked up a mine worker in Lari, the town neighboring Madrigal, and gave him a ride back to Corporaque, another village on the north side of the valley. The Americans had recently sold the mine back to the Peruvians, he told us. Labor problems and then sinking prices on the metals markets had pretty much done in the mine in the middle 1980s. Once there had been 600 workers at the mine, including 400 day laborers. It was a hard life. Forty workers had died on the job over the past decade and a half; the last one was electrocuted. Now the number of mine workers was down to 180. There's not much money for spare parts. Some ventilators in the mine shafts have broken down. The risks were mounting as the money ran out.

We seemed to be caught in a time warp—in a place where there was no electricity but there were videos, or where there was electricity but six thousand hectares of untilled soil. The Spanish, having mined what they needed from this place, were long gone, but their neatly laid-out towns, their churches, and their language remained. Project Majes had come and gone from this place: the roads were good, the mountains were wired, the motel rooms had showers, and water coursed through solid rock toward the desert coast. The Americans had come and gone, mined what they could and left chalky stains for the winds to whip into a frenzy.

What was now in store for the valley of the Colca, for this place where condors wheeled through a rain of zinc, copper, and lead?

At Corporaque we gave a ride to another man. He was going to Chivay. As we approached Chivay, I asked him about a landing strip we could see off in a field. It dated from the days of Project Majes. I asked him if it was still used at all. Not much, he said. But last week the army came in helicopters. They said they were looking for outsiders, people they said are terrorists, people from the Sendero.

Erasmo had led us up to Yanque Viejo. Here the lower terraces were still used. It was a bright Sunday, and a lot of people, sometimes as whole families, were out working their small plots of land. They had regular jobs during the week, many of them, but they would not consider not working the family *chacra*, or plot of land, even those who made enough to buy their own basic foodstuffs. It was not a matter of money to them.

At one point, working our way up to Yanque Viejo,

Erasmo came across a series of old holes that had been dug in the ground and lined with rocks. He hesitated, somewhat self-consciously. They were old graves, he said. He whispered that he was a little afraid; you could get an *enfermedad*, a sickness, around here. I helped him around the holes, and we moved on.

We stood in front of the old church. Sometime before he was born, Erasmo said, a villager rummaging through the rock piles had found a statue of Nuestro Señor de Huanca, a local saint, and a church bell. The villager took the image across the river to Yanque Neuvo. The family of the villager who moved the statue is gone—every single member. They all died off. People who desecrate Yanque Viejo get sick, said Erasmo. They dry up and die.

If you plant crops up here at Yanque Viejo, said Erasmo, you have to pay. The man who planted this corn in and around the church and the churchyard pays once a month. He leaves his offerings under that big tree. He leaves canihua or quinua—two types of cereal grains—or he leaves a newborn pig.

We were quiet for a while, the three of us. We listened to the dry rustling of the corn in the warm breeze. Down the valley a puff of bitter dust floated over Madrigal. Slowly, after a while, Erasmo told us about the night the moon died and the dead danced.

CHAPTER SEVEN
Bolivia: Tears from the Tin Mines

EUSTAQUIO PICACHURI'S NEW JOB as a security officer is to try to keep what is left of the tin mountain at Siglo XX from collapsing. The Bolivian government has all but closed the mine, which for much of the twentieth century was the largest in the world. For decades, miners chiseled, drilled, and scraped away at the treeless, humpbacked mountain. At its height, the mine produced 10 percent of the world's tin and made one of the world's great rags-to-riches fortunes for "the King of Tin," Simón Patiño. Now all that remains are the free-lance miners—the *cooperativistas*—who have moved in for one last whack at Siglo XX's vanishing riches.

Faded architectural drawings, tacked to the wall at the mine security office, make it clear that there is not even much rock left to hold the mountain up. Cavernous galleries have been blasted and drilled into the mountain, along with a fragile network of tunnels and elevator shafts and air vents. What's left looks in the drawings like a brick warehouse gutted by fire: a thin outer shell of rock supported by a latticework of rock pillars. To tap the remaining anemic veins of tin, the free-lancers are gnawing away at the rock-face and the pillars. Day after day they breathe in the white dust that breeds silicosis, brave weakened tunnels and downed electrical power lines, and threaten to bring the whole mountain down on top of themselves.

Making his morning rounds, Picachuri sloshes in his black rubber miner's boots through six inches of opaque water laced with an acid that would eat away at leather or jeans. He passes under a gaily decorated statue of La Virgencita de Concepción at the *bocaminas,* the mouth of the mine, at Nivel 650 (the level at 650 meters below the top of the mountain). Outside the entrance is a growing junk pile of rusting miniature railroad cars, a jumble of discarded track, an incipient ghost town of dilapidated, abandoned-looking wooden outbuildings, and huge, dun-colored piles of tailings that stretch into the blue-sky distance like a small mountain chain. In front of him 7,217 feet of narrow-gauge railroad track juts straight into the darkness.

A few light bulbs hang limp and dark in the air. The power to the mine has been shut off. The *cooperativistas* have pirated other power lines into the mine to run the elevators and their drills. Picachuri has no way of knowing which of the bare cables festooning the tunnel are alive and which are dead. Up ahead he catches a glimpse of a few dim yellow lights, floating and bobbing in the dark: the battery-powered helmet lanterns of free-lancers on their way to work. Other miners, negotiating the water-filled trenches to each side of the track or traipsing surefootedly from railroad tie to railroad tie, pass him on the left or right. The miners' helmet lanterns nod jauntily up and down by way of salutation. On their backs they wear burlap rucksacks. The packs are stuffed with old clothes for the work deep in the mine, coca-leaf chaws to numb the gums and make it bearable to work in the dank cold at 14,000 feet above sea level, cigarettes, a soft drink or two, maybe some food, and a miner's hammer.

Most of the free-lancers are campesinos with little or no experience. Some—perhaps 30 percent—are miners who chose to stay in their line of work even after the government shut down the mine. They belong to cooperatives to which the government has granted mining concessions. This is all done with winks and nods by every party in the arrangement. What the *cooperativistas* are really doing is sheer *juqueo,* or thievery. They belong to the co-ops, but they sell their meager hoards of tin to *rescatiris,* shadowy middlemen who act as brokers for the legitimate buyers of tin that will be resold on the world market.

Because they are not salaried, as miners used to be at Siglo XX, and because they are paid by weight for whatever they can extract from the mine, the free-lancers are working feverishly against time. The government is playing a hands-off role. Controls have been lifted. Safety and security measures are virtually nonexistent. The free-lancers are attacking the face of the interior galleries with pneumatic drills—but without spraying water to keep the rock dust down. They are inhaling dangerous amounts of rock dust, including the silica that causes what the miners call *mal de mina.*

Picachuri has been working in the mine for ten years, since he was twenty years old. His lungs have yet to succumb to silicosis, mainly because he stayed away from block work. (In a mine like Siglo XX, explosives are used to cave in large blocks of rocks inside the mountain. Attacking the resulting rubble with pneumatic drills is known as block work.) When Siglo XX was up and running, miners who worked the block made the most money—perhaps six hundred bolivianos a month—and inevitably died young. Picachuri's father worked the block, and died after barely ten years on the job. Picachuri himself stuck to tasks away from the swirling dust. He made 150 to 200 bolivianos a month.

As part of its effort to jump-start the stalled Bolivian economy and halt runaway inflation, the belt-tightening government in La Paz adopted a package of shock measures in the mid-1980s. Taming the notoriously inefficient tin-mining industry was a principal objective, and when world prices for tin, the country's leading export, crashed in 1985, the government closed seventeen state-owned mines, including Siglo XX, and threw twenty-three thousand of the country's miners out of work, keeping on only skeleton crews, such as Picachuri's security group at Siglo XX.

The government made a strong push to relocate the miners to more promising parts of the country. It made lump-sum payments to the miners, which usually amounted to a few thousand dollars, and urged them to leave the bleak, wasted mining towns of the Bolivian altiplano. The rocky expanses of the altiplano had yielded all they could yield. They had enriched the Spanish, the English, the Americans, and a few lucky Bolivians. Now they were spent. Maybe it would be possible to get the Japanese to come in and extract what is left out of the tailings—maybe even get them to level the hollowed-out silver mountain at Potosí, once the richest in the world, and sift the rubble for what riches remain. But for now, the government told the miners, go east to find work, down into the fertile, underpopulated lowland tropics of the Amazon basin.

The resulting migration was a tragedy. The altiplano miners—barrel-chested Indians for the most part, men inured to the thin air and hardscrabble life of the highlands—streamed down into unfamiliar territory. There were those who used their government checks to buy taxis in Santa Cruz, a hot boomtown on the windswept plains east of the Andes that has become Bolivia's second city. There, in their too-heavy clothing, they cruised the recently paved streets, hoping to put their lives back together. Some made it, successfully absorbing the culture shock, fending off typhoid and hepatitis, acclimatizing themselves to the thick, oxygen-rich tropical air.

Most could not make a go of it. One who never could make the switch was Sinforozo Rivera, forty-eight, who had lost his job in June of 1986 after two decades in the mines. While Picachuri sloshes daily through the now nearly empty tunnels at the Siglo XX mine, Rivera is camped out in protest at the San Francisco Cathedral in La Paz. During the day he and hundreds of other miners demonstrate against the government's relocation plan and present their own to reactivate the mines with union workers. At night they huddle in woolen blankets and ponchos in the wet chill of the church, left in the wake of the country's austere economic modernization plan.

In the 12,000-foot-high city of La Paz, a chill still pervades the church all day. At night it deepens into a mountain cold. Rivera is wearing woolen pants, a sweater, and a suit jacket, the usual uniform of the miner outside the mine shafts. He is short and stocky. As he sits on the church pew, his feet don't quite reach the stone floor; his legs swing a little, like a young boy's halfway through Sunday mass. He had fourteen hundred bolivianos in savings right after he lost his job nineteen months ago. Now he's got four hundred left. He despairs at the thought of being unable to provide a future for his wife, Alina, and their seven children, whom he's left back home in Siglo XX. He sits in a sea of bedrolls and cardboard suitcases that spreads from wall to wall in the cathedral. He stares down at the cracked leather of his ankle-high boots, then gloomily surveys the scene at the cathedral. "This is the pay of the miner," he says.

The Indian women in the church, their long black hair running the full length of their backs, carry small bundles of food, occasionally dispensing sugary cakes to the children in their tow. As Rivera walks toward the church doors on his way outside to have a cigarette, he passes two city women; they wear cardigans and carry small leather purses and have their hair cut short in the manner of the city. One of the city women jabs a finger in the direction of an Indian woman squatting amidst her children and belongings. *"Hedionda!"*—Foul-smelling woman!—mutters the city woman, just loud enough for Rivera to hear her. "That," says Rivera, "is the pay of the miner."

The miner was once a heroic, or at least feared, figure in Bolivian life. In 1952, the miners helped to bring about a genuine revolution in Bolivia, one of the most thorough and deep-rooted that Latin America has ever known. Bolivia had by then experienced 170 palace revolts or coups since its independence from Spain in 1825. But the 1952 upheaval was a real social revolution. It led to the expropriation and nationalization of the mines, the breakup of the vast haciendas, a redistribution of the land among the peasantry, and universal suffrage.

Wretched economic conditions for the vast majority of

Bolivians and the privileged lifestyle of the tiny upper class had turned the country into a tinderbox by 1952. Only 31 percent of the 2.6 million people were literate. In the whole country there were only 706 doctors and some 1,500 lawyers. In 1950, the country's universities granted only 132 degrees. Seven out of ten Bolivians made their living off the land. But most of the land was in a few hands. A mere six hundred or so estates—one of them sprawled over more than six million hectares—encompassed about half the farmland, and most of that the big landowners let lay fallow.

The strongest sector of the economy was mining, but it too was fraught with tension. All but 20 percent of the industry was in the pockets of three families who composed the *superestado minero,* a mining superstate, that ran Bolivia's economy and politics. Chafing for decades under backward, dangerous, and unhealthy conditions, the miners had grown increasingly restless and radical. Militant unionism was countered by militant management: with the miners armed, the tin barons brought in the Bolivian army. The mineowners paid the soldiers their salary, gave them free Derby cigarettes, let them into the company-town cinemas at no charge, and offered them the same discounts as the miners at the company commissaries.

The first big instance of military intervention came in 1923, when the government put down a strike at Uncía, down the road from Siglo XX, killing eight miners. In the summer of 1942, in the dusty expanse of a field between the Siglo XX mine and the town of Catavi, army troops put down another strike, this time killing thirty-five protestors. Among those killed were some women who came to the aid of the men after the first staccato explosion of machine-gun fire; since then, women have traditionally marched at the front of miners' demonstrations. By 1952, the Bolivian miners' union had become one of the most militant trade unions in the world.

Also setting the stage for revolution was the Chaco War of 1932–35, which would become, after the Civil War in the United States, the costliest war in men and matériel in the history of the Western Hemisphere. The Chaco is a lowland plain the size of Texas that spills into Bolivia, Paraguay, and Argentina. Prior to the outbreak of the war in mid-1932, Bolivia and Paraguay had skirmished for territory in the northern Chaco. By the time the war ended, Bolivia would have sent more than 10 percent of its total population—250,000 soldiers—off to fight. At least one out of every five died, killed mostly by thirst and disease; another 20,000 were captured and imprisoned in camps until the war's end. Though outnumbered, Paraguay, which lost about 35,000 troops, outstrategized the Bolivians and won three-quarters of the Bolivian Chaco.

The experience was a cathartic one for the Bolivian people. Most of the frontline soldiers were Aymara- and Quechua-speaking Indians. The war instilled in them a sense of nationhood they had never known, one that would allow the revolution that was to come two decades later to skip across old ethnic and geographical boundaries. The soldiers from the altiplano met people from the cities for the first time. Talk of politics filled the night. The Indians learned how to handle firearms and became familiar with the language of the cities, Spanish. Foot soldiers and officers from the cities, in turn, learned of life and death in the mines.

When the revolution came, it was not as bloody as the

only real revolution to come before it in Latin America, the Mexican Revolution. But it did begin to transform Bolivian society, even if in the end it did not reach all of its goals. In that sense it was like the Mexican Revolution and the only two other genuine revolutions in Latin American history, the Cuban and Nicaraguan revolutions. In Bolivia, change came fast. A fraudulent presidential election in 1951 led to a military coup; the coup led to popular uprisings in La Paz and elsewhere. The real winner of the 1951 election, Víctor Paz Estenssoro, took over the government in 1952. He would guide the country through twelve years of reform; the greatest victory of the revolution, he would say later, was that the Indian no longer bows when he greets a white man. He was overthrown in a military coup in 1964. A general confronted Paz: "I am taking you either to the airport or to the cemetery. Which do you choose?" Paz chose the airport.

The greatest single transformation of the revolution was the nationalization of the tin industry. On October 31, 1952, Paz and Juan Lechín Oquendo, the leader of the mine workers, came to Llallagua, the town at the edge of the giant Siglo XX mine. They announced that the government was paying twenty-seven million dollars—not a princely sum but more than two-thirds of Bolivia's foreign exchange reserves at the time—to buy out the tin barons. Sixty-three mines, thirteen companies, annual production of twenty-seven thousand metric tons, twenty-nine thousand workers: the state gobbled them all up. Patiño, Aramayo, Hochschild: the big names of Bolivian tin fell with a stroke of a pen.

That day the ethereal blue of the altiplano sky rang with the celebratory fireworks of local militia rifles. It thundered with the sound of exploding dynamite taken from the mine warehouses. And yet for all the fuss and fanfare, the halcyon days of tin mining were already over. Production had begun to wane. Other metals, plastics, open-pit mining would conspire against the price and perils of mining inside mountains two miles high. It was already over, and the Patiños, the Aramayos, and the Hochschilds, as they must have suspected at the time, did well to get out when they did.

On his deathbed in Buenos Aires in 1947, at the age of eighty-six, Simón Patiño, creator of the family's global tin empire, seemed to see what was coming. Speaking to his cardiologist about a minor expropriation by the Argentine government of a building next to his hotel, Patiño said: "You see the way things are, Doctor: in the old days, kings governed the people and administered their affairs by divine right; now those who govern have themselves elected by the people so that they can take away what the people have." Within a few days, the King of Tin was dead, and the Bolivian government, still respectful of the tin barons in those days before the 1952 revolution convulsed the country, declared a national day of mourning.

During the 1890s, Simón Patiño, a son of the altiplano with a rakish smile, hammered away with little success at the granite batholiths beneath the Andean landscape southeast of Oruro. This land offers rock and little else; when the early miners cut a dirt road into the mountains, it looked like a nail scratch on cowhide. Scraped clean by the wind, these lands would be drearily forbidding were it not for the magnificent backdrop of the vast sky. It did not go well for Patiño at the beginning.

Patiño's luck changed with the turn of the century. In 1900 he struck a vein of tin so pure that the small band of miners who were then working for him insisted it was silver. The strike was at Patiño's La Salvadora mine, a four-hectare precursor to the great mining complex that he would call with unabashed optimism Siglo XX, the Twentieth Century.

The optimism was deserved. By 1906, Patiño was able to set up his own bank, Banco Mercantil, with more capital than all of Bolivia's other banks put together. He issued his own currency; the fifty-boliviano note was engraved with the likenesses of his two daughters. By 1920, he controlled 40 percent of Bolivia's tin production, and the family fortune was estimated at half a billion dollars. When the Patiños traveled to New York they took a floor at the Waldorf and received visits from the great U.S. tycoons of the day.

The richest days of the Bolivian tin-mining industry occurred during the first two decades. Patiño would go on to build a worldwide empire—with heavy mining interests in Malaysia, processing plants around the world, and more than one hundred subsidiaries outside of Bolivia—while the Bolivian piece of his pie got smaller and smaller. In 1925, when the Bolivian government raised Patiño's taxes from 7.5 percent to 15 percent, he reincorporated his company in Delaware and, along with his family, began to spend less and less time in Bolivia.

And now? The rusting tin roofs of Patiño's mines and schools and company stores and hospitals flap in the wind at Siglo XX, Catavi, Llallagua, Uncía, Huanuni. On the short stretch of road from Llallagua to Catavi, where in 1949 thousands of uniform-clad schoolchildren lined up for several miles to bid welcome to Patiño's widow and her daughters following the death of the King of Tin, check-points have been set up to search scavengers who might be carting away a few kilos of ore or a bit of scrap metal from the idled machinery at the mines. At night, when in the old days the hillsides would glow like amusement parks with the brilliant lights of the ore-concentration plants, the tin mountains are pitch black and dead quiet but for the sound of bar music as a few ex-miners pass around liter bottles of pilsener beer.

At Catavi, the concentration plant, the railroad tracks, and the roads in and out of town are all eerily quiet. The town of Catavi is separated from Llallagua and the Siglo XX mine by a broad open space. The expanse is called the Fields of María Barzola, after the first woman to be shot dead when the miners clashed with the military during the bloody summer of 1942.

On one side of the fields is the old Catavi Golf Club. A few sheep and some goats graze on the dusty fairways, which faintly recall the days when foreign mine executives played the course. On the other side of the fields is the Siglo XX–Catavi cemetery. Yellowing posters commemorate this deadly event or that. Says one: LEST YOU FORGET. NOVEMBER 1979. THEY ASSASSINATED 400 INNOCENT BO-LIVIANS. But the most striking thing about the cemetery is the preponderance of tombstones that mark the graves of men in their twenties, thirties, and early forties, men who died not at gunpoint but from disease or accident.

Catavi would be a less ghostly place if there were no people at all. There is just enough life to make the town seem even more haunting. Unexpectedly, an old pickup truck clatters over the old railroad tracks and wheezes down the main street. The windows of the old Catavi hospital, named after Simón Patiño's wife, Albina, are coated with a film of dust that blows off the nearby slag heaps. In the interior courtyard, a clock is stopped at 12:36. There is a telephone booth in the classic English style, but painted green instead of red, its glass panels missing. It dates from World War II days, when tin mining flourished in the frenzy to supply the Allies and the miners' union was demanding a daily minimum wage of thirty-two cents for adult male workers. Hospital-green operating rooms, with ancient equipment on museumlike display, are padlocked. Not a sound. And then a nurse in her crisp uniform walks down the hallway, her rubber-soled shoes squeaking on the tiles.

Just a few years ago thirty-three doctors made the rounds of three hundred beds. Now there are three doctors, three nurses, one technician, three nurse's aides, three orderlies, and one half-time biochemist. Twelve patients—two on the men's floor, ten on the women's floor, half of them maternity cases—are housed in the newer annex behind the older main hospital building. The newer section was built in 1962 and is called, in the equalizing, leveling language of postnationalization, El Minero. The rains washed away the pipes a while back; there's still no running water in the hospital, and the staff doesn't expect the government to do anything about that anytime soon. Further up the hill is the children's hospital. Like the silent ore-concentration plant it looks down on, the children's hospital is closed nowadays.

Llallagua, hard by the Siglo XX mine, is a busier place than Catavi and there are more people around, but it too is in its death throes. The town looks like a city in wartime: it is a city of old men, women, and children; most of the men are in La Paz, camping out in the cathedral and at public schools, making their case before the government. At mass on Sunday, the churchgoers in Llallagua sing the hymns they have sung for decades: "God calls on us to make / Of this world / A table of equality / Struggling and working together. . . ." And at communion: "To fight alongside the worker / For a just salary / That is love. . . ." The people of Llallagua hold on to their small company houses, many of them under threat of eviction, and wait.

For what? They are waiting for the miners to take back the mines. That is the way it has always been done. In a plaza surrounded by the neat rows of company housing, near the union meeting hall and the cinema that in the boom days would get a first-run movie before the theaters in La Paz, stands a statue that has long symbolized the special defiance of the Siglo XX miners: a courageous miner lifts his muscled arms into the air, holding aloft his rifle in one hand, his pneumatic drill in the other.

That is the way it was always done. Above the town looms another symbol of defiance: the red-and-white broadcast tower of Radio Pío XII, named after Pope Pius XII and known as "La Voz del Minero" (the Voice of the Miner). The miners of Siglo XX were wary when they heard, in the years following the nationalization of the mines, that the foreign missionaries were coming to town. But when the Oblate priests arrived, they came dressed in beige cassocks; the people took it as a good omen that the priests were not dressed in black, the color of vultures. Still, in the early years, the Voice of the Miner was a moderate, even conservative voice. The priests soon veered left. Their radicalism hardened with time, and in recent years, the Voice of the Miner has stood firm even when the miners themselves felt beaten.

The radio station has been bombed from the air,

booby-trapped by saboteurs, blown up by demolition teams, and has come under attack by ground troops. For months on end the priests of Pío XII would sleep with their passports at their side. Padre Roberto—a tough, committed New Hampshire priest who makes a point of speaking only Spanish with visitors—had to bolt with his passport in 1980. He walked for several days through the bleak land before meeting up, as prearranged, with a teacher who had brought along a jeep loaded with sticks of dynamite and extra cans of gasoline. After a bad nighttime crash in the hills, Roberto finally made it to Cochabamba, where he hid out for six months, waiting—in the Bolivian way—for the government in La Paz to change hands.

That is the way it has always been done. Pío XII would rally the miners, help organize their protests. The miners would make a stand against the tin barons or the government. Women would die in the fields by the golf course. Or the men would march en masse to La Paz, clogging the highway between Oruro and the capital. They would flex their muscle, make their case, and get at least part of what they wanted.

But last year, after the government closed the mines and began trying to relocate the miners, the big march on La Paz ended differently. The marchers were met by troops on the Oruro–La Paz highway. They didn't have the strength to punch their way through to the capital. They turned, and headed home. People in Llallagua remember that when the marchers straggled back into town, some of the miners were crying. Padre Roberto had never seen that before. He had never seen the men of Siglo XX cry, not like that, not in defeat.

It was economic reality more than the government

troops that took the fight out of the miners. Between 1981 and 1985 the state mining company had run up $700 million in losses on top of $400 million it owed previously. That was before tin prices really started cascading. Afterward the state monopoly was chalking up cash deficits of $9 million a month—not to mention loans, which were piling up like so many slag heaps. At Catavi–Siglo XX, the government was spending ten dollars for every dollar of tin it produced, and nearly five thousand mine workers were producing only 30 metric tons a month, compared to 750 a month in 1952. And so it was that Víctor Paz Estenssoro, the president who came to Llallagua in 1952 to sign the tin-nationalization documents, back in office again, had begun closing the tin mines in 1985. Tin mining, the way the Bolivians had done it, was dead: that is what took the fight out of the miners and what made some of them cry.

After the failed march on La Paz, car-and-bus caravans of miners streamed out of Llallagua toward the "red zones" that the government had identified as relocation areas for the miners. For a while Llallagua was all but abandoned. Then came the failures in Santa Cruz and elsewhere, and the disillusioned started coming back. Sinforozo Rivera had spent $2,000 of his $2,500 severance paycheck for a little used car. He planned to have a taxi business in Cochabamba. But his new car was a two-door, and in Cochabamba, taxis had to have four doors. So he left the car with one of his sons and brought the family back to Llallagua— to wait.

Like Rivera, hundreds of other miners came back, waiting to see if the government would accept the union's reactivation plan. The plan is a fairly modest one, involving six hundred workers and only the tailings—not going back into the tin mountain. But the government could not accept it, and would not. The government knows that only machinery can do efficiently what the Bolivian miners had done for centuries—for the Spanish, for the Americans, for the Patiños, the Aramayos, and the Hochschilds. The government doesn't have the capital to buy the machinery. The only answer is privatization and foreign investment. And to do that, the government knows, it has to kill the miners' union: the specter of a Bolivian miner wielding a rifle along with his pneumatic drill is too much for a foreign investor to bear.

Near the statue of the defiant miner, by the roadside and behind a low rock wall, there's a garbage dump. A car stops. A man gets out and tosses a bag of trash over the wall. Four pigs, three young boys, and one woman scurry toward the pile. On a wall across the road there's some graffiti: VIVA LAS COOPERATIVAS MINERAS. Long live the mining cooperatives.

At Sinforozo Rivera's home at Mining Camp No. 6, his eighteen-year-old daughter, Rocío, a pretty girl with her hair cut short in the manner of the city, presides over a pot of noodle soup on the stove. Row after row of concrete-block houses line the hill that leads up to the mine. Sinforozo's family had been working the mines for long enough so that the family has managed to fashion a single home from two side-by-side houses (his and his father's), a total of four rooms for Sinforozo and Alina and the six of seven children who are still living at home. Some 45-rpm records are hung on the green walls as decorations: "La Minerita": "The Little Mining Woman." "Los de Uncía": "The Ones from Uncía." Songs of romance and defiance.

Rocío is at home alone today. Sinforozo is still at the cathedral in La Paz. The rest of the family is out and about. The family always leaves somebody at home these days. Three or four times the authorities have come by to try to evict the Riveras. The ones who come by don't really have their heart in their eviction work—they're from this harsh mining country, they know the story behind the Fields of María Barzola, how María and the other women picked up the Bolivian flag dropped by the miners and walked straight into the path of the machine gun—so if anybody's home they can usually be turned away.

At Radio Pío XII, the broadcast booth is empty, the microphones and antenna tower dead—shut down for a political meeting. A murmur, rising and falling, floats down the tiled hall from a meeting room where the Pío XII staff has gathered for a session of *autocrítica,* Marxist-style self-criticism: how do they help the miners take back the mines? Greeting a couple of visitors in his plain, clean office, Padre Roberto reflects on the struggles of the past. He speaks of how the men who worked the block were always the hardest, the furthest to the left politically. He remembers the time he escaped an army ambush by hiding in a casket and then riding an ore cart through darkened shafts to the other side of the mountain. He recalls how the marchers came back, some of them crying, from the last march on La Paz. "And to what end has all this been done?" he asks in Spanish. "To fill the cemeteries." His thoughts are noble, but they seem divorced from the reality that the miners and their families must cope with someday.

On his security rounds, Eustaquio Picachuri walks deeper and deeper into the mine, his boots loudly slapping the black water. In the tunnel there is one section that is particularly weak. It was repaired two weeks ago, and already some of the beams are giving way again. Picachuri worries that there will be a great accident someday. Inside the mine, the wooden beams rot fast; they seldom last more than two years. They're not being replaced anymore. All the repairs are makeshift these days, designed to buy a little time.

The race is on to dismantle the tin mountain. In the murky darkness a mile into the main tunnel, Picachuri surveys what's left of the old mining-company offices. He remembers when the offices had shiny wood floors and real lamps and desks and filing cabinets, and when the accountants would sit at their desks and fill their ledgers as railroad cars laden with glistening rock lumbered down the track and out of the mine, and when, across the way, the miners would stop briefly to sit on the wooden benches at the chapel inside the mine dedicated to La Virgencita de Concepción.

Now government crews huddle over rusting equipment. Mechanics armed with wrenches and blowtorches are taking apart the giant winches, immobilizing the forearm-thick cables, silencing the large elevator cages that service the great open galleries higher up in the mine. And the *cooperativistas* are picking over the skeletal remains of the old mining-company offices and busting up the benches at the chapel, scavenging furiously for wooden planks to use as crutches to bolster weakened beams before the mountain either collapses or yields its last tin. "It's sad," says Picachuri. "It makes you cry."

Up ahead an old mining cart that has been shanghaied back into service by the *cooperativistas* rumbles lightly along on the track on bootlegged electrical power. The miners who are on a board glance at Picachuri and turn away again; as they do, the watery light from the lamps on their helmets appears and then disappears. The old mining cart ducks down a spur and out of sight, a pirate ship slipping into a cove.

CHAPTER EIGHT
Chile: Traffic Lights in the Desert

ARICA, CHILE. Nov. 4, 1987. Superimposed on the Chilean desert like a strip of black electrical tape, the Pan American Highway south from Peru is an escape route from the Third World. We have abruptly crossed over into a Latin American Almost–First World, where highways are sleek lanes of glistening asphalt, complete with stripes down the middle and road signs. There were times on the trip, picking our way through Guatemala or Peru along stretches of highway, when we would know we were on the right road only because we would blow past a frowzy café called El Panamericano. Now, here in Chile, in the desert, where the empty highway meets a lonely side road, there is, of all things, a traffic light.

Soon enough, I would miss the invigorating chaos and endearing no-rules informality of the Latin America that lies to the north. But for the moment I enjoy the sense of homecoming a gringo feels when he returns to Main Street and McDonald's after a long absence. I can feel organization and order crashing over me, great foaming breakers of familiarity. Drink the water. Eat the salads. Joggers—European-looking here where the Indian imprint fades—in flapping turquoise shorts, bicyclists on sleek ten-speeds, pastel-colored apartment complexes. A video drive-in in the desert called Polyvan: in the cool of night, waiters in tight blue waistcoats and black bow ties serve food and drinks on little car-window trays as the clientele stares at an oversize outdoor TV screen that has never known the wetness of a raindrop.

What a strangely familiar place Chile is for an American. It's an elongated, antipodal California, five thousand kilometers of upside-down Pacific coastline fringed on the east by the Andes, from Aconcagua on the northern Argentine border—the highest mountain in the world outside of Asia—to the last nubs of the great cordillera as it sinks into the southernmost seas. Driving north to south, from sand dunes to ice floes, is like going from the sterile outback of Baja California to the far reaches of Alaska.

But this is not California. This is Chile. General Pinochet is still in Santiago. And on the outskirts of Arica in the morning, the crack-and-thud of rifle shots echoes from the seaside military firing range. And in the bars in the late afternoon, over glasses of the country's most popular brandy, a pisco neatly named Control, politics are still discussed in a whisper. And in the evening the army recruit on the way to his barracks talks mechanically about going after the *comunistas*. And in *El Mercurio*, a thick and rich *Los Angeles Times* look-alike whose front section carries more society news than foreign coverage, a page-one headline sets the theme for Pinochet's Chile:

ECONOMIC DEVELOPMENT
DOES NOT ALLOW
POPULIST ADVENTURES

Arica to Iquique. Nov. 5. The Atacama Desert
stretches south from Arica for 775 miles down the coast to
Copiapó. The Atacama, cooled by the Pacific, is a broad,
flat stairstep that drops in a series of pink-brown cliffs to
the rocky coast below. This is one of the driest places on
the face of the earth; in some spots, no rain has ever been
recorded.

At the foot of one such cliff lies Iquique, the first city
south of Arica. Iquique, like the other coastal oases in
northern Chile, is artificially sustained by water lines from
the Andes. Food is brought in by ship or over the highways.
It is a pleasant enough place whose gaily painted Victorian
buildings and slightly faded quality suggest the glorious
mining past of the desert.

Inland the demise of this region as a mining center is
starkly apparent. From the highway, we can see ghost town
after ghost town: Humberstone, Buena Ventura, Rica Ventura, Alianza. The names themselves recall the nineteenth-
century English influence and the strike-it-rich aspirations
that fueled the boom days. The short history of each town
is nailed shut with unmistakable finality by its cemetery,
which seems far too densely filled to have been populated
by the small town next to it until you remember how
mining can kill.

Humberstone, one of the largest of the ghost towns, is
at the Pan American Highway turnoff to Iquique. The
wood of the abandoned buildings with their punched-out
windows has been buffed glass-smooth by the gritty desert

wind. Long-idle machinery has rusted to a purplish brown. A honky-tonk bar and the old Teatro Humberstone sit frozen in time, dead and mute but for the creaking of floorboards underfoot.

This used to be Bolivia. Then came the War of the Pacific (1879–83), which established Chile as the great warrior state of South America. Chile's sea power gave it the edge it needed to exploit first the rich guano deposits off what was then the Bolivian and Peruvian coastline. As those deposits were mined to exhaustion, Chile mined the beds of nitrate, another fertilizer as well as a source of dynamite, that lay just beneath the bleak surface of the Atacama.

With the backing of British capital, Chile soon gained control over all known South American sources of natural nitrate. In 1879 it solidified its grip by a military occupation of the main Bolivian mining centers along the Atacama coast, and as it edged northward toward Lima, began to challenge the authority of Peru as well. Before it was all over, Chile actually occupied the Peruvian capital for a time. The Peru-Chile territorial wrangles were not resolved diplomatically until 1929, and even today they continue to be a source of friction at the border between Arica, Chile, and Tacna, Peru.

As for Bolivia, it lost its crucial gateway to the Pacific for its mineral exports. The idea of recapturing a path to the ocean continues to be a driving force in Bolivian politics and, judging from army recruiting posters that show Bolivian soldiers and tanks roaring over the Andes to the crashing waves of a Pacific beach, an argument for the existence of Bolivia's armed forces (including a vestigial navy that for now must stick to patrolling Lake Titicaca). Knowing this helps clear up the confusion of befuddled tourists in the Bolivian capital who sit at 12,000 feet, battling altitude sickness and puzzling over the slogan printed on the spine of the La Paz telephone directory: BOLIVIA DEMANDS ITS RIGHT TO A PATH TO THE SEA.

Chuquicamata. Nov. 6. There is enough heavy infrastructure traversing the desert to suggest that something of moment exists in the foothills to the east. A good, wide road. A railroad line off in the distance. And humming electrical cables looped over gargantuan towers. They are all headed for the largest copper mine in the world.

The mine, developed by the U.S. company Anaconda but now state owned, is responsible for more than half of the copper output of Chile, the world's number one producer. The open pit has reached a depth of more than 1,000 feet. The annual production at Chuquicamata— roughly half a million metric tons per year during the 1980s—is accomplished with legendary Chilean efficiency. Until Bolivia shut down its tin mines, Bolivia's Siglo XX– Catavi tin operations and Chile's Chuquicamata mine each employed about four to five thousand workers; yet Chuquicamata mined as much copper in a week as Siglo XX–Catavi mined tin in a year's time.

On the edge of the pit is a company town of thirty thousand people. It is spruced-up Orwellian, an orderly community where all the streets have names. It's our third day in Chile, and I still cannot get over even the gas stations: Exxon red-white-and-blue service islands in a lake of black asphalt; metal canopies overhead to protect us from the sun; blue-uniformed attendants darting among gleaming pumps that aren't empty, dispensing gas that isn't watered down. Already, however, the cool efficiency of the place, so much like home, is disconcerting: where's the magic and the mystery that shone through the surface disorganization of the Latin America we had come to know on the trip?

We pick up some lunch for the road and follow the power lines and the copper-laden railcars back down to the coast, to the formerly Bolivian port of Antofagasta. It is an hour before sunset by the time we pull up to 7 Cabañas, a funky little motel outside of town. My little bout with disorientation in Chile continues: the motel is across the road from a beach named after Huáscar, the Inca; our host, the owner, is a tall white man named Guillermo E. Flynn. He turns the whole motel over to us on the condition that we not make him turn on the generator for electricity. He goes into town to shop for our dinner and breakfast. I start up the grill. Flynn and his wife return with chicken and onions and eggs, a bottle of Gato Negro red wine (a cheap table wine palatable enough to hint at the promise of the rich vineyards down south), even a silver candelabra to get us through the evening.

Caldera. Nov. 7. On the road from Antofagasta to the iron-ore port of Caldera, billboards keep welcoming us to the Atacama region, "where the desert blooms." Ordinarily such hyperbole would be written off as Chamber of Commerce boosterism. This spring it is gloriously true. The southern reaches of the desert have gotten the kind of rain that falls only once in a generation. For mile after mile, softly undulating fields of wildflowers cover the desert floor with a profusion of color. It looks like God's nursery.

At night, while we're camped at a cabin at Bahía Inglesa, the shortwave picks up a BBC report about how the English spend relatively little money on their children compared with what they spend on their pets. On a Voice of America rebroadcast of some weekend news panel, one of *Newsweek*'s White House correspondents is explaining that some Reagan Supreme Court nominee was doomed when it was discovered that he had smoked marijuana as a young man. Hmmm. More strange news from the First World.

La Serena and the Elqui Valley. Nov. 8–14. We are headed from the superb shellfish restaurants of La Serena into the northernmost of Chile's grape-growing regions. Only now are we getting a sense of Chile's potential as a world agricultural power. Swift streams fed by thick mountain snowbeds course through vast stretches of untilled land that has the look and feel of a proto-California: with irrigation, the northern half of Chile would bloom with a lot more than the wildflowers that come with the once-a-generation rains. Whereas so much of the terrace agriculture in Guatemala and Peru has a spent look, here in Chile, where the farmland is much less densely populated, time seems to be on the country's side.

At Vicuña, the retail center of the valley, a dirt road cuts south into the most agriculturally productive section of the valley. The sky here is astonishingly clear. It looks scrubbed clean, and is redolent with the sweet smell of young brandy from all the pisco distilleries. This town was jammed with comet-watchers in 1985: on the plaza there's even a tavern called Halley. With its dry, cool nighttime air, minimal ambient light after dark, and a mix of foliage that reduces reflection from the ground up, the region is famous as an astronomical center; just this past year, a spectacular supernova was spotted from this vantage point. The roaming, domed eyes of several observatories peer up from the mountains; at the largest, the Cerro Tololo Inter-American Observatory—which has a four-hundred-centimeter reflecting telescope, the largest in the Southern Hemisphere—and the European Southern Observatory, a total of nineteen telescopes scan the heavens.

The valley from Vicuña south is long and narrow, a lovely cleft in the earth. It's hot today at midday, but there's snow on the high ridges. Just last week the grape growers in the valley awakened to a gleaming frost that blanketed their vineyards. The best pisco in Chile comes from the valley, which yields grapes much higher in sugar content than the delicate wine grapes south of Santiago. The Elqui grapes that don't go into making the bracing, clear brandy are exported as table grapes or become wonderfully plump raisins. Down the road from Montegrande, where a tidy little museum marks the birthplace of the Nobel laureate poet Gabriela Mistral (she wrote with great affection of the Elqui's "gardens fed by the very sap of the hills"), is the center of the grape-growing area, Pisco Elqui. Many of the vineyards in the valley are members of the two big Chilean pisco cooperatives, Control and Capel. Some of the growers, like RRR and Tres Cruces, which would be called "boutique vineyards" if they were in California's Napa Valley, produce their own pisco.

We fill our silver flask with Tres Cruces and head further down the valley, past Horcón and on to Alcahuaz, in search of a campsite for the night. We dine under an enormous weeping willow. As darkness falls, the clamor of the Elqui's water at our side seems to get louder and louder. Standing on a nearby small bridge I notice that when Venus comes up it is so bright that it casts a shadow from my hand onto the bridge railing. Thus distracted, I am startled when I hear the scrape and clatter of horse hooves from the other end of the bridge. I yell a too-loud greeting—¡hola!—which in turn surprises the horse. The horse bolts. In the pitch black of the night a stirrup snaps sharply and the rider has to dismount abruptly, spurs jangling, boots clicking on the bridge.

So it is that we meet Ramón Luis Alvarez. The *huaso,* or cowboy, leads his Chilean barb over to us by the reins. A conversation lasting nearly an hour—it is so dark we never see more than an outline of Ramón Luis and his horse—yields an invitation to come by his small ranch in the morning. We get directions and hope we will be able to recognize our host when we meet up with him again in the light of day.

We manage to track down Ramón Luis with little problem. He is in his early thirties, short and well built, with a quick smile. Except during lunch in the dining room of his compact ranch house or when we clambered up the hillside to look at some Indian rock paintings, I never saw him more than five yards from one of his three horses. The horses have chewed and stomped away every blade of grass around the house and the corral. The rest of the property—five acres or so—is fenced in and planted with grapes, whose chief raison d'être is to make a little money to buy more horses.

Someday the corral will be the site of Ramón Luis's *media luna,* the typical Chilean half-moon-shaped riding arena where horses are broken and trained, and where parties and rodeos are held. The media luna is a riding ring built of stones and stripped logs and poles. Media lunas were originally rectangular, but were rounded at the edges over the years so that the huaso could better work the cattle. They must be stout enough to withstand the full charge of a barrel-chested barb as it performs a bone-cracking *ata-jada:* ramming a yearling calf and then pinning the animal for a split second against the timbers. The media luna in Chilean horse country is what the swimming pool became in the United States in the post–World War II era: a status symbol among the upwardly mobile. At the end of his workday, Ramón Luis climbs the hill behind his house; he ignores the petroglyphs and, as the vineyards darken to a green-black in the fading sunlight, daydreams about his media luna.

Someday. For now, he's got his modest corral and stables. He keeps his tack locked inside oil drums that have been cut in half and hinged. He works out of a small office under the stare of dark-eyed Chilean blondes clinging to wall calendars advertising a tractor dealership in La Serena. There's another calendar on his desk; it is filled with photos from Chilean rodeos, a pictorial parade of huasos draped in colorful woven *mantas,* or shawl-sized blankets, and astride quick-stepping barbs. Dusty sample-size bottles of Pisco Control line a shelf. Condor feathers with sharpened nibs lie beside an inkwell. A saddle in midconstruction decorates a pedestal in the middle of the small room. Strewn about the floor are bits of felt, leather, and metal. An assortment of star- and asterisk-shaped silver spurs, some of them blood tipped, hangs on the wall.

We spend much of the day with Ramón Luis. I try to get him to talk about politics. In my own mind fragments of recent history race by like clouds: in 1970, Salvador Allende becomes the first democratically elected Marxist president in the world; a rush to socialism wrenches the economy out of shape, polarizing the population and setting the stage for military intervention; when the coup comes, in 1973, Allende dies in his burning palace; under Gen. Augusto Pinochet, the new regime unleashes wave after wave of repression, executing thousands of Chileans with a scarifying lack of discrimination and jailing or forcing into exile tens of thousands of others. Twice during the day I broach the subject of the coup and the subsequent era of government repression with Ramón Luis. The first time, he politely changes the subject. The second time, he is equally noncommittal. He acknowledges that he is paying attention to what I am saying and then adds: "But let's not talk about those days."

Ramón Luis goes a bit further on the second full day we spend with him. It is late in the day. We've been up and down the valley on horseback. Against our sunburned skin, the air turns cool and sharp. I bring up the subject of the Pinochet coup again. He will very quickly change the subject again, but before he does, he says: "It was bad, 1973, but not so bad."

It would be easy to pigeonhole Ramón Luis. He seems the type who fits a standard-issue caricature of the Chilean people: hard workers who have been seduced by the measure of prosperity that the Pinochet era has brought to much of the country, softened enough by relative wealth to lower the heat of their indignation at Pinochet's boot-heel tactics; people who have come to prize, like their government, economic stability above all else, even civil liberties— economic development over populist adventures. There is some truth to that, but it ignores the great stigma of the brutality that brought Pinochet to power. As a people

Chileans often seem locked into silence and submission by some secret terror—like grown-ups who as children witnessed something so awful that they have repressed its very memory. That is why they don't want to talk about how a democratic people not particularly coup-prone or repressive before 1973 could allow the brutality of the Pinochet era to take place.

Santiago de Chile. Nov. 15–18. It wasn't that long ago, back in New York, that I was looking through some photographs that had come in for a story we were doing about Chile. In Santiago's poorest neighborhoods, demonstrators held empty pots and pans aloft to show that Pinochet's radical laissez-faire economic policies had cut millions of Chileans out of the money loop. Water cannons bore down on protestors. In one particularly memorable photos, a riot-police attack dog was lunging at a fleeing youth; in the mind's eye the dog's teeth connected with the youth's leg a split second later.

This is not that Santiago. Ours is sun dappled and becalmed. There are a fair number of brown-uniformed police around, serious and alert. Their presence is so low-key that they soon become part of the scenery, vaguely threatening monuments to street rioting I read about in the past and may well read about again. In our Santiago, conformism, not terror or fear, is in the air. Except for a smattering of opposition voices, the media are gushing with happy talk. Government television sticks to smiley-face pleasantries, General Pinochet ribbon cuttings, Mrs. Pinochet hospital visits. *El Mercurio,* grown fat on government loans, remains relentlessly slick and upbeat, or not quite relevant: the Sunday paper's "Wiken" section (as in "weekend") carries a jaunty article on *yins* (jeans).

The message is: hey, we're okay, really, we're okay. And maybe they are. In a couple of years, after all, Pinochet will turn his presidential sash over to Patricio Aylwin of the moderate opposition, the military will have promised to respect the will of the people, and the exiles, many of them anyway, will begin to return. But right now, in the fifteenth summer of Pinochet's rule, this country is still healing. Chile is not okay, not really. Over the past decade and a half Chile lost a lot of people to death and to exile, and with them—the artists and the dancers and the professors and the others—went a chunk of the people's soul. Something is missing.

One night in Santiago we walk from our hotel hard by the lush green of Santa Lucía Hill over to the ballet at the Municipal Theater. *Santiaguenses* in all their warm-weather finery are marching up the broad staircase and into the porticoed front entrance. With our two-thousand-peso (not quite ten-dollar) tickets, we are politely ushered away from the pricier doors, around to the side entrance, and then up into the balcony seats. We have come to see *Le Papillon,* a nineteenth-century French ballet about love and freedom. Chile is like the ballet as it is performed before us tonight. This *Le Papillon* is admirably staged and lush-looking. But there is something missing: the exiles. Not one of the key dancers is a Chilean.

Santiago to Marchihue. Nov. 19–21. We saunter southward through a countryside that grows more and more beautiful each day. This is Chile's wine country. In the Maipo Valley, a sea of vineyards glistening green is almost unbroken but for an archipelago of whitewashed islands: the winery buildings that house gleaming stainless-steel tanks aboveground and, below, the cool, aromatic cellars of Santa Rita or Concha y Toro. The region bespeaks tradition, from the ancient thick trunks of the vines to the rosebush hedges that divide the fields. (More sensitive than the vines to blight, the roses serve as an early warning to the growers.) The lifestyle of the wine country seems to preclude mediocrity. At even common roadside restaurants it's hard to get anything less than a fine grilled chicken or cut of beef—and a good glass of wine.

During a two-night stay at an out-of-the-way motel in San Vicente, we learn that a Chilean rodeo—something we had wanted to see ever since Ramón Luis whetted our appetite—is to be held on Saturday at Marchihue. We drive in the cool of the morning, get to Marchihue early, and settle in for twelve hours of equestrian fanfare. Much of the time is spent choosing and feting the dark-eyed queen, who along with her rivals has been coyly courting the crowd all morning long. Once the rodeo itself begins, in what soon becomes a blur, prizes are handed out to the contestants in the various rodeo events (I remember fifth prize: a six-pack of motor oil). There are leather belts and leather harnesses and woven-leather lariats for sale. At mealtime, everybody eats and dances the *cueca*.

But the centerpiece of the marathon fiesta is the atajada, the fearsome bit of horsemanship that had been described to us up in the Elqui Valley. Distilled from the workaday task of cutting (or sorting) cattle in the pens for branding or sale, the atajada has evolved into an elaborately choreographed contest that becomes a full-time occupation for the huasos who are best at it. On the dusty arena of the media luna, two riders in short capes rein in their horses, waiting. A *novillo*, a bull two or three years old, is released from its pen. The bull charges counterclockwise around the ring, herded by the two huasos on horseback. One rider, from behind, coaxes the novillo forward. The second rider, at the same breakneck speed, moves his horse smartly sideways at nearly right angles to the bull and the wall. At this point only two or three seconds have passed. Within the next second or two—before reaching a specially designated point along the media luna's inside wall—the sideways-galloping rider must charge at the bull. At full speed, he must ram his horse's chest into the novillo, punch the animal up against the wall and, if he can, pin him there for a split second. I think I will never tire of watching this stylish sport, but I do. By midevening the rodeo itself starts winding down. The dancing will go on well past midnight, we are told, but we've had enough, and leave.

Salto del Laja. Nov. 22. The land and the climate are changing fast. Yesterday at the atajada it was all dust, the jangle of four-inch silver spurs, hooves pounding into a carpet of dust that thickened as the day wore on, and the mentholated scent from cut eucalyptus branches used to shade the bleachers. This evening there are deer, wildflowers, and buzzing squadrons of postwinter insects cavorting in the warmth. We are reentering familiar latitudes, and I experience a strong rush of nostalgia during a late-afternoon walk to the 150-foot waterfall after which this town along the Pan American Highway is named. I am reminded at every turn of Bartholomew's Cobble, a nature preserve near a home we used to rent in Sheffield, Massachusetts, where the northernmost vestiges of trees typical to the U.S. South mingle along the Housatonic River with the southernmost of cold-country pines and maples. It strikes me, wistfully, that it's nearly Thanksgiving, that we've been on the road for six months now, and that, as far away as home is from this antipodal Chilean spring, we'll be back in the States in three months.

Villarrica. Nov. 23. This town anchors the northwest corner of one of the world's great lake districts and rests on the edge of the district's most famously beautiful lake, Villarrica, a sweep of cobalt blue edged by wild roses and deep-green forests and set against a snow-capped volcano. There is a Germanic cast to this part of southern Chile. The architecture—the steep pitch of the roofs, the eaves jutting out over mullioned windows, the dark-stained wood—is reminiscent of towns along the Rhine. There is something Germanic, too, about the Chilean penchant for organization. On a seventeen-mile bike ride around one side of the lake to the quaint village of Pucón, we come across various road crews meticulously repairing what would be considered an ultramodern superhighway in a more downtrodden Latin American country. I count at least a hundred workers deployed in platoon-size contingents along the road. Each wears a hard hat color coded to his or her task, be it tar spreader, supervisor, or flagperson. On this autobahn, even cyclists are expected to heed the flagpersons; to fail to do so would incur a flurry of remonstrative headshakes. Each flagperson brandishes an oversize ping-pong paddle, flipping it green for "go," red for "stop." Here, in a technique unsettlingly suggestive of police practices at the scene of a murder, each pothole is outlined in white paint. And numbered. West to east. Villarrica to Pucón. No. 1 through No. 404. It is chilling to think that a country that circles and numbers potholes on a rural road will never know how many Chileans were summarily executed in soccer stadiums and basements in the first weeks of Pinochet's rule.

Nilque. Nov. 24–26. It is off-season in the mountains. High above the lushly foliated woods around Nilque, the cavernous old ski chalet at Antillanca is empty except for a Harvard-educated Chilean entomologist and his wife. (He is here to investigate a recurring plague of giant horseflies that over the past few years has decimated the summer tourism business hereabouts for two weeks before and after Christmas.) Only at the uppermost reaches of the ski runs, where the slopes flatten before dipping down into the old volcanic crater, is there any snow. At the Hotel Termas de Puyehue's indoor pool, a single dive into the 115-degree spring water echoes raucously through deserted locker rooms. We leave the lake country behind in order to keep a date in Puerto Montt: Thanksgiving dinner with our friends from Costa Rica, the Dyers, who have come down to Chile for a meeting of the Inter-American Press Association. Our holiday fare is appropriate to the latitude of Puerto Montt: spring lamb.

Puerto Montt. Nov. 27. This alpine-looking port is the beginning of the end in Chile. Early in his regime, to replace the old system of twenty-five provinces, Pinochet divided Chile into twelve regions, numbered north to south, and one metropolitan area. Puerto Montt is the capital of the Tenth Region. A third of the country lies to the south still, but it is in Puerto Montt that populated Chile ends. This gives Puerto Montt a wonderful feel. It is the sort of place Melville and Conrad liked to write about. The railroad ends here. The road system ends here (with one exception, as we will soon find out for ourselves). From here, supply ships head out each week to deliver groceries, hardware, and dry goods to remote settlements to the south. Cruise ships sail south down the coast into the glaciated fjords. Planes hopscotch down to Punta Arenas in Chilean Patagonia and on past Tierra del Fuego to Puerto Williams, the most southerly place in the world with a permanent population.

Chiloé Island. Nov. 28–Dec. 2. South of Puerto Montt lies archipelagic Chile. The Tenth Region is like a pane of shattered glass on the South Pacific; this fractured landmass is a fantastically wild jumble of virgin forests, cragged mountains, spectacular glaciers, icy fjords, heavily wooded islands, and deep, dark channels. As beautiful as it is, as rich as it is—in fisheries, lumber, and petrochemicals, to mention just a few things—the land resists human habitation; only 3 percent of Chile's twelve million people live south of Puerto Montt. The region's great bond is water. The channels and rivers and bays are roadways; boats and ferries are the principal modes of transport. Water rushes everywhere from all directions. Glacial streams and aquamarine rivers pour into the ocean. The ocean feeds the sky. The sky returns its bounty; in some parts of archipelagic Chile as many as two hundred inches of rain fall each year.

On Chiloé, the largest of the islands (155 miles long, 31 miles wide), the weather is stormy more than three hundred days a year. The brooding weather merely enhances the beauty of the island, whose name means "the land of the sea gulls." The green of the fields and the trees is indelible, the green of Ireland, or of the Guatemalan mountains in the rainy season. The gravelly roads are perpetually wet and shiny, the people routinely swathed in wool from local sheep. The rare glint of sunlight on the water or a sheep pasture pops off the canvas, like the extraordinary wildflowers we saw up north in the Atacama. When we get off the ferry from Puerto Montt, Ancud is between storms—not sunny in the least, but handsomely enveloped in great capes of mist and drizzle. It is cold and damp, and the gray shrouds make the world seem very compact all of a sudden. Were we not just in the desert? How long ago was it that we were driving at 16,000 feet in the Peruvian Andes, when the sky seemed frontierless?

The fishing villages on Chiloé—their pastel buildings stubbornly colorful against the gray of the water and the sky and the green of the land—all boast fine wood-shingled churches. The churches were built by the Jesuits who came to the island right after the first non-Indian settlers arrived 257 years ago. One of the finest is on Achao, which is the largest of a cluster of satellite islands off Chiloé and is reachable by a bright orange four-car ferry from the town of Dalcahue. Chiloé remains almost exclusively Catholic. On our return from Achao, at the church in Dalcahue, Julith asks two boys if there are many Protestants—*protestantes*—hereabouts. They have no idea what she is talking about. She begins to explain how Protestants differ from Catholics. "Oh," says one of the boys, "you mean *contrabandistas*."

Set on the far side of Chiloé, away from the other villages, is Cucao. When you come to a place like Cucao, on the violently windward side of Chiloé, after driving along a road that turns to dirt track, passing a pair of big wind-whipped lakes and stalwart woods and outcroppings that face the wind like giant chisels, and you get to a place where teams of packhorses are moving cargoes of rubbery tubes of algae up from the beach en route to the Japanese food industry, and you see through misty veils bare-chested men out in the thunder of the rough surf scooping up armloads of shellfish, and you look out to sea beyond the horses, the men, and the frothing surf along a nine-mile beach and you see nothing else—when you come to a place like Cucao, you understand how it is that a Spaniard could have dragged himself to such a place and thought, as he later recorded in his diary: That's it, there's nothing more, the edge that I see is where the world stops.

Puerto Chacabuco. Dec. 4. We have reached the southernmost point in our journey. We came overnight—an eighteen-hour trip—in the ferry from Quellón, a port in the south of Chiloé. We spent our last night on Chiloé in Chonchi, to my thinking the handsomest of the island's fishing villages. My impression may well be skewed by our stay there at the Antiguo Chalet. The hotel is an old mansion that belonged to a Chonchi timber baron who exported lumber to the Argentines back when the Argentines were rich. It is a place of high ceilings, tall windows with weathered shutters, Victorian furniture, and glass prisms that catch the light from the crackling fire, the one noise in the house. The owners serve us salmon and *licor de oro,* a homemade liqueur laced with vanilla and egg yolks that in any setting other than the Antiguo Chalet we would find too sweet to drink.

The following night we shared the last of the *licor de oro* with a French couple we met on the ferry. I spent midnight alone on deck, taking in the awesome quiet as we neared what looked vaguely like land on this clearest of

black nights. I could just barely feel the thrumming of the
ferry's engines under my feet and through my hands as they
gripped the cold steel of the railing. The water was black.
Blacker still were big, looming humps on either side of us—
the slopes, feathery black with indistinguishable pine trees,
of mountains that dropped down into the water. For two
hours I waited for the moon. I had seen two lighthouses,
and I saw one other light, the light of a house probably, a
single jewel sewn onto a black-velvet mountain. Now there
was not a single light anywhere. And then, preceded by a
faint glow on the rise of one mountain, came the moon, a
full moon, rising into the black night, moving with the
stealth of our ferry.

Puerto Chacabuco, for all the grandeur surrounding
it, is a sadly dog-eared port. We are drawn to it because it
is near the southern terminus of the southernmost highway
in Chile. The highway is an undeniable feat of engineering
in this daunting landscape, but it strikes us as typical
Pinochet hype and egocentrism that this slip of a road—a
single lane of packed dirt—should bear the grandiose name
Carretera Austral Gen. Augusto Pinochet. Most southern
chilenos, however, do not begrudge the president his privi-
lege. The Pinochet government has done much to develop
Chile south of Puerto Montt and to exploit—often reck-
lessly—its considerable resources. Because of this, Pinochet
himself is noticeably more popular in the south than he is
elsewhere in the country.

Our plan was to loop back up north on the Chilean
mainland and then cross at Futaleufú into Argentine Patagonia. We had no idea what the road would be like. Only
one isolated stretch of it had been completed, well south of
Puerto Montt—a 420-kilometer stretch that went from

nowhere to nowhere. We were put off a bit by what we had read in our guidebook: allow up to ten days for this journey between Coihaique, just south of Puerto Chacabuco, and Chaitén, an overnight ferry trip from Puerto Montt. At Puerto Chacabuco, we stop in at the local headquarters of the national police—the *carabineros*—to check on road conditions. The road sounds okay, but while we are in the office I catch a glimpse of one of those grim Chilean reminders of the fanaticism that courses beneath the surface in Pinochet's Chile. There's a poster on the wall. "Wanted for Murder: These Communists." (The word "Communists" is in bright red.) Then eight photos. Three of them are covered over with brown paper.

The Carretera Austral is a one-lane corduroy road, built of logs laid side by side transversely and covered with the dark loam of the region. It snakes through countryside that even to our eyes, accustomed by now to almost daily explosions of scenic beauty after so many months on the road, seems preternaturally beautiful. When the Carretera Austral is not cutting through forests that have never known the blade of an ax or the teeth of a chain saw, it navigates a thin lip of land between deep blue fjords on our left and on our right, thickly wooded hillsides, roiling brooks that slip through corrugated-tin ducts beneath our little road, and mountains frosted with light blue glaciers.

During two days of driving—it would not take us ten, thankfully—we run into only two cars on the road. One of them we run into all too literally. I had been lulled into carelessness by the sights and sounds, and by the absence of anybody else on the highway. Suddenly, I see a jeep coming at us around a bend in the one-lane road. There's a fjord on the left, a wall of rock on the right. Neither one of us is going very fast. We both downshift fast and step on the brakes. A split second before the collision, I recognize the vehicle heading into me: a carabinero jeep. Fortunately, the carabineros—organized, if nothing else—have fastened a spare tire to the front of their jeep. We are going slow enough so that when our two war wagons collide, it is just a tap that sends the jeep lurching back a bit. (Later the local people would tell us that they drive the road only at night; with their headlights on, drivers coming from opposite directions can spot each other from a long way off.)

Man's presence here is minimal, but growing. After several hours on the road, it is jarring to see men on horseback. They wear cowboy hats, heavy vests, and fleecy sheepskin chaps, and are driving a herd of cattle from the lowlands around Mañiguales to summer pastures up in the highlands of El Emperador. The human presence is more intrusive where settlers have moved into their wood-frame houses. *"Gran Bingo Campesino,"* says the poster in Mañiguales (first prize: a braided lasso; second prize: a pair of reins). Nearby, where trees have been felled for lumber, the buzz saw has left the flat tops of waist-high tree trunks gleaming a lifelessly pale yellow. Up the road, houses that have just recently been painted green are clustered around a schoolhouse in midconstruction. A sign along the road identifies the place as Villa Amengual. Next to the word *"Habitantes"* (Inhabitants), the space where a number will go someday soon has been left blank for now.

Puyuguapi. Dec. 5. "A person can rest easy at night."

It is the eve of our last day in Chile. By tomorrow we will be crossing into Argentine Patagonia. But for now we are listening to Ursula Flack, who is telling us why she admires Augusto Pinochet. Señora Flack runs the finest boardinghouse in Puyuguapi, a quaint village at the end of a very long fjord, about halfway through our south-north jaunt along the general's highway. There are hints of Rhineland and alpine architecture in the village, especially in the bigger houses, the ones where the German immigrants live. Señora Flack's pension is called the Residencial Alemana (for "German"). She came to Puyuguapi thirty-eight years ago with her husband and his two brothers. Señora Flack was recently widowed, but she's making the best of her new life. Her boardinghouse now comes more highly recommended than the Bavarian-looking farmhouse run by Nora Winkler.

"Pinochet is a man of vision. He has done things. Other politicians just talk, talk, talk. He's given us potable water, schools, a gymnasium with showers and bathrooms. By next October we will have electricity and telephones."

Upstairs carpenters are banging away. It's a prosperous sound. Señora Flack is redoing her guest rooms for the summer season. There's still a chill in the air at this time of year, even at lunchtime. Thanks to her extensive greenhouse out in the backyard, we're enjoying an exquisitely fresh salad of lettuce and radishes. At night Señora Flack fires up her new woodstove. The town generator provides electricity during part of the evening and, to go with it, videotapes from Santiago over a closed-circuit television network that is wired into all the houses.

"When Allende came into office, some Chileans here went to the new *intendente*, the local commander of the carabineros, and complained about the gringos, as they call us Germans. The intendente said, 'I'd rather have ten gringos than a hundred Chileans working for me anyday.' So much for that. Still, those were not easy times. We had to buy cooking oil on the black market in Puerto Montt. Now it's different. We can buy things now. They come on the boat once a week from Puerto Montt. You place your order, you wait a week, and you get it."

Señora Flack, a large-boned woman of ruddy complexion, must have been about twenty years old or so when she came to Puyuguapi. From pioneer to entrepreneur, she has apparently thrived on her life at the end of the fjord. She is still a strong, attractive woman. Her auburn hair has a sheen to it, and one can imagine her brushing it, counting to one hundred, as her last act each night before bed. She must have been quite beautiful in her youth—a suitable match for her husband. There is an old photograph of him on a shelf in the dining room. He's in his Nazi uniform, fair skinned and blond.

"The Carretera Austral is not just a backcountry road. To the people who live here, it's a highway. Life is better here because of it. Pinochet is a man with vision. From Puerto Montt to the south, let Pinochet be the candidate for president. From Puerto Montt to the north, let them have another candidate."

CHAPTER NINE
Argentina: The Shrinks of Buenos Aires

GONE WITH THE WIND is playing at one of the grand cinemas on Lavalle Street. It is a slow, sultry day in January in Buenos Aires. The people with real money are gone; the papers in the capital carry daily stories about their doings in Mar del Plata and Punta del Este. The psychotherapists are off; *Uno Mismo (One's Self)* and other magazines, like the *New Yorker* in August, run cartoons about angst-ridden patients muddling through the month without their accustomed couch time. For those who are left behind there are long afternoons at the movies and cafés of sun-bleached paneling and polished brass, and late-night dinners of pasta and wine thinned with soda water. The women standing on line for *Gone with the Wind* are mostly elderly and mostly overdressed in a quaint, appealing way; over their arms they carry cherished old cashmere sweaters to stave off the chill from the air-conditioning inside. Ensconced in slightly threadbare velvet seats, surrounded by the sort of lavish theater decor that died in the cinemas of most cities three or four decades ago, the women every so often murmur lines from the movie. They know them by heart, and they speak them in the proper British English they learned in their youth at the best academies in Buenos Aires. It is impossible not to imagine that, as Atlanta burns on the screen, the women do not think of some bygone greatness in their own lives in this once-great city.

When you approach Buenos Aires by road from the west, you see where the promise of Argentina and its capital first flourished. Grassland, unrelievedly flat and straw colored at this time of the year, stretches as far as the eye can see. The great breadth, from horizon to horizon, barely hints at the full scope of the Argentine pampas—a two-hundred-thousand-square-mile expanse the size of Kansas, Iowa, and Missouri combined. The Spanish crown paid little attention to the potential of the pampas; the Spaniards were interested in metal, not stalks of wheat. Spain bestowed a trading monopoly upon Lima because Peru was where the gold was, and Argentina was consigned to its place as a backwater colony while Buenos Aires, for all its advantages as a deep-water port, was cut off from sanctioned trade routes and turned instead to piracy and contraband. In 1750, when Lima and Mexico City were great cities, Buenos Aires was a seedy port with twelve thousand inhabitants.

All this began to change in the mid-1800s, when Argentina had just a little over a million inhabitants. Political stability afforded by a constitution fashioned broadly after that of the United States coincided with the first great waves of European immigration and with innovations such as barbed-wire fencing and the modern windmill water pump to turn the pampas into one of the world's most productive breadbaskets and cattle-grazing lands. The earth of the pampas is famously rich and well suited to growing grain; agronomists have found alfalfa roots growing in stoneless soil to a depth of fifteen feet. The impact of the agricultural boom on the Argentine economy was phenomenal. In 1876 the country exported a mere twenty-one tons of wheat. By the turn of the century annual wheat exports exceeded two million tons. On the eve of the Great Depression, from which Argentina recovered faster than many other countries, grain and beef exports had helped to turn the economy into the world's tenth largest. During World War II, Argentina's total grain production rose to ninety million tons a year.

Already, though, cracks had appeared in the Argentine economy, mainly in the area of modernization. There was a spurt of industrialization during World War I, but it was not sustained, nor was the development of energy resources, and Argentina continued slipping far behind countries that it had once regarded as economic rivals—the United States, Britain, Germany, and France. With the Depression came a military coup that marked the beginning of a half century of frightful swings between civilian and military rule, between governments that were legitimate and illegitimate, proproletariat and proaristocracy. In the process, economic development suffered disastrously from a lack of coherent policy.

Following a series of fraudulently elected governments in the 1930s, the country seemed on the verge of turning over power to pro-British conservatives during the war years. Though the military would switch sides near the end of the war when it became clear Germany and Japan would lose, it began the war as pro-Axis. It intervened against the pro-British threat and took power. High up in the power structure was an ambitious and astute colonel named Juan Domingo Perón. As the country began another spurt of industrialization and rural Argentines moved from the country, where landownership was concentrated in relatively few hands, to the city, Perón championed the cause of the burgeoning class of urban workers, the *descamisados,* or "shirtless ones." Increasingly wary of Perón's populist threat, the military threw him out of the government and into prison in 1945. Perón's wife, his former mistress, the ex-actress Eva Duarte Perón, rallied the descamisados, who took to the streets and won his release. Perón was elected to the presidency four months later.

Perón was a visionary who saw Argentina as a dynamic industrial power that could stand on its own, independent of Europe and the United States, as the leader and economic powerhouse of Latin America. To accomplish this, Perón set up a state trading monopoly that purchased surplus agricultural products as cheaply as possible and resold them overseas at inflated prices, dramatically adding to state revenues. Argentina had also accumulated large foreign exchange reserves during World War II and for a time, as much of the industrialized world recovered from the war, Perón's policy worked. With its surplus cash, the government nationalized foreign-owned companies, promoted a new generation of industries, and passed out substantial wage increases to the working class.

In reality, Perón's economic measures would soon prove shortsighted. His farm-price policy discouraged production; by the early 1950s grain production had slumped to nearly a third of what it had been a decade earlier. The economy was racked by massive inefficiency, as epitomized by the obese state bureaucracy (between 1945 and 1955 the number of government employees nearly quintupled). In addition, the military, which Perón had managed to co-opt for a while, was stirring in opposition to his highly personalized, authoritarian presidency, and the *peronismo* movement lost a large measure of its charisma when Eva Perón died from cancer in 1952. Three years later, as Perón was threatening to arm his descamisados to hang on to power, he was toppled by the military and sent into exile.

Perón left Argentine society more deeply riven than it ever had been in this century. Under his rule, the lot of Buenos Aires's working class improved dramatically, but he had done nothing to better the economic conditions of small farmers and the rural poor while at the same time he was profoundly alienating the aristocracy. In the aftermath, labor unrest was chronic and violent, and economic policy lurched back and forth between nationalist (anti–foreign investment) and internationalist (pro–foreign investment) tendencies. Outlawed at first from political participation in the post-Perón years, the Peronistas were gradually destigmatized during the 1960s and accepted back into the electoral fold. In 1973 Perón, in delicate health, was elected to the presidency in a landslide. He would die eight months later, but even before his death the seeds had been sowed for a horrific decade-long nightmare from which Argentina is still recovering.

The steam heat of January recalls August in New York; the emptiness, August in Paris. In the listlessness of late afternoon, before the café or the cinema, before the strong, warm wind, sometimes steady, sometimes gusting, floods in from the broad Río de la Plata, Buenos Aires residents who have been left behind by the holiday exodus browse in the conditioned air of the great bookstores of Buenos Aires. Amidst the translations of British and American thrillers and tables groaning under the ubiquitous tomes on or by Sigmund Freud and his apostles or apostates—only in Buenos Aires can one imagine such a wealth, in bookstore after bookstore, of psychological literature—there are stacks of a rust red paperback titled *Nunca Más* (*Never Again*). This book, in its fifteenth printing this summer, is the report issued by the National Commission on the Disappearance of Persons. *Nunca Más* is a compilation of what it meant to be a *"desaparecido"* during the seventies and early eighties in Argentina:

> "The soles of the feet, after the torture, were left burned and layers of hard skin formed that later fell off. Evidently, the skin burned with the electric shocks. . . ."
> "The one they called 'Julián the Turk' began to hit me and beat me with chains and later with a lash, while he yelled and insulted me. . . . I could feel my whole body burning and hurting, the more so because they threw brine on my skin. . . ."

Enough. The book goes on for 490 pages. The most chilling words in *Never Again*—indeed, the ones that most throw into question the simple declaration "Never Again"—come from General Roberto Viola, who, as part of a whirlwind succession of military leaders in Argentina during the seventies and early eighties, ruled the country from March to November of 1981. At the time, a reporter asked the general whether it was necessary to conduct an investigation into the problem of the desaparecidos. Viola said:

"It seems to me that what you mean to say is that we should investigate the security forces, and that shall never happen. In this war there are victors, and we were the victors and rest assured that if in the last world war the troops of the Reich had won, the judgment would not have been held at Nuremberg but in Virginia."

The war the security forces won was the so-called Dirty War. When Juan Perón was returned to power in 1973, Argentina was already plagued by terrorist acts, most of them by a numerically small but headline-grabbing Marxist guerrilla group, the People's Revolutionary Army. In exile, Perón had hardened into a rightist, and with his return the spiral of violence widened. His new stamp repelled left-wing Peronistas. Many joined or at least sympathized with an increasingly powerful group of urban terrorists called the Montoneros, so named after a group of nineteenth-century independence fighters. Perón was succeeded in office by his second wife and vice-president, the former cabaret dancer Isabel Perón. Her top adviser was a mystic and purported soothsayer named José López Rega, who decided to take on radical leftists inside and outside *peronismo* by forming a rightist death squad, the Triple-A, or Argentine Anti-Communist Alliance. In less than two years, when the political survival of Isabel Perón seemed threatened by political and economic turmoil, the military cast her aside and took power itself. It institutionalized the campaign against subversion. Thus began the Dirty War.

Just who was and was not "subversive" was very much in the eye of the beholder. Imbued with a frightening randomness and lack of discrimination, the Dirty War became much more than an antisubversive campaign; it became an instrument of official, personal, or political vendetta. Students, union members, psychoanalysts and journalists, infants and pregnant women and old men, nuns and priests and lay workers—the Dirty War swept up thousands of Argentines and deposited them in hundreds of clandestine torture centers and jails. Before the Dirty War wound down in 1980, it left at least eight thousand Argentines dead.

In the grand apartments of the Barrio Norte, the heavy drapes are drawn closed against the lugubrious summer heat. As a repository of wealth and elegance, the Barrio Norte has done its best to fend off the ravishments of hard times. It is a silk-stocking district with a run in it. The warm evening gusts rise off the coppery surface of the Río de la Plata, an estuary as broad as a sea. They buffet closed windows and balcony doors, causing them to shudder. The apartments and the basement garages are mostly empty. Summer has taken the neighborhood on holiday. In the newspaper *Clarín* each day, the special Punta del Este and Mar del Plata pages chronicle the far-off social whirl: the actress espied at the disco in Mar del Plata, on Argentina's Atlantic Coast; the rumors of a big loss at 21 in the cavernous casino in Punta del Este, the glitzy Uruguayan resort preferred by Buenos Aires's richest citizens. Many of the shopkeepers in the Barrio Norte are also gone. As befits their class, they are summering on the tepid café-au-lait-colored canals in Tigre, one hour away by derelict train, where the mighty Paraná dumps its silt-laden water from the tropical north into the Río de la Plata.

In the morning in the Barrio Norte maids from that tropical north air out an apartment or two. The master or the mistress may be back for the day on the crowded commuter flight from Punta to the Aeroparque Jorge Newbery, conveniently close to the Barrio Norte. They would be in to change money—dollars for australes, to take advantage of the tumbling exchange rates—or to keep an appointment with their psychoanalyst if he happens to be planning to be in town the same day.

The papers are filled with dreadful economic news: all the more reason to change money in smaller quantities more often as the austral declines in value. In *Clarín* one Saturday, the headlines on page 2 alone are a litany of troubles: TELEPHONE WORKERS: ANOTHER PROTEST SET FOR MONDAY. TEXTILE WORKERS DRAW UP BATTLE PLAN. TELEGRAPH WORKERS KEEP PRESSING THEIR DEMANDS. The putative good news on page 2 is bad news in disguise: BANK EMPLOYEES SUSPEND WORK STOPPAGES ANNOUNCED FOR NEXT WEEK. HOSPITAL STRIKE ENDS. Page 3 of the morning's *Clarín* is turned over to a labor conflict between the oil workers' union and the famously inefficient state oil monopoly, YPF. (One of the Hunt brothers from Texas, describing the moneymaking potential of the petroleum industry, once said that the most profitable company in the world is an oil company that is well run; the second most profitable company in the world, he said, is an oil company that is poorly run. YPF is the exception to the Hunt rule.) The *Clarín* story says that gasoline shortages have already been reported around Buenos Aires and on the Atlantic Coast.

Argentina is a country of the newly poor. Its inflation rate this past year (175 percent) was higher than Peru's (114.5 percent), but Buenos Aires's poverty does not stand out stark, grim, and irreversible like the metastasizing shack cities of straw and sticks on the desert outside Lima. Peru has been growing poor for half a millennium; Argentina has been in decline for less than half a century. The British-built trains of Argentina are losing over a million dollars a day, but when they are not on strike at least they run, carrying suburban commuters from Buenos Aires's still-sizable middle class in and out of the city.

Though more infrequent now than in the past, the *asado*—the traditional Sunday cookout featuring great slabs of beef and flowing bottles of red wine from the fine vineyards around Mendoza—still seems to be within reach of a surprising number of Argentines. One Wednesday there's a short item in the business pages of the English-language *Buenos Aires Herald,* a paper that has seen better days. It reports that livestock prices have fallen so far that they are now 6.4 percent below 1960 levels. "In November," says the *Herald,* "[beef] consumption in Greater Buenos Aires was 88 kilos [193.6 pounds] per person per year, which represents a 12.94 percent decline over the same period [in 1986]." Regrettable, perhaps, but not exactly a starvation diet.

In other ways, the stamp of past wealth is fading with astounding speed. The youngest generation of working Argentines—visitors to the wine capital of Mendoza would buy shoes from a sociologist; in the Barrio Norte, they would meet an MBA selling shirts at James Smart—know that time is running out, that history is coming full circle. By the hundreds of thousands, Italians emigrated to Argentina in the second half of the nineteenth century and the early years of the twentieth, seeking a better life. Now the reverse is happening. In 1990 Jacobo Timerman, the Argentine journalist, would tell the story of how the Rome government sent emissaries to Argentina to recruit forty thousand orderlies for Italian hospitals. By the thousands, Argentines signed up to leave home. That was telling enough. But the bitterest fact of all was that most of the would-be orderlies were Argentine medical doctors.

Not far from the Plaza de Mayo, where not so many years ago the mothers of the disappeared would stand in silent protest and hold aloft sun-faded snapshots of the son who didn't make it home one day from the university or the daughter whose bloody high-heeled shoe was found in the park, summer inflicts a stifling calm on the financial district. The exceptions are the money-exchange houses. At noon, during one of what seems to be a half dozen slots set aside each workday for a meal or a pre- or post- or in-between-meal snack or coffee, passersby can find islands of shade along streets like Tucumán and Reconquista. Over-head, giant cobwebs of black wire block out the sunlight. These are phone lines. A few legal wires strung (no doubt grudgingly) by the state telephone company, another fa-mously inefficient government monopoly, entwine with a fuzzball of illegal lines. The rest of the Argentine economy may be in a slumber, but this miasma of wires is alive with the one aspect of Buenos Aires business that never sleeps: money-exchange talk.

A white telphone rings in an office four floors up in a building along Tucumán. "Yes, Doctor. . . . It's at four twenty-five, four thirty to the dollar." The austral's down-ward slide continues. The white phone again. "Three hun-dred thousand lira? I don't know. Wait a minute." Chacho reaches for the brown phone, the one with no dial. He picks it up. "Hey, Pepe, three hundred thousand lira, what's that worth?" The white phone rings again. Chacho makes an appointment to meet a regular customer for a three-thousand-dollar exchange, australes to dollars. The client has come in that morning from Punta. They'll meet for coffee.

The brown phone in Chacho's office is a hot line hooked up directly to a money table in another building down the street. On the ground floor in many of the buildings are open, legitimate money-exchange houses. Upstairs are the money tables, which do legitimate and illegitimate deals. Here the black market meets the open market. These so-called money tables—*mesas de dinero*—look like phone-bank boiler rooms operating at the breakneck speed of a commodities brokerage house. Then there are offices like Chacho's.

"This office is 'black.' It's supposed to be a travel agency. I have papers that say so. In fact, I can write airline tickets. But I don't spend much time writing airline tickets. I make a living working the margins, a point here and a point there. I do so discreetly. Discretion is the capital of this business."

Tracing the graceful curve of the beach at Punta del Este, sleek high-rise condominium apartment buildings stand like sentinels between the open waters of the Atlantic and the cool pine forest. This is the *playa brava,* the rough beach. Set with good taste and discretion back in the woods are the second homes of hundreds of summering *porteños,* as the people of Buenos Aires call themselves. On the other side of the town itself are the calm waters of the bay. That is the *playa mansa,* the tame beach. Punta del Este, more than any other single place in the world, is the resort that debt built.

A whole new layer of glitz—the highest high-rises, the fanciest restaurants, the most imposing of the residences set back in the pines—has been added to Punta, mostly on the playa brava side, in the last decade. As soaring oil prices fattened stores of petrodollars, American and European bankers stalked the capitals of the Third World in search of borrowers. They found plenty. Those were the days of *plata dulce* (sweet money, in the Argentine phrase), not only in New York and Zurich and London, but also in Mexico City and Brasília and Buenos Aires. In ways legal and otherwise, government officials, industrialists, bankers, union barons, and military brass made fortunes large and small. Many got rich off the great economic boom that the explosion of cash triggered. Others got rich off the loan transactions themselves, off fees and commissions, off moving money around, shaving percentage points, making a little here and a little more there. They were working the margins—big-time Chachos.

Even before the bottom fell out of the petroleum market and a chain reaction of other events—from plunging prices for key commodities and soaring interest rates on their debt—sent Latin American economies into a tailspin, the new money began leaving the economies where it had been made. Driven by worries about inflation and the whiff of political instability, but mostly by doing what comes naturally to money—seeking the safest and most profitable haven—the new fortunes made tracks. This capital flight did wonders for the U.S. economy. It helped kick off an investment frenzy in Miami that drug money would keep going long after the petrodollar boom died down. Investors who sought luxury to go along with some security had much to choose from. While Mexicans were scooping up vacation homes on Padre Island, on the Texas coast, and in La Jolla, on the California coast, porteños did not have to look far beyond the Río de la Plata they could see from their office windows. Punta del Este boomed.

Punta del Este is quietest before noon. Only a few cars move along the coastal road; maids sweep the front walks back amid the pines. The nightlife is demanding, and the vacationers sleep in. After an asado, at about midnight, the older Argentine kids head to the discos and their parents go to the casino. The couples pair off at the gaming tables. The husband bets. His wife stands at his side, dispensing or collecting money: his banker. One sees this back in Buenos Aires, too: the woman carting around the man's wallet.

By late morning, the gleaming strip of sand along the playa brava begins to fill with people. It is that way one Monday in January as beach radios broadcast the latest reports on some irksome news from home. A couple of days ago a rebel lieutenant colonel named Aldo Rico mounted a putsch against his superiors. Now the radio reports a new, related uprising at the military base in San Luis. There's also a report that a group of Rico partisans have stormed the air-traffic control tower at the Jorge Newbery Airport; on the beach, this news is particularly disconcerting to a Buenos Aires toy retailer and his wife, as they had planned to fly home the next day to run some errands.

As distracted as they are by the comings and goings of other beachcombers on this particular morning, listeners gathered around one radio catch a smattering of reports on the bad news back home.

11:05. The announcer reads a communiqué from the

estado mayor—the joint chiefs of staff—that in San Luis the "third focal point" of the insurrection was successfully put down by troops loyal to the government. Ten rebels were arrested. In Monte Caseros, the military base where the insurrection began, there would have been heavier fighting than there has been so far, the radio reports, if so many troops had not been on vacation.

11:10. Following a lengthy discussion about how much it is raining at Monte Caseros, the announcer and a reporter at the scene speculate about whether the bridges in the area have been wired with explosives.

11:20. The announcer reads a communiqué about a truck that ran over a land mine, injuring the driver and a passenger.

Although the porteños in Punta will not get the word until later in the day, the insurrection is on its last legs even as they pack up their beach things to go home for lunch. At 1:00 P.M. or a little earlier on that Monday, the newspaper *La Nación* would report the following weekend, Rico had contacted the commander of the loyal troops who were advancing on the rebel position and offered to give himself up at 6:00 P.M.

A couple of weeks after the Rico rebellion was put down, Chacho the money changer is out to dinner with his wife, a psychologist who writes a mental-health column for a monthly magazine, and some of their friends. "I knew it, I knew it!" he exclaims, boasting that he had been able to pinpoint the moment when Aldo Rico contacted the commander of the loyal troops and offered to give himself up. Chacho explains. The austral had been falling like crazy all summer long. The four-to-one ratios he had quoted the doctor over the phone not so long ago were already history.

The outbreak of the Rico affair sent the currency into an even dizzier tailspin. But then on "Rico Monday," the 18th of January, Chacho noticed a strange blip on the money market. Chacho is careful to watch for such things: he knows that government big shots often trade on inside information. Sure enough, on Rico Monday the austral at one point stopped falling and began climbing, however briefly. Between 1:00 P.M. and 1:30 P.M. Chacho saw the austral go from 5.80 to 5.63 to the dollar. "This is how I knew Rico would turn himself in," says Chacho.

The psychiatric *consultorios* that line the streets around the Plaza Freud—smallish office suites announced by dignified brass plaques—are mostly dark, all but abandoned to Buenos Aires's summer heat. At one edge of the park the Confitería Snack Bar Plaza Freud is into its slowest month of business; the tables lined up expectantly under the awning look forlorn and unwanted. The plaza is a leafy square in a quiet residential quarter of Buenos Aires. Since the Dirty War, its official name has been all but forgotten. It is popularly known as Plaza Freud because of its location, at the heart of the city's *psico*—or shrink—district. During the Dirty War, the shrinks of Buenos Aires were among the first groups to be persecuted. This happened for a number of reasons—because of the supposed preponderance of Argentine Jews in the profession, because of biases that linked the psico and Jewish communities alike to leftist political tendencies, and because the shrinks supposedly had confidential information about other Dirty War targets that might be useful to the authorities. The designation "Plaza Freud" didn't even really enter the urban vernacular until after the Dirty War. Today, the Confitería Snack Bar

Plaza Freud doesn't hesitate to stamp its cocktail napkins in brown ink with the likeness of Sigmund himself.

Since the Dirty War the shrink community has made an astounding comeback. Psychology has long held sway among the Argentines. Psychiatry and, in particular, psychoanalysis have been prestigious and popular fields of study in Argentina since Maria Langer and other eminent disciples of Freud emigrated from Central Europe to Buenos Aires in the face of Nazi repression in the 1930s. The post–Dirty War shrink renaissance has been so strong that it has caused something of an identity crisis within the community. The numbers alone were cause for introspection.

The cover story of the current issue of *Uno Mismo* is an article titled "Psychologists: Why?" It says that at the University of Buenos Aries, where as recently as two years ago the schools of law and medicine had the highest enrollment, the registrar's list at the school of psychology has since that time surpassed both of the other schools. While other schools at UBA chalk up flat or declining enrollment, the school of psychology will graduate a record ten thousand students this year. This wouldn't necessarily mean that much (you can study psychology and not be a practicing shrink) except that an inordinate number of the graduates—the "vast majority," according to the article— actually go on to do clinical work in private practice.

The shrink-to-population ratio in Buenos Aires at the very least puts the city up with Manhattan and Beverly Hills. According to Enrique Saforcada, the vice-dean of UBA's psychology school, there are about sixty thousand psychologists in Argentina, or one for every five hundred Argentines; most of them are practicing some form of psychotherapy and most of them are doing it in Buenos Aires. In all of the United States, there are about sixty thousand practicing psychiatrists and psychoanalysts. The psychotherapy phenomenon may well affect precious few Argentines; as Saforcada wrote recently, if all the country's shrinks went on strike (Argentines always have strikes of one sort or another on their minds), nobody would care except for the urban upper-middle and upper classes. But the sense of angst emanating from those elites would be considerable—especially among porteños.

In Buenos Aires, more so even than in Beverly Hills or Manhattan, the wealthy talk often and casually about therapy and their analysts. Among the professional classes, porteños who are not married to a shrink are almost surely friends of somebody who is. The daily newspaper *Página 12* runs a special psychology page. Magazines carry cartoons lampooning psycho-esoterica that would be virtually incomprehensible in any other city; six years after his death, cartoonists in Buenos Aires continue to pen inside jokes about the controversial French psychoanalyst Jacques Lacan (who broke away from classic Freudian theory by espousing therapy sessions lasting just five or ten minutes instead of fifty, and then, late in life, returned to the Freudian fold). The visit to the shrink is a perfectly ordinary event in Buenos Aires, something you squeeze in between shopping at James Smart and meeting a friend for ice cream at Freddo.

One reason for the plethora of psychologists, psychiatrists, and psychoanalysts in Buenos Aires is the emphasis placed on white-collar professions in a country that is notoriously disdainful of manual labor. Practicing psychotherapy is relatively inexpensive. Porteños joke that all it takes is a degree from the state university, a couch, and an answering machine. It is also a profession that feeds on itself. As Enrique Saforcada has written, it is like a "Persian market" where everybody is both a seller and a buyer, where therapy dispensers are also therapy consumers. In keeping with classical Freudian theory, which predominates in Buenos Aires, therapists must themselves be in therapy. Under those circumstances, psychoanalysis becomes something like a chain-letter scheme at $37.50 per fifty-minute session—four times a week for hard-line Freudians.

Another reason is that history has dealt Argentina strong cause for introspection. Introspection is not a trait that non-Argentines, particularly in Latin America, would immediately equate with the people of Buenos Aires. The classic porteño is seen as arrogant, someone whose stereotype mimics other, equally distorted ones—the braggadocio of a Texan, the parochialism of a New Yorker, the snootiness of a Parisian. And yet the haughtiness, though it lingers still, was tempered by the challenge of decades of seemingly avoidable economic decline. That gave rise to a universal question: What went wrong? How could such a country—blessed with tremendous natural resources, a relatively well educated and small (thirty million) population, and a vast territory (Argentina is the fourth largest country in the Americas, after Canada, the United States, and Brazil)—fail?

That question—the subject of countless academic studies and popular books—has never resonated as strongly as it has in this decade in Argentina. Whatever was left of the Argentines' feelings of superiority was shaken to its foundations by the ignominy of the Dirty War and by the humiliating loss to the British in the Falklands/Malvinas

War. Increasingly, introspection mixed with self-doubt—
fertile ground for psychoanalysis.

Throughout the history of Argentina, porteños were
the self-appointed keepers of Argentine pride. Their pride-
fulness especially rankled Latin Americans, for it was tinged
with racism. Forty percent of Argentina's population is of
Spanish descent. Another 40 percent is of Italian descent.
Less than 2 percent of the population is mestizo or Indian.
Since its founding, Buenos Aires ignored or put down the
rest of Latin America as inferior, and, like many great ports,
looked outward across the waters for its cultural roots, its
tastes, and its fashions.

The eighties stripped away the last bit of pride that the
Argentines, and in particular the porteños, had left. While
Wall Streeters were busy sating their greed and talking real
estate, porteños during the 1980s were asking themselves a
single question: What went wrong with us? Not just, What
went wrong? but, What went wrong with *us*? During the
decades of economic decline they had wrapped themselves
in the hand-me-down shawl of dignity, just as Buenos Aires
had quaintly kept up appearances with its grand architecture and broad avenues and elegant cafés, and now the
shawl was in tatters.

On a summer Sunday, on a hot street corner in the
neighborhood of San Telmo, a lissome couple—the woman
in red, the man in black—dances to a tango recorded by
Carlos Gardel. Gardel, who died in a plane crash in 1935 at
the height of his international fame, was in his day, and for
many porteños remains to this day, the symbol of Argentine
dreams. The dancers have set up a cassette player and
speakers on the street. Nearby there's a box, lined in deep
red velvet, for passersby to toss money into. San Telmo is

one of Buenos Aires's oldest neighborhoods; in the early part of this century, three out of every four adults in San Telmo were European-born. Gardel is singing the anthem of his city's incurable nostalgia, "Mi Buenos Aires Querido" ("My Beloved Buenos Aires"). As the song ends, he sings: "My beloved Buenos Aires, when I see you again, there will be neither pain nor forgetting."

All around the dancing couple, across the street on the Plaza Dorrego, up and down the streets of San Telmo, are the remnants of that beloved Buenos Aires. Well-oiled chests of antique silver flatware that was never used. Toy lead soldiers carrying miniature metal Union Jacks. Tiffany lamps. Lead-crystal vases. Art Deco mirrors. Antique automobiles that seem destined for Hollywood movie sets. And, at booth after booth on the Plaza Dorrego, stacked high in brown paper jackets, old 78s of every single tango ever made when the tango, like Buenos Aires, was in its heyday.

On a summer's day at La Chacarita, the great, sprawling cemetery in suburban Buenos Aires, heat shimmers up in waves from the black asphalt of dozens of streets. The family vaults—some of them with dust-filmed windows of beveled glass and curtains of old, yellowing lace—are lined up like row houses on streets that are numbered. At the corner of Sixth and Thirty-third, as if braking for phantom pedestrians, a big black hearse from the 1950s comes to a full stop, then proceeds. At that corner, at the grave of Carlos Gardel, someone has come by just minutes ago to place, as people do, a cigarette in the right hand of the glossy black statue in his likeness. Gardel stands at ease. His left hand is in the pants pocket of his dapper three-piece suit. His brilliantined hair gleams in the sunlight. He smiles his handsome signature smile.

An elderly woman walks up to Gardel's tomb. She is carrying a single white carnation. She places it at Gardel's feet, where a few dozen other flowers lie wilting in the heat of a Buenos Aires January. She runs a gentle hand along the raised letters of his name on the tomb. She had obviously done this many times. The ritual is pleasing to her—a reassurance grounded, like so much of Buenos Aires, in the past. In Gardel's right hand, which he holds elegantly at his side, waist-high, is a marigold, fresh, its lush orange color not yet faded in the sunlight. In the same hand he holds the cigarette; from the still-lighted end a ragged ribbon of smoke curls upward. The woman, squinting at the bright sky, looks up at Gardel. "He's always smiling," she says. She lingers awhile and then slowly walks away.

CHAPTER TEN
Mexico: Churches atop Temples

WE LEFT BUENOS AIRES at the end of our slow, delicious summer there and flew home to a blur of culture shock. The Miami airport was awash in Mickey Mouse hats, the big black rodent ears bobbing in a sea of Sony boom boxes. A sizable percentage of Latin America seemed to be heading home themselves following the pilgrimage to Disney World and the Miami shopping safari. Flotillas of groaning luggage carts destined for Caracas and Bogotá cruised past our bags, in which we had safeguarded treasures of our own: the whisper-soft alpaca overcoats fashioned by Argentine tailors from Peruvian wool, the fine Bolivian weavings.

Back in my parents' kitchen, in the retirement community where the streets have golfing names, I was confused. Was that electronic beep I was hearing the microwave or the computer-programmed clothes dryer? One day not long after returning home I was walking the aisles of a grocery store near our house in Ashfield when I was startled by the sudden whoosh! of an automatic sprinkler system as it watered the vegetable bins. And the prices! The Decade of Greed would wind down soon enough, but money seemed to have slipped free of its moorings. *Newsweek* put us up at a New York City hotel for a couple of weeks—the tab was larger than what we had spent for lodging during seven months on the road. This is home?

We had no time to absorb this onslaught of North Americana. The job in Mexico City was waiting. The Mexican presidential elections were coming up in a few months. There was work to be done. So we headed south once again. It felt good: though I crave convenience and things that work as much as those Latin Americans passing through the Miami airport, I was already missing the chaos and surprise, the romance, that have not yet been leeched from the land from Mexico south.

I found the first time we drove through Mexico, during that summer of 1987 heavy with anticipation, that I did not sense I was really getting into Mexico until after we left Mexico City and headed further south. There is magic and mystery in northern Mexico, but the people of the north bear the strong imprint of the United States. The border itself is an inconvenient dotted line that binds residents of both sides together more than it keeps them apart. In the big Mexican border cities, much larger than their twin cities on the other side, people have even adopted the driving habits of the Californians and Texans: they stop at stop signs and at traffic signals in the desert. The sprawling assembly plants growing like Topsy in northern Mexico—a nascent Taiwan or Korea of cheap wages—look as "American" as industrial parks in Detroit or Saint Louis. From here in the north, to no one's surprise, came the political pragmatism and economic conservatism that would soon dominate the Mexican bureaucracy and forge ties between Mexico and the United States that would have been unthinkable a generation ago.

In the south I felt I had come upon a Mexico with more pronounced ties to its pre-Columbian past. South of the Valley of Mexico and the polluted miasma of Mexico City, past where the two gnarled branches of the Sierra Madre come together, I crossed what seemed to me the cultural equivalent of the continental divide.

It was our first day driving south from the capital. We were groping our way through heavy fog along a range of mountains between Puebla and Oaxaca. We were negotiating switchbacks so sharp-angled that at every curve there were giant white arrows painted on the asphalt instructing vehicles to switch lanes. This was so that larger vehicles, trucks and buses, could make the turns. If you were climbing you would cross from the right into the left lane as you approached the curve; the same if you were coming in the other direction. If you did what the arrows suggested, you had to trust that oncoming traffic would do the same. It was unnerving to trust so much to fate.

As we climbed, the fog thickened. The headlights of oncoming vehicles would become visible at ten yards: dim, watery moons floating toward us. Finally we saw a cluster of lights up a way and off to one side, lights other than headlights. If that's a hotel, any hotel—we agreed—we're stopping. Approaching it was like sailing; we tacked from curve to curve. Suddenly there it was right in front of us: not a hotel, but a giant roadside shrine. It was the biggest shrine I'd ever seen. I was accustomed to the little crosses, plastic flowers, and flickering candles marking the exact spot where some poor busload of Mexicans had careened off the side of a mountain. Or the gaudy Vírgenes de Guadalupe standing guard at taxi stands and parking garages. In the fog this mountain shrine we had come upon looked like a garish Notre Dame, strung with Christmas lights, surrounded by a large parking lot—a monument to fatalism.

From that point south it seemed to me that the balance between life and death was somehow different among the people we would meet; it would not change back again until we got into countries like Chile and Argentina, where the populations are largely of European descent. Here at this cultural divide death began to become a more powerful force than I would ever sense it to be in the United States, its pull more powerful, magnified by what is left of great civilizations.

Life seemed now more tenuous. It was to be lived fully and with great joy at times, but death when it came was not a surprise, not an assault on the senses the way it is for many of us who grew up in the United States. For somebody from the United States, the change is unsettling. It is as if the cargo has shifted in the hold of a ship: the vessel keeps on going, but something essential about the voyage has changed.

And of course something about our own voyage *had* changed for me. I was paying more attention. In countries less far removed from their agricultural roots than the United States is, the cycles of life and death, of sowing and harvest, are much more transparent in day-to-day living. When you harvest corn, the crop dies in order to give life to those it will feed. A simple precept such as that becomes a driving force in an agricultural society, and helps to give it an order that advanced industrial societies seem to lack.

It is not without reason that a fascinating controversy has grown up in Mexico around the dueling celebrations of Halloween and the Day of the Dead. Both are end-of-the-harvest celebrations, though under the heavy clutter of commercialism we in the United States have all but buried the origins of Halloween. U.S.-style Halloween parties—where costumed suburban kids wind up at McDonald's after a night of trick-or-treating (*"Quiero mi Halloween,"* they say when they come to your door: "I want my Halloween")—compete mightily with traditional Day of the Dead celebrations—where offerings of food and incense and prayer to one's ancestors are interspersed between joyous, elaborate meals. Much to the chagrin of the Mexican intelligentsia, the line between the two celebrations—between McDonald's and mourning the dead—is becoming blurred. The writer Carlos Monsivais gave me one of my favorite totems from my time in Mexico, a plastic toy that perfectly syncretizes Halloween and the Day of the Dead in modern Mexico: a skeleton with a pumpkin head.

We crossed the befogged mountain range and went through a mountaintop town with the lovely name Puerto del Cielo (Port of Heaven). Soon we were in the state of Oaxaca. This place has stubbornly resisted change. It doesn't matter that the Spaniards built their cathedrals atop Mixtec temples, as they did at Mitla and at countless other sites, or that the hills are dotted with telephone microwave towers. Here Zapotec is the language spoken in most rural homes. Spanish is the language of trade, of the city, the official language. Customs old and new are layered atop one another in splendid confusion, but the deep past is what matters here.

My son Shayne lived for a while in Oaxaca city, the

state capital. He told me a story once about meeting an old Zapotec woman in a village outside the city. "We have been conquered by many people," she said. "But the Zapotecs will never change. The Mexicans are here now. They will leave. Others will come. We will still be here." A people's roots have to be sunk very deep into the land for a woman to dismiss "the Mexicans" (by which she means any outsiders linked in some way to the central government in Mexico City), who have ruled Oaxaca for eight generations, as a conquering horde as fleeting and impermanent as the Spanish, who ruled it for over three hundred years.

I got a sense of just how deep those roots can be at San Juan Chamula, one of the last Mexican towns we visited on our trip before crossing into Guatemala. Here deep in southern Mexico, the present is a thin veneer over a culture whose very ancientness is foreign to a visitor from the United States, where everything is so relatively young. San Juan Chamula's very name bears the familiar tattoo of Spanish conquest: the Catholic name prefixed to the original Indian one. But as the old Zapotec woman suggested to Shayne, neither Catholicism nor the Spanish ever really conquered Chamula or the rest of Mexico. The conquerors' marks, like wax imperial seals, seeped into what was already there; they did not destroy it.

The countryside around Chamula foretells the deep greens of Guatemala. There is water here, at last, in contrast to the vast highland stretches of parched soil north of Mexico City, through the northern deserts, and into the U.S. Southwest. Here in the south, great curtains of rain fall all summer long and leave the mountains wreathed in misty halos. On the mountainsides, deforested scabs alternate with patches of pine. In these hills around San Cristóbal de las Casas, Chamula is a rare flat place surrounded by graceful slopes.

The guidebooks warn you not to take pictures inside the Catholic church at Chamula, a dazzlingly white building at one end of a plain square; they say two tourists were killed for doing so. Even that warning did not prepare me for what I saw inside the church. I had been reared in a traditional Catholicism, the Catholicism of Spanish priests in the Dominican Republic, of Benedictine monks who tended sheep and boys at a boarding school in Rhode Island; in my view at the time, Catholicism old and new divided over whether you wanted the mass said in Latin or in your own language. What I saw in the church in Chamula added a startling chapter to all I had learned.

I walked in at noon, and the adjustment my eyes had to make to the interior darkness magnified the effect of the place on me. I could not see clearly at first. I could only hear: chanting in a Mayan dialect. Then I saw: the flickering flames of scores of candles. The candles were stuck with their own wax to the floor. The floor seemed to be in permanent soft-focus: it was covered with a blanket of pine needles. At first the place seemed strangely open and empty. Of course: something was missing; there were no pews. As my eyes adjusted to the darkness, rocking bundles on the floor became people. They clustered together in groups: families. They prayed and chanted and talked; the atmosphere inside the church was that of a subdued picnic. They would snack—I could hear the crinkling of little plastic bags, like at the movies in Mexico City—and they would drink from shared bottles of Coca-Cola that they passed around like communion wafers.

From the ceiling hung brightly colored drapes, huge

and medieval-looking. Along the side walls there were statues of saints I recognized and saints I did not, popular saints that would not show up in any traditional Catholic hagiography. They were clothed in velvet the color of blood. Their faces were an unfamiliar gray-brown, the color of sweating stone. Up at the front of the church, there was an altar that nobody was paying attention to. It seemed an afterthought.

It was important for me to have at Chamula that feeling of being culturally adrift. Eduardo Galeano, the Uruguayan writer and radical historian, believes that Latin America's great weakness is "the usurpation of its memory" by conquistadores ancient and modern. The memory lies buried beneath the monuments of the colonizers, in the rubble of destroyed ancient temples beneath Catholic churches, in the tailings of gold and silver mines, in the leached soil of banana plantations. But the memory is not dead. It may be buried deep sometimes in the cultural sedimentation of Latin America, but the traveler who pays attention comes across it, like rock formations exposed by road cuts. It is alive in the old tongues and the stories they tell. It is alive in the cuisines and in the way of carrying firewood down from the scarred hills. It is alive, too, in the "nationalism" that underlies Latin America's revolutionary movements. I could feel its presence, even if I couldn't always understand it.

As an American, I was a foreigner as soon as I crossed the thin ribbon of the Rio Grande. As we moved further south, the human terrain, the native languages and different lifestyles, had seemed more and more alien; the familiar receded. As I discovered for myself a new America, I was more and more a stranger. It was not an unpleasant feeling. I felt like a swimmer in the dark: the strokes were the same; but the sensation was different. Only in that way did I feel myself beginning to learn.

A Mexican traveling through the United States, as Octavio Paz has noted, is struck by its "novelty," its modernity. An American from the United States traveling south is struck by the archaism, the profound antiquity, of Latin America. The United States was driven forward; it still is. Much of the rest of the Americas is pulled backward. The United States, Paz says, was born as a "categorical criticism" of the past. It was rejecting its European past— the religious and political and economic strictures—and barely noticed its American Indian past as it trod across it, east to west, ever pushing against the frontier.

The Spanish experience in Latin America was entirely different. Whereas the Europeans who settled New England and pushed west came for the most part to stay, the Spaniards who came to make their fortunes in Mexico and to the south came for the most part to leave. The mining of America was keeping Spain alive as an empire. The gold and silver were paying for the wars against the Moors and against the Protestant Reformation of Martin Luther. They were subsidizing the crown's European past. The Spaniards were not pushing across vast, undeveloped regions; they were coming up against big, entrenched civilizations. The Aztecs' Tenochtitlán (now Mexico City) and the Incas' Cuzco were among the largest cities in the world in the sixteenth century. The population of Mesoamerica alone— from the Ulúa River in Honduras to the boundary between agriculture-based Indian civilizations and the wandering tribes of northern Mexico—was more than fifteen million people.

The America south of Tenochtitlán was conquered. The America north of Tenochtitlán was settled. Brazil is the exception that proves the rule: if it is the Latin American country most like the United States, that is because it was settled, not conquered, and it shares the energizing force of a frontier. The word itself—*frontier*—is a clue to the profound differences that divide the Americas. To somebody in the United States, it has a clear meaning that transcends a mere boundary line: it is the horizon, open spaces, something out there beyond what already exists, something hopeful and filled with promise. In Latin America, *frontera* says what it means: "border." It is a limit.

The ways in which the past pulls Latin America and the future drives the United States explain much about modern relations between American states. Those forces have for centuries exerted a historical gravitational force on the Americas, and they will continue to do so. We were seeing glimmers of this historical lode as we headed south. Here, climbing through the deep green pine forests of the state of Chiapas, as in Oaxaca to the north, the divisions between pre- and post-Columbian America became clearer. The Spanish tried to destroy the past: they constructed their churches atop the old temples; they burned the old codices. As much as they were able to disrupt things, and as much as they managed to take away, they failed to destroy the past. What they left behind of themselves is important and permanent, but it amounts to little more than a veneer over what was already there.

After our journey through the Americas, we returned to Mexico to live. In 1989, while I was doing much of the writing of this book, we spent part of the summer and many weekends away from our home in Mexico City and in a beautiful mountain town to the south called Santiago Tepetlapa. In the capital during the week, over long, disputatious lunches—the equivalent of the intelligentsia's salon for Mexico's *clase política,* its "political class" of people in government or in a position to influence it—I got part of my education about Mexico. Much of the rest I got out in Santiago, a town with one cemetery, one cobbled street, one telephone, and two out-of-order water-well pumps. Here, and around this place, I could riffle at my leisure through the confusing layers of conquest and cultures that have made Mexico such a baffling, rich, and appealing place for me.

Our house enjoyed a splendid isolation. To the west a curtain of steep, crumbly hills separated us from the larger town of Tepoztlán. At night, after the slender metal cross atop the highest of the hills had disappeared along with the setting sun, Tepoztlán existed only as a thin aureole of light that traced the jagged shape of the hills. To the north, behind stands of *tejocote* trees that blocked our view of distant mountains, all we could see of Santiago was the blue neon cross over the single Catholic church; the lighted cross struck me as garish at first, but over time it absorbed the dignity of its surroundings. To the east a network of stone walls and irregularly shaped cornfields, which made a racket in the evening breeze, shielded us from the occasional light of a nearby farmhouse. To the south, beyond the clumps of oleander and bougainvillea, and poinsettia plants the size of fruit trees, lay a broad valley that invited contemplation.

At twilight that summer we could count on a daily *son-et-lumière* extravaganza as the storms rolled in over the distant mountains. Across the valley, thirty miles off in the distance, bright veins of lightning flashed in the darkening sky as it changed from an aqueous blue to blue-black. As the storm neared, the metallic scent of wet air mingled with a surging cool. The corn to the east strained like boat sails against sheets of water borne on gusts of wind. To the north, between blowtorch explosions of lightning and the crack of close thunder, the neon cross atop the church dimmed and flickered and sometimes died as the town's electrical power faltered in the storm.

If the storms came from the north, sneaking up on us from behind the distant mountains, their harbinger was much more subtle. We would hear a swelling sound as rushing water from the uplands filled the town's extensive network of narrow stone irrigation canals—veins and arteries coming to life as they filled cisterns and soaked into the parched soil of bean fields and cornfields.

Along the old road from Tepoztlán to Yautepec, the turnoff to Santiago was designated by a rusting sign that had only a few months more of life left in it. In the daylight there were almost always two small clumps of people waiting at the intersection—one group waiting for the bus into Tepoztlán, the other for the bus to Yautepec. Yautepec, which lay down in the valley among tomato fields and sugarcane, was a few hundred meters lower in altitude than Santiago. Though Yautepec was only a twenty-minute bus ride away, the people of Santiago spoke of this warmer, lower town in what they called the *tierra caliente*—the hotlands—as if it were in some distant hell.

Santiago is a town of less than a thousand inhabitants. The main street, Calle Morelos, runs from the intersection to the concrete archway of the church with the blue neon cross on top. It is a distance of three or four football fields.

Calle Morelos slopes steeply down into the town, and would wash out quickly were it not cobbled with heavy cut stones. It is barely wide enough for two VW bugs to pass each other, though heavy traffic is the least of Santiago's worries. What commends Calle Morelos and gives it its stature is that it is fully paved, unlike the other streets in town.

Calle Morelos—the street itself—is an interesting measure of civic pride and responsibility. A number of years ago, the town's most prominent resident, a senior diplomat in the Ministry of Foreign Relations who had long kept a house in Santiago, donated truckloads of cobbles to the town so that the townspeople could repair Calle Morelos, which had been falling into successively worse stages of muddy disrepair with each rainy season. The arrangement was that each family would then recobble the stretch of Calle Morelos in front of their house. When we arrived, the work had been done, and we found a street in various telltale stages of repair: a smooth, handsomely cobbled stretch here, a lackadaisically paved part there, and in between, a road from hell that seemed little more than a knocked-down pile of stones.

Perhaps twenty homes border each side of Calle Morelos. For the most part they are invisible behind high walls painted gray or blue or green. Through some of the gates you can see small yards guarded by a dog or two and some chickens. Some of the houses—ostentatious amidst the simplicity of a mostly poor town—are strikingly different from the others. These are the *casas dólares* that can be seen in any Mexican town. They are built by families who are earning dollars as undocumented workers in the United States. Their dollars have spawned an architectural style:

two-story redbrick homes with lots of gold-metal-trim windows; rather than the old-style thick walls, which obstruct the view, these houses are surrounded by lacy perimeters of wrought iron and slender arches that allow the neighbors to get an eyeful of new wealth. In this way, the United States leaves its own imprint on Mexico, a layer as plain and often as revered as all the churches atop temples left behind by Spain.

There are a half-dozen casas dólares along Calle Morelos. In Mexican towns to the north, in states like Jalisco and Michoacán, there would be many more. Just as the United States has had its railroads built, its deserts turned into irrigated agricultural miracles, and its dishes washed by Mexican labor over the course of the twentieth century, Mexico, too, has benefited hugely from the migrant tide. In countless towns, the ebb and flow has deposited a thick layer of dollars: TV antennas, pickups with license plates from Texas and Arizona, Sony Walkmen, dirt bikes, houses built, farms kept afloat, hospital bills paid. In these towns, at the appointed hour each weekday, long lines of anxious women stand outside small post offices, waiting for word and money from Chicago and Saginaw, Seattle and Dallas—just as they do in Santiago, albeit in smaller numbers down here in the south.

A gringo friend of mine tells of being in one of these dollar-economy pueblos when some migrant families were back in town for the holidays. The kids had grown up in the States. A girl who looked as if she had just descended from East L.A. saw my friend on the street. Do you speak English? she asked—in English, of course. Yes, he said. Thank God! she said, emitting a sigh accented in fluent California ennui.

When a town like Santiago celebrates the feast day of its saint—the grandest fiesta of the year—it swells with residents returning from the United States for a visit. At the food and carnival booths up and down Calle Morelos, the kids from the States—prodigal sons and Valley Girls— are easy to spot in their faddish haircuts, the California jams down to their knees, Sea World T-shirts, and Reebok high-tops that cost the equivalent of a Mexican's factory wages for a week. A week or two later, the visitors will be gone. In their wake you will see a new TV flickering through a window that used to be dark, and a young cousin of one of the visitors walking up Calle Morelos from the corn miller's in the cherished Disneyland T-shirt.

A third of the way down Calle Morelos from the intersection is Alejandro's house. He lives there, in three rooms, with his mother and an extended family of six or so; his father is long gone, though how, to where, and under what circumstances are not clear. Alejandro was seventeen when we lived in Santiago. He's a painfully shy, lanky boy whose hair is home cut; he dropped out of high school in his junior year to become a gardener. He is valued because he can read and write, and we were paying him more each month to keep up our garden and pool than his teachers earn. In exchange, Alejandro was out watering the pots and gardens by seven-thirty in the morning; the sand-papery shuffle of his sandals on tile patios and the splash of water onto the shrubbery were like a pleasant wake-up call.

Halfway down Calle Morelos a sign—a blue bell on a white background—hangs over the gated entrance to Don Francisco's house. This is where Santiago's lone phone resides; behind a locked metal door, beneath a wall calendar bearing the image of the state of Morelos's best-known hero, the revolutionary leader Emiliano Zapata, the instrument sits alone on a desk in this tiny one-room building. It is a source of power and extra income for Don Francisco—a dollar or two for calls to the capital, ten dollars or more for a brief call to the States.

Don Francisco is the town fixer. He's a trim man of fifty-five or so. His short-cropped gray hair and bright eyes give him a sagacious, distinguished look. To outsiders the fact that the town's single phone line landed in his residence suggests rich political connections and a keen comprehension of the mysterious ways of rural Mexico.

City slickers are convinced that without Don Francisco's support they will be lost in Santiago, and few dare to test this notion. Don Francisco's chief nontelephonic responsibility is as liaision between weekend *santiagueños* and local plumbers, electricians, water haulers, butane gas suppliers, glaziers, pool servicers, carpenters, roofers, and others who stand between a weekend of rest and a lot of tiresome chores or, worse, a flooded bedroom or a pool pea green in algae growth. He makes a pretty peso in commissions.

Don Francisco spends much of his time surveying the virtually nonexistent traffic on Calle Morelos. Looking rakish in his signature straw cowboy hat, he leans jauntily up against his whitewashed gateway. As for his phone—the town phone—it is mostly out of order. Exactly why is never clear. Finding out why would not necessarily get it fixed. So it stays out of order. Eventually the cars belonging to the city people who used to stop by to call their offices in the morning stop stopping beneath the blue-and-white sign. And, to no one's surprise in Santiago, life goes on.

At the bottom of Calle Morelos, in the house on the

left just before the gate at the churchyard, lives Cleotilde. Cleotilde shares a comfortable, Spartan home with her parents, her son, Omar, who was twelve when we met him, and a handful of other family members who come and go. I never saw Cleotilde's father; all I knew about him was that he caused a rift in the family by joining a Protestant congregation in town. Cleotilde, as much by way of pragmatic compromise as out of conviction, became an agnostic. Cleotilde's mother is a handsome woman who wears her waist-length hair in a long braid down her back and is often dressed in the checked gingham apron favored by poor women in the Mexican countryside. Omar is a polite, hardworking boy whose sense of fun is stifled somewhat by his mother's determination to make a better life for him than what she now has. I never heard where Omar's father went, or why.

Cleotilde is a tireless entrepreneur. If she were a man, I could imagine her taking the route to success that Don Francisco has taken. As a woman, that route is not open to her. She will take another one, and perhaps get farther. Cleotilde is in her mid-thirties. She happens not to be a pretty woman, but she is very smart and wise in the ways that she will need to get ahead. She is proud enough not to bow and scrape in the manner of too many Mexican poor people. She is not deferential when she does not need to be, and she has the easy smile of an intelligent, self-assured woman.

Cleotilde makes fifty dollars a week teaching a double shift at a public school in the southern slums of Mexico City. The second shift she "purchased" from a retiring teacher for fifteen hundred dollars. At four-thirty each Monday morning she hustles her tanklike body up Calle

Morelos in the dark to the intersection in order to catch a bus to Mexico City. She spends her weekday nights in a tiny shared apartment near her school. For several years she has needled and cajoled her teachers' union, which is the largest union in Latin America and runs the schools from top to bottom (weirdly, administrators as well as teachers belong), for a job closer to her home and her son.

After school on Friday she returns to Santiago in time for a late meal at home. By the time she is walking down Calle Morelos from the bus stop, most of the town's lights are off. By eight the next morning, when we lived there, she was scrubbing a floor or thumping sofa pillows at our home. Her Saturday job with us paid her eight dollars. On Saturday nights she would make superior tamales late into the evening with her mother's help; the next day she would take them to the market in Tepoztlán and sell them, steam rising up from their banana-leaf or corn-husk wrappings.

In November 1990, as I finished writing this book, Julith received a letter from Cleotilde and with it two "death poems," one for each of us. The letter's warmth, its eloquence, and its elegant writing style moved us. Its grace and thoughtfulness, not to mention the bright flash of Cleotilde's humor, took me back to Santiago, smiling. As a piece of correspondence in these days of deep personal communication via telephone answering machines, the letter is pleasantly old-fashioned. As for the death poems, they are known as *calaveras*, or "skulls"; they are more celebratory than morbid, and are frequently part of the Day of the Dead ritual in Mexico. Cleotilde's death poems took my breath away when I first read them; they are gracious, unsettling, and beautiful at the same time. Her letter was dated November 2 (especially in rural Mexico, the celebra-

tion of the "Day" of the Dead can extend over several days).
Her handwriting was clear, fluid, and handsome, exhibiting
the penmanship of a good teacher.

2 November 1990
The Day of the Dead
Santiago Tepetlapa

Dear Julie,

From the beautiful town of Santiago, at the foot
of the mountain of the cross, I greet you with
affection, hoping that you and Stryker find yourselves
well. I want to excuse myself for not writing earlier
but I have been working full days since February and it
is very hard for me, but I have not forgotten you, nor
do I think I will forget you for a long time. The house
where you lived is still full of reminders of you. The
dried flowers are still in the living room, the amate
tree that you had planted has become very lovely, the
poinsettias have begun to flower, and since it has
rained a great deal the garden has turned very green.
Since February the house has been occupied by a
family (a couple and three children) but I have not
worked there since the twentieth of October because I
had problems with them and I sent them you know
where. I am very sad that I can't be in the house
anymore because I had grown very fond of it. But, on
the other hand, the work tired me out. Now I will
dedicate my free time to Omar [her son], whom I
have neglected badly.

As you know our dead come to visit us every year
and in the offering there is everything that your
husband loves to eat; it is a pity you are so far away,

but I ate for you, and I also wrote you a death poem; I hope you like it.

It has been impossible for me these days to make the wreaths of chiles because the heavy rains have damaged the chile crop and they are very few and expensive. I hope I can make them next year.

My family sends you many greetings, and so do Alejandro and Omar. All of us would be very happy to see you again, even just for a visit. But me especially, next time I see your family, I would like to see not just two people but three. Merry Christmas. Don't forget the sermon of the Christ Child.

She who remembers you with great fondness,
Cleotilde

DEATH POEM FOR JULIE
Julie was about to go out
when death arrived.
She remained motionless
and her husband remained, crying.

DEATH POEM FOR STRYKER
Stryker was eating
tamales from Vera Cruz
when death came in running.
Stryker fell to the ground
in the form of a cross.

We lived on the outskirts of Santiago in more ways than one. We would always be outsiders. As neighbors, the Mexicans we met in Santiago and elsewhere were hospitable, often beyond their means, but not readily intimate. When a Mexican opens her door to you, you see her home but little of the person; man or woman, you feel welcome to go so far and no further. We had some Chilean friends in Santiago. We would laugh about Santiago, and they would recite for us a Chilean saying that they thought was particularly appropriate: *Pueblo pequeño, infierno grande.* Small town, big hell. Our Chilean friends left to return to Chile when it returned to democratic government. We would eventually leave too, but it was only in jest that I could agree with their assessment of Santiago as a big hell.

For all its seeming isolation, Santiago afforded me a grand view of modern Mexico. I was close enough to Mexico City—it was less than one hour's drive away—to feel keenly the pull of that powerful urban maelstrom. In the quiet after the rain I could hear the distant throaty roar of Mexico City–bound buses as they climbed over the mountains—a reminder that only a single, massive hump of mountains separated us from the polluted southern reaches of the world's largest metropolis. From the vantage point of Santiago I could see how the lifestyle and economy of the big city intruded into the rich, if by some lights "backward," ways of rural Mexico, how the present and the past melded, sometimes appealingly, sometimes not.

The mix was particularly evident in Tepoztlán, the larger town beyond the line of hills to the west of Santiago.

Tepoztlán is five kilometers from Santiago, back down the road to Mexico City. It enjoys the climate of the region, which is famously mild; "eternal spring" is the descriptive phrase that keeps insinuating itself into guidebooks and Sunday-newspaper travel sections. The heat of May, hardly extreme, gives way to a summer of evening thunderstorms. The rest of the year is relentlessly agreeable. Bright, sunny days are a welcome counterpoint to the ozone-laced smog of the capital; the setting of the sun brings cool, starry nights. In the wintertime those who can afford the luxury fire up the gas heaters for their swimming pools, or in the evening light wood fires to take the chill out of the air.

During the week Tepoztlán is like many other Mexican towns that, by escaping heavy industry and the glass-box office-building architecture of recent decades, have retained the look and feel of previous centuries. The one asphalt-paved road leads to the central square, segues into a roughly cobbled street, and then on the outskirts of town turns back into asphalt again on its way to Santiago. A very uneven grid of cobbled or dirt streets extends outward from the square. The streets are hemmed in by thick adobe walls painted in dark colors along the bottom to camouflage mud splatters. The walls keep secrets from passersby: only the cognoscenti know whether behind the wall there is a modest brick home with chickens scratching in the yard or the elaborate weekend retreat of Mexico's former minister of tourism.

On Wednesday the town market springs to life between the town square and the cathedral. Beneath a patchwork canopy of plastic sheets that bathes everything in a petrochemical blue and forces anybody under five feet ten into a permanent stoop, there is a never-ending labyrinth of stalls: freshly killed meat so designated by a red flag, chickens barely dead, ripe tomatoes with the thin skins and real taste that have vanished in the States, bananas and pineapples from the coast, sugarcane from the nearby lowlands, apples and pears from Washington State, grapes from California and Baja California, wood carvings, bright cotton dresses and polyester ones, machetes and nails, a dozen different kinds of chiles from slender crisp green fresh serranos to crinkly mahogany-colored dried mulatos to skinny hot fire-engine red chiles de árbol, string beans, dried beans, tortillas made the night before from bleached corn, blue corn, purple corn, plums, peaches, rice, incense, dried herbs, fresh herbs, pork skin, tin soldiers, ceramic pots, flatware, ironware, lye, lard, and candles.

Just as there is a hierarchy of prices—tortillas are one thousand pesos (forty cents) a dozen for outsiders, eight hundred for the locals—there is a hierarchy of vendors. The poorest women sell only one thing: nopales (the rabbit-ear-shaped leaf from the nopal cactus that, sliced and boiled, tastes vaguely like green beans) or scallions. The women from the nearby hill towns like Santo Domingo or Amatlán sell blackberries, home-made charcoal, spindly fresh mushrooms called "little brooms," or resin-rich chunks of ocote wood that are cut with axes from high-mountain pines and leave ugly blood-red wounds in the tree trunks.

On weekdays in Tepoztlán there is barely a hint of the transformation that takes place on the weekend. Around the corner from the public market there is a store that sells chemicals and gadgets for swimming pools. At 11:00 A.M., when the morning papers have arrived at the town square newsstand from Mexico City, a few patrons show up at a trendy little café called El Pan Nuestro (Our Daily Bread) to sip espresso and fresh orange juice and read the left-leaning *La Jornada*. By midafternoon the French journalist who lives in town and is writing a novel about the Spanish Conquest might take his family to Los Colorines, a fine restaurant down the street from the police station.

On the weekends the character of Tepoztlán and its market changes. The market spills onto neighboring streets, where you can buy mango ice cream, clothing made in

Guatemala, cashews and pistachios, and Batman T-shirts. Alleys overflow with VW Corsars and Ford Topazes bearing "D.F." plates from the Federal District. On Saturday whole families from the capital who might have been eating McDonald's hamburgers last night gather around market-stall charcoal braziers for incomparably fresh tacos of hand-made corn tortillas and wild mushrooms. Girls in tight Guess? jeans and spiked heels navigate the cobbles. Antlike columns of backpacking Boy Scouts, who are en route to the Scout camp between Tepoztlán and Santiago for an overnight stay, seem to be carrying enough gear for a week in the wilderness. Catty-corner from the busy miller who grinds corn for tortillas, El Pan Nuestro does a bang-up business selling "European" pastries and plate-size oatmeal cookies.

The hierarchy of resentment against the tawdrification of Tepoztlán goes something like this: as far as the native *tepoztecos* are concerned, anybody who was not born in Tepoztlán, whether he is from Cuernavaca or Queens, is an *extranjero* (foreigner); Mexicans born outside of Tepoztlán, Europeans, South Americans, and (to a lesser extent) Americans who "discovered" Tepoztlán years ago and are now year-round residents resent the part-timers; part-timers who own homes in Tepoztlán and spend whole seasons in Tepoztlán resent the weekenders; weekenders who own homes resent those who rent, and all of these groups, of course, resent the day-trippers.

In this way, Tepoztlán is a Mexican mix of Santa Fe and Southampton. Steeped in both history and trendiness, removed from Mexico City and yet accessible to it, Tepoztlán is as much New Age as it is pre-Columbian. It is both a gem and a bauble. It sits up against an especially cragged ridge of mountains whose strange shapes, eroded over time by rain and wind, have long lent the site an air of mystery and magic. Shrouded in the heavy clouds of the summer rainy season, dark promontories and glinting blades of rock threaten the town below. Later in the year, covered in the green furry down bequeathed by the rains, the hills take on strange shapes—a phallus here, a bird there.

Not surprisingly, Tepoztlán has long had a reputation as a place of special spiritual significance. High in the Ridge of Tepoztlán is a pre-Aztec pyramid. Spanish priests hurled an idol from the temple down the mountain; it didn't break, so they smashed it. They did not build atop the temple, but Dominican priests constructed a thick-walled church down in the town. On September 8 each year, one side of the market area is set aside for a reenactment in Nahuatl of the final days of the supremacy of Aztec gods in these hills and the valley below, while at the cathedral people celebrate in Spanish the Day of the Virgin. City folk seek out noted shamans to cleanse their minds and bodies. Others come because they have heard that the local rock formations have special magnetic properties. And still others come to eat macrobiotic food, to practice yoga, or simply to stare into the night and marvel at the great strange shapes of the special hills that have attracted such diverse people and spirits to this place.

One day just before we left Santiago Tepetlapa for good, we went to Amatlán, a town higher in the mountains that is reputed to be the birthplace of Quetzalcoatl.

The story of Quetzalcoatl is profoundly Mexican. Quetzalcoatl—the name in Nahuatl means "feathered serpent"—is an ancient Toltec deity. The Toltecs also gave the name Quetzalcoatl to a ruler (it is not clear if the ruler and the deity were the same) who is said to have discovered maize, which until this day is the nutritional pillar of Mexican society and permeates its art and culture the way rice does in many Asian countries, and who brought the arts and sciences to the Toltecs. Quetzalcoatl, as the god of civilization, represented the forces of good and light. He was identified with the wind and the planet Venus, the first star in the night sky.

The Aztecs took the name for one of their major deities. (The Mayans, whose god Kukulcán was also represented by a feathered serpent, may have done the same.) Most disastrously, Moctezuma, the Aztec emperor at the time of the Spanish Conquest, mistook the invading Spaniards as heralds and hosts of the returning Quetzalcoatl. The word *Quetzalcoatl* itself has the power and scope of *Jesus* or *Allah*. It is one of those words that help to define a culture; it explains why people live the way they do and die the way they do, and why they go to war.

It is December when we visit Amatlán, midway between rainy seasons. At home in Santiago, with water from our eight-thousand-gallon cistern, our poinsettias are as big as trees, their flowers as red as Christmas church vestments. In Amatlán, the open spaces have been scorched dry by the sun; in the shade beneath the trees there are islands of cool and green. Amatlán—"the place of the amate tree"—is where the Aztecs manufactured parchment for codices from the bark of the amate. For all its local fame, Amatlán has somehow retained its dignity. There are no tour buses, no vendors hawking sun-faded postcards of the very spot on which Quetzalcoatl was born, not even a restaurant.

Over the past several months we had on a number of

occasions walked up in the mountains beyond Amatlán. One trail follows a stream through the outskirts of town; here, the land is parklike, its grass clipped short by livestock grazing in an orchard of deep green tejocote trees. A half-hour walk through a narrow canyon leads to a grassy defile. Pine trees tower overhead. Pinpoints of red and yellow and blue wildflowers peek through the grass. The scent of ocote, of giant pine trees bleeding, is in the air. The untrammeled earth is several inches deep in pine needles. It smells like the church in San Juan Chamula.

From up in the mountains you can look down on Amatlán, a smudge down below of green, white adobe, and bright laundry. It does not necessarily look like the birth-place of a deity, as handsome as the place is. But there is magic around here. Up in the hills, they say, Zapata took refuge in those caves. The sun shines into the entrance of another cave, they say—pointing high into the mountains— only on New Year's Day. I believe all these things because Mexico has taught me to believe first and disbelieve second.

One of the very few indications that Amatlán is any different from any other appealing Mexican mountain vil-lage is a sign as you enter the central part of town: HERE QUETZALCOATL TOOK HIS FIRST STEPS IN HIS SANDALS OF GOLD. A statue of Quetzalcoatl stands next to the white-washed church. Otherwise, life goes on as usual, as in most Mexican towns. Families tend their fields of corn. Men and boys look after the livestock. Girls haul water up from the creek. Women, who here as in the rest of rural Mexico do most of the buying and selling, go to the market in Tepoz-tlán. What is unusual is subtle: each home displays a plaque with its name in Nahuatl, a quiet acknowledgment of the past. The church also has its name posted above the doorway: Teocalli, possibly a synthesis of the Latin and Greek for "god" and the Nahuatl word for "house," *calli*.

Today we are walking not up into the hills but down into the valley. The sun has done its work; everything I see is the color of straw. Finally we find a deep canyon cut by a stream; you can smell the water. We clamber down a trail to a pool. It would be much deeper and cleaner during the summer rains. Now it is shallow, and the stream, reduced to a trickle, barely moves the debris that is collecting around the edges of the pool. Along the banks, scraggly grass reaches upward. Spindly vines reach down toward the pool, plumbing for the remaining water. The water itself is greener than one would want it to be: too many living things are sucking on its oxygen. Up high, trees embrace to keep out the sun—cottonwoods, scrub oaks, the yellow-barked amate trees. This, they say, is the spot where Quetzalcoatl was born.

There is a modest hill nearby. It is surrounded by tumbledown stone walls; where there are gaps in the wall, prickly cactuses and thorny branches are piled up as make-shift gates. A dog, not much of a dog, scurries down the hill to meet us and protect his master from us. This is more than just a hill. The shape of the hill gives it away: beneath the scorched earth is a pre-Aztec temple. It is known as Cinteopa, the Temple of the God of Corn.

Atop the temple lives its self-appointed guardian, Emilio Corrales. Don Emilio lives in a two-room stone house on the flat top of the ancient temple. Though stooped and feeble—he shambles around his property with a walking stick—Don Emilio has a full head of snow white hair. He has set some beans out to dry in the sun. The dog, scrawny and straw colored like the few stalks of corn left in

Don Emilio's field, guards the beans from the pair of intruders.

Don Emilio says he is about ninety-three years old. He bases his estimate on the fact that he was fifteen or sixteen years old when he fought in the Mexican Revolution of 1910–20. He tried to sign up when he was even younger. *"Acabas de mamar!"* someone told him. "You're practically still nursing!" He remembers that when he left home to go off to war, his parents cried. It was years before he returned. His parents were convinced he was dead; for a number of years on the Day of the Dead, they would place on an altar in their home an offering to his surely departed soul.

Don Emilio says he rarely runs into anybody who fought in the revolution anymore. Some time ago, he says, he went to the *zócalo* down in Yautepec. Time was when a trip to the *zócalo*—the main plaza—would have turned up a cluster of old men talking about their days in the revolution. "The last time," says Don Emilio, "I found nobody."

There was a time—one time only—when Don Emilio's soldiering during the revolution took him to Mexico City. He remembers seeing the vast zocalo, the cathedral, and the elegant Government Palace. He's never been back; though he lives practically in a suburb of the capital now, he's never had reason to return.

His life is here at the Cinteopa. There's a quiet nobility to what he has chosen to do on what he repeatedly refers to as *tierra sagrada,* "holy land." Though he wears trousers made from gunnysacks and sandals of leather cracked like his brown skin, there is something priestly about this simple farmer. Behind his house, because this is holy land, some-one erected a simple altar. It is little more than a piece of slate atop a small pile of stones. Scattered on the slate are some chunks of incense, a handful of dried flowers, and a tiny ceramic bowl in which someone has placed bird feathers. All of which serve as a reminder: this is one temple the Spaniards did not conquer.

Don Emilio lives in a very Mexican world. For him the wall between life and death, between reality and fantasy, is most porous. With childlike guilelessness, he tells us of a dream he had. The spirit of a dead man appeared in his dream and spoke to him. When he quotes the spirit, Don Emilio speaks in Nahuatl. He assumes we understand him. Eventually Don Emilio switches back into Spanish and over the course of our conversation, we gather what he had said. The spirit told him to take his hoe and dig in a certain spot in his cornfield. Don Emilio did, and found a carved and painted stone. This piece, like many others Don Emilio had found over the years, was stolen by thieves who know the great value of such things.

Don Emilio also tells us about meeting Satan one day. "Not here," he is quick to say. "This is tierra sagrada." He talks about this casually, as if he had had a nasty turn with the postman. These figures are as real to Don Emilio as the old men who swapped stories about the revolution with him at the zocalo in Yautepec. He was walking along the creek bed about a half kilometer from his home. Satanás came out of a cave. He was brandishing a sword. Don Emilio shook his fist at Satan. *"¡Soy un hombre de Dios! ¡Váyase!"* "I am a man of God! Go!"

For Don Emilio, Quetzalcoatl and Jesus Christ are one and the same. He speaks of them interchangeably as "Our Father." Toward the end of our visit, he pulls two beloved books of Bible stories out of a plastic bag he keeps stashed somewhere in his house. He can't read, but he recognizes the pictures. In one, Jesus is shown below a star in the heavens. Don Emilio points to the star with affection. He talks of how he sees Quetzalcoatl in the sky—as the first light in the night. He says he sometimes sits here outside his home and watches Quetzalcoatl's progress across the sky as Venus. As he tells us this, Don Emilio, noble guardian of Cinteopa, gently presses the tips of his fingers together in a gesture of prayer.

Don Emilio's faith is especially appealing because it is not anchored to a single tradition. The melding of the old beliefs with Catholicism seems perfectly natural here on a sunbaked hill outside Amatlán. I had found the syncretism at San Juan Chamula unsettling. Here on Don Emilio's *tierra sagrada* it is not that way. Don Emilio is living proof that the "usurpation" of Latin America's memory by the conquistadores of which Eduardo Galeano wrote is not total. Don Emilio knows instinctively what I had to learn: that not all of Mexico and the rest of Latin America was conquered, and that what was *not* conquered is what attracts so many of us to it.